W9-BKS-745

DISCARD

Insidious
Foes

Insidious Foes

The Axis Fifth Column
and the American Home Front

FRANCIS MacDONNELL

New York   Oxford
OXFORD UNIVERSITY PRESS
1995

Oxford University Press

Oxford   New York
Athens   Auckland   Bangkok   Bombay
Calcutta   Cape Town   Dar es Salaam   Delhi
Florence   Hong Kong   Istanbul   Karachi
Kuala Lumpur   Madras   Madrid   Melbourne
Mexico City   Nairobi   Paris   Singapore
Taipei   Tokyo   Toronto

and associated companies in
Berlin   Ibadan

Copyright © 1995 by Francis MacDonnell

Published by Oxford University Press, Inc.
198 Madison Avenue, New York, New York 10016

Oxford is a registered trademark of Oxford University Press

Library of Congress Cataloging-in-Publication Data
MacDonnell, Francis.
Insidious foes : the Axis Fifth Column and the American home front
/ Francis MacDonnell.
p. cm.   Includes bibliographical references and index.
ISBN 0-19-509268-6
1. Subversive activities—United States—History—20th century.
2. Espionage—United States—History—20th century.   3. World War,
1939–1945—Secret service—United States.   4. Spies—United States—
History—20th century.   I. Title.
E743.5.M15   1995
973.917— dc20   94 – 44379

1 3 5 7 9 8 6 4 2

Printed in the United States of America
on acid-free paper

for

Kenneth MacDonnell, Sr.

and

Ann Marie MacDonnell

PREFACE

This book is an anatomy of a spy scare that gripped the American public mind in the period preceding the Pearl Harbor attack and continuing through the first year of United States intervention in the Second World War. *Insidious Foes* considers why so many Americans publicly professed fears that an Axis Fifth Column had penetrated the nation. We know now that the threat of a totalitarian Trojan Horse of enemy agents, saboteurs, rumor-mongers, and dupes was largely chimerical. Nonetheless, responsible voices in the White House, Congress, the intelligence community, and organizations of citizens voiced genuine alarm that democratic government might be undone by those who bored from within. Motion pictures, radio programs, novels, pulp fiction, comic books, and posters contributed to the hysteria. *Insidious Foes* seeks to recapture the spirit of thrilling anxiety and dread that permeated the country between 1938 and 1942. The book examines factors that led to the rise and fall of the panic and outlines the significant legacy of the Fifth Column scare both for the Second World War period and the years that followed.

This is not the first historical study to touch on the Fifth Column problem. Louis De Jong's pioneering work *The German Fifth Column in the Second World War* explored the gap between the reality of the threat and public perceptions. This analysis emphasized the way in which the existence of some actual Fifth Column activity combined with the speed and totality of Germany's blitzkrieg advances in 1940 to heighten fears internationally. De Jong's work discussed the emergence of a Trojan Horse panic in Europe and in North and South America. The breadth of his study left him only a few pages to treat the panic in the United States.[1]

Specific aspects of the Fifth Column scare in America have been dealt with thoughtfully by historians other than De Jong. Richard Steele has written an important and compelling piece on Franklin Roosevelt's efforts to use the Fifth Column menace to undermine his foreign policy critics. A chapter in Leo Ribuffo's *The Old Christian Right: The Protestant Far Right from the Great Depression to the Cold War* entitled "Brown Scare" echoes many of Steele's criticisms of Roosevelt's failure to protect civil liberties adequately. Geoffrey Smith's *To Save a Nation: American Countersubversives, the New Deal, and the Coming of World War II* has noted that the support Charles Coughlin, William Dudley Pelley, and Fritz Kuhn voiced for nonintervention tainted the entire isolationist movement with treason. Similarly, Wayne Cole's various studies of isolationism have shown that movement's difficulties in overcoming the Fifth Column label. Richard Gid Power's masterful biography of J. Edgar Hoover discusses ways in which the FBI chief may have helped contain popular panic at the start of World War II. Bradley Smith has argued that the establishment of the Office of Strategic Services was integrally connected to the notion that the United States needed to develop a capacity for irregular warfare.[2]

Despite such work, there has been no overarching survey made of the Fifth Column scare in the United States. In this book I attempt to provide such an account and offer the kind of sustained treatment of a public panic available in Robert K. Murray's *Red Scare*, the classic account of America's post-World War I anti-Bolshevist panic, and Richard Fried's more recent study of Cold War hysteria, *Nightmare in Red*.[3] I have drawn on sources located in the Franklin Delano Roosevelt Presidential Library; the National Archives and Records Administration; the Library of Congress; the Federal Bureau of Investigation reading room; the Public Record Office in Kew, England; the Warner Brothers film archive at the University of Southern California; the Naval Historical Center, Washington, D.C.; Churchill College, Cambridge University; Sterling Library at Yale University; and the Houghton and Widener libraries at Harvard. Extensive use has been made of contemporary newspapers and magazines, as well as published microfilm and documentary collections. I have also drawn upon the superb secondary literature available on the First World War, American extremist groups, anti-Communism, Japanese internment, German Fifth Column operations, the Roosevelt administration, and American intelligence.

I am indebted to Professor Ernest May, who led me to this topic while I was a graduate student at Harvard University and supervised the ensuing project. Charles Ameringer read the entire manuscript and helped me correct errors and deepen my analysis. Suzanne Keen provided invaluable assistance in editing the text. Akira Iriye, Thomas Schwartz, and Leonid Heretz offered several useful suggestions at important moments throughout the project. Stephanie Sakson improved the manuscript in innumerable ways. Andrew Albanese guided the project through Oxford University Press. I am indebted to Vince Tompkins, Mark Peterson, Steve Biel, Dean Grodzins, Gerry Prokopowicz, Karla Goldman,

Bruce Venarde, and Tim Naftali for their critical suggestions and friendship. I received support from many members of the Quincy House community at Harvard, including Evan Mandery, Blanford Parker, Mary Ledwell, Jody Gho, and especially co-masters Michael and Rosa Shinagel. Family members offered constant encouragement, especially my mother and father.

New Haven   F.M.
January 1995

CONTENTS

Introduction 3

ONE   Prelude to the Fifth Column Scare:
The Lessons of World War I   11

TWO   Dangerous Demagogues, Men on Horseback,
and Native Fascists   29

THREE   The Opening Alarm:
The Rumrich Spy Case   49

FOUR   Other Fifth Columns:
Italy, the Soviet Union, and Japan   73

FIVE   "Perfidious Albion":
Great Britain and the Fifth Column   91

SIX   The Fifth Column in Europe   107

SEVEN   Keeping the Panic Alive:
*German Propaganda, Espionage, and Sabotage
in the United States*   123

EIGHT   Franklin Roosevelt and the Fifth Column   137

NINE   J. Edgar Hoover versus the Nazis   157

Conclusion   185

Notes   193

Bibliography   229

Index   239

Insidious
Foes

For it is clear enough that under certain conditions men respond as powerfully to fictions as they do to realities, and that in many cases they help to create the very fictions to which they respond. Let him cast the first stone who did not believe in the Russian army that passed through England in August, 1914, did not accept any tale of atrocities without direct proof, and never saw a plot, a traitor, or a spy where there was none. Let him cast a stone who never passed on as the real inside truth what he had heard someone say who knew no more than he did.

WALTER LIPPMAN, Public Opinion (1922)

Introduction

From 1938 to 1942 stories of the Axis Fifth Column inundated America. Fears about a hidden enemy boring from within and preparing the way for a hostile invasion extended from the White House to the public at large. In reality, Axis operations in the United States never amounted to much, and the Federal Bureau of Investigation easily countered the "Trojan Horse" activity that did exist. Nevertheless, by the time of United States entry into the Second World War the Fifth Column scare had deeply penetrated the nation's psyche. This study outlines the origins, evolution, and collapse of the hysteria, and it explains the causes and consequences of the panic.

The term "Fifth Column" originated during the Spanish Civil War. It was said to have first been used by the Nationalist general Emilio de Mola. During a radio broadcast in September 1936, Mola allegedly announced that four separate columns were advancing on Madrid, one from the south, another from the southwest, a third from the west, and a fourth from the northwest. He added that a fifth column was making ready to erupt from within the capital city.

Foreign agents, domestic traitors, and enemy dupes would form the backbone of a Fifth Column force. It would employ espionage, sabotage, and subversion in order to leave its host country demoralized, divided, and militarily unprepared for war. In the event of an actual invasion, Trojan Horse operatives would assist the enemies' regular troops. The Fifth Column came to be viewed as a favorite technique not only of Franco's Nationalists but also of several totalitarian regimes. At one time or another, the world press accused Italy, Japan, the Soviet Union, and Germany of seeking to undermine their adversaries from within.

While many authoritarian powers were thought to employ a Fifth Column, the term was most strongly associated with Nazi Germany. Hitler's series of triumphs, especially his blitzkrieg victories in the spring of 1940, seemed explicable to many observers worldwide only as the product of Trojan Horse treachery. Historian Louis De Jong has shown that fear of Nazi espionage, sabotage, and subversion was an international phenomenon affecting nations in Europe, North America, and South America.[1] De Jong notes that to some degree the "Fifth Column did most certainly exist." In Austria, Czechoslovakia, and Poland, the Nazis had relied on ethnic Germans to help their cause. However, the significance of Trojan Horse tactics in other Nazi victories came to be grossly inflated.

It is understandable that England and other European nations succumbed to a spy hysteria, given the proximity of the German threat. Latin America's concerns about the Fifth Column also make a certain amount of sense, given the number of fascist sympathizers throughout the region. The hysterical response of the United States, however, to a modest Fifth Column threat is more puzzling. Hitler viewed America as a low priority. Though the Germans practiced espionage, sabotage, and subversion in United States, their efforts were modest and almost uniformly unsuccessful.

Nonetheless, Americans have long felt vulnerable to conspiracies launched against the republic, and historians have frequently noted the central role that fears of subversion have played in our national past. The American Revolution resulted, at least in part, from widely held fears that Britain intended to enslave the colonies. Throughout the nation's earliest political contests Federalists and Republicans saw one another as secretly plotting to undo the triumphs of the Revolution. The Jacksonian period witnessed fears of anti-democratic conspiracies by Mormons, Catholics, Masons, the "Monster Bank," and "King Andrew." Before the Civil War, northerners condemned the shadowy maneuverings of the slave power, while southerners denounced the clandestine schemes of the Black Republicans. In the 1890s, the Populists sought to explain their changing world in terms of hidden combinations by big business. Through the early decades of the twentieth century, many Americans doubted the loyalty of new immigrants from eastern and southern Europe. Red scares shook the United States after both world wars.[2] The Axis Fifth Column scare thus fits into a historical pattern of national hysteria.

Conditions of life in the United States made the existence of a Fifth Column threat plausible. America is an enormous country with long and highly permeable borders. Once here, enemy agents would find a society lacking strong central institutions to monitor and order its citizens' lives. The tremendous geographical mobility characteristic of the nation's population would allow hidden foes to move from place to place without attracting suspicion. America's diversity afforded opportunities for clever adversaries to encourage domestic upheaval through "divide and conquer" tactics. Since the United States is a heterogeneous mix of ethnicities, races, and religions, the possibility that certain treacherous individuals would give their first loyalty to an alien creed or a foreign nation always existed. Perhaps even honest Americans might be manipulated by threats against relatives still trapped in the Old World (for example, government officials occasionally justified U.S. restrictions on refugees from Nazi Germany by pointing out the vulnerability of such individuals to Gestapo threats).[3] The major defining quality of American nationality has been an individual's acceptance of the principles embodied in the United States Constitution and the Bill of Rights. Yet beliefs are hidden from the world; Hitler's Fifth Columnists might fraudulently claim allegiance to republican principles while secretly aiding the Third Reich.

Prior to World War II, the American public tended to believe in its own innocence and in the decadence of Europe. Americans generally perceived themselves as a gregarious, trusting, open, and naive people. Germans, on the other hand, were thought to be sophisticated, clever, and ruthless. These attitudes led many Americans to worry that a Nazi Trojan Horse campaign might gravely weaken the United States. The Third Reich's efforts to spread fascism placed Germany on a collision course with the United States. Americans saw their nation as the providentially designated homeland for freedom. If Hitler sought a fascist world empire, he would undoubtedly try to undo the "last, best hope" for democracy. Fifth Column tactics would allow the Nazis to soften up America before a conventional military attack. Moreover, the Fifth Column seemed a peculiarly appropriate modus operandi for the Reich. Like the serpent in Eden, Hitler would seek his objectives through guile and fraud. Only the resort to such insidious tactics would allow fascism to triumph over democracy.

The supposition that Hitler's secret service would attack the United States was partly a product of the lessons of history. Before 1917, the Germans had engaged in a range of hostile operations within the United States. Such actions included efforts to disrupt operations at defense factories and the planting of incendiary devices aboard merchant ships. For Hitler to target America even before making a declaration of war would be in accord with Germany's past behavior. During the First World War, United States material and human resources had tilted the balance against the Kaiser's drive for empire. For many it was axiomatic that Hitler would seek to neutralize America as a decisive player in world affairs so as to avoid the disastrous results of World War I. In the thirties and forties these fears were partly justified by the revelation of actual cases of Fifth Column intrigue by the Nazis. Government investigations broke several German spy rings, exposed clumsy Nazi propaganda efforts, and thwarted enemy sabotage missions.

The mass media played a pivotal role in persuading the public that America was a playground for agents of the Reich. Newspaper features, magazine articles, personal memoirs, novels, comic books, radio pro-

grams, and motion pictures all ballyhooed the menace that subversive
forces allegedly posed to the republic. The media gave extensive coverage
to stories of German espionage, sabotage, and subversion. In part, the
media was simply covering legitimate news stories; actual cases of
German Fifth Column activity uncovered by American intelligence de-
served press coverage. The apparent danger posed to national security
by native fascist groups such as the German-American Bund also fasci-
nated journalists. Additionally, events in Europe seemed to confirm the
fact that subversion was one of Hitler's favorite tactics in subduing his
foes. Reports fed back to America from reliable sources on the continent
identified Trojan Horse tactics as a key component of Germany's early
conquests. Newspapers, radio networks, and film studios also wanted to
please the public, and next to sex scandals few stories were easier to sell
than the Fifth Column.

Officials in the American government did nothing to discourage the
media from believing that the United States was vulnerable to German
subversion. The White House, Congress, and the FBI all proclaimed the
Fifth Column a dire threat to national security. Franklin Roosevelt, Martin Dies (Chairman of the House Committee on Un-American Activites),
and J. Edgar Hoover all genuinely believed in the danger posed by internal Nazi enemies, yet each had reasons for overstating the scope of
the problem. Conviction and convenience were happily married to one
another.

President Roosevelt and his cabinet members consistently spoke out
on the need for vigilance in the face of a Nazi Trojan Horse offensive
against America. The Fifth Column proved a useful security threat for
the White House. Before America's entrance into the war, interventionists in the Roosevelt administration contended that the Nazis had already
begun a secret attack on America and that Hitler would not stop until
he had destroyed democracy everywhere. There could be no more compelling a refutation of isolationism than the demonstration that a
German Fifth Column was in the process of subverting America.

The House Un-American Activities Committee and its chairman Martin Dies proved to be the most important congressional commentators
on the Fifth Column. Though the committee principally focused on Soviet Fifth Column activities, it was also very much involved in investigating and denouncing Nazi intrigue. Dies and his colleagues used the
spy menace in order to win free publicity. The conservative members of
HUAC also saw the Fifth Column problem as a way to attack the Roosevelt administration.

The FBI repeatedly cautioned Americans that Fifth Columnists had
penetrated every aspect of the nation's life. Though the Bureau discouraged hysteria and vigilante spybusting, J. Edgar Hoover described the
Trojan Horse in a frightening fashion. Such an approach made sense:
the FBI was a small organization entrusted with the enormously difficult

responsibility of domestic counterespionage. Hoover depended on public vigilance and public cooperation. Hence, he worked to ensure that the nation took the threat of foreign intrigue seriously. Moreover, the Bureau ensured that it received adequate funding and manpower to fight the Fifth Column by stressing the severity of the problem. It was safer to err on the side of overestimating the threat. In the event the Nazis actually did get away with some particular act of terror, Hoover could simply say that the problem was so big that it could not be completely contained.

Great Britain also calculated its behavior to heighten America's fears about the Fifth Column. It suited London's interests to have the Americans feel directly threatened by Germany. British policymakers knew that evidence of Nazi intrigue in the Western Hemisphere would push the United States closer to the Allies. Beginning in 1940, the British established a major intelligence organization in the United States, British Security Coordination (BSC). This agency exposed German covert activities in North and South America. BSC also generated rumors suggesting the presence of widespread disloyalty in the United States. Additionally, London passed along its own concerns about German penetration of the British Isles to the United States. Britain's warnings regarding the Fifth Column menace augmented America's own fears. Finally, British suspense novels and films helped to create in America an image of Germans as master spies and subverters.

Fear of German Fifth Column activity in America went through several distinct phases. Prior to 1938 the doings of the German-American Bund and various native fascist groups aroused only modest concern. In 1938 everything changed when the FBI uncovered a major German spy ring in New York City. A celebrated espionage trial presented evidence which proved that Hitler's government was running covert operations in America. This case received national coverage and helped generate a new awareness of the spy problem facing America.

Throughout 1939 and 1940 the nation's Fifth Column jitters intensified. With the fall of Denmark, Norway, Belgium, the Netherlands, and France, a full-blown spy scare gripped the country. Anecdotal accounts started to appear in the press, suggesting the onset of a public panic. In June 1940, *Time* reported that a Michigan man had murdered his neighbor because he suspected him of being part of the Fifth Column. The same magazine told Americans of a group of middle-aged matrons in Manhattan who had organized the Molly Pitcher Rifle Legion, "pledged to target practice once a week. Purpose! to pick off descending parachute troops, when and if."[4] Such anxieties were not merely confined to a lunatic fringe. In June of 1940 *Life* magazine proclaimed that "the destructive ability of the German Fifth Column in recent weeks has made Americans justifiably suspicious of Nazis living in their midst."[5] In August 1940, a Gallup poll indicated that 48 percent of Americans believed their own communities had been infiltrated by Fifth Columnists. Only 26 percent believed their neighborhoods were free of subversive forces, while 26 percent were not sure either way.[6]

The public began to flood the government with reports of suspected cases of espionage. The increase in such complaints is striking. Between 1933 and 1938 the Federal Bureau of Investigation received an average of 35 complaints per year; in 1938 the figure was up to 250; in 1939 it reached 1,615; and on one day in May 1940 the number was 2,871.[7] Some of the complaints sent into federal officials were clearly from unbalanced individuals. For example, a California man wrote the State Department the following bizarre note:

> My wife and I have some friends or rather she has a girl friend who is married to a German who we suspicion [sic] is a German spy. I have been trying to check up on his movements and try [sic] to catch him. Right now by mental telepathy I have the information that he is sending messages to Germany on a very low short wave length from a cave on the out skirts of the little town of Vencill New Mexico.[8]

Other correspondence came in from Tom Sawyer-types eager to become players in the Great Game of espionage. A man from Yonkers, New York, sent the following letter addressed to "Secretary of War" (actually Secretary of State) Cordell Hull:

> If you send me five men of experience who do not put their church ahead of God. Home and Country I will produce evidence of destruction of America from within. Please send identifications. Also they must come from you or the United States Secret Service.[9]

Most letters were received from sane, apparently sincere citizens, who were disturbed by unusual events that they perceived as evidence of possible subversion.

In the autumn of 1942, fears about the Axis Fifth Column declined precipitously. The Allies' move to the offensive, the failure of any effective domestic spy threat to emerge, and the reduced intensity of government warnings to the public calmed home-front anxieties. Stories of the German Fifth Column never entirely disappeared, of course. In fact, they continued long into the postwar era. Fugitive Nazis, relocated in the western hemisphere, became the stuff of suspense novels and films. More important, as the Cold War developed, the German Fifth Columnist of the early forties reemerged in popular cultural forms as the Communist spy of the fifties.

The Axis Fifth Column's heyday lasted no more than two years. However, the scare produced changes of great importance for the World War

II and Cold War periods. The FBI's manpower, funding, and authority rapidly expanded. The British and American intelligence communities established close ties of cooperation. The United States developed its own capacity for Fifth Column operations in the form of the Office of Strategic Services (OSS) and later the Central Intelligence Agency. Congress passed important security legislation and took an active part in investigating alleged domestic subversion. Isolationism lost credibility as a viable foreign policy option for the United States as the America First movement was tainted with the stigma of disloyalty. These changes fostered American internationalism abroad while accelerating the creation of a powerful intelligence establishment at home.

ONE

———⚮———

Prelude to the
Fifth Column Scare

The Lessons of World War I

On April 2, 1917, Woodrow Wilson asked Congress to declare war against Germany. The President argued that Berlin's resort to unrestricted submarine warfare undermined freedom of the seas, violated the rights of neutrals, and jeopardized American lives and property. Though Wilson focused principally on Berlin's submarine warfare as the source of conflict between the two nations, he also cited as a casus belli the Imperial Government's willingness to run espionage, sabotage, and subversion campaigns in America:

> One of the things that has served to convince us that the Prussian autocracy was not and could never be our friend is that from the very outset of the present war it has filled our unsuspecting communities and even our offices of government with spies. Indeed, it is now evident that it spies and sets criminal intrigues everywhere afoot against our national unity of counsel, our peace within and without, our industries and our commerce. Indeed, it is now evident that its spies were here even before the war began; and it is unhappily not a matter of mere conjecture but a fact proved in our courts of justice that the intrigues which have more than once come perilously near to disturbing the industries of the country have been carried on at the instigation, with the support, and even under the personal direction of official agents of the Imperial Government accredited to the Government of the United States.[1]

During the period from 1914–17 the Central Powers mounted repeated acts of intrigue against America. The German and Austrian embassies supervised this clandestine warfare. It included attempts to forge passports, blow up bridges, incite labor unrest, disrupt munitions production, and plant incendiary devices aboard merchant ships. Plots were devised to set Mexico at odds with the United States and to use America as a base from which to attack Canada. The Wilson administration, with considerable assistance from British intelligence, fought against Germany's covert warfare. Over time, Berlin's incessant intriguing enraged the White House and solidified public support behind America's entrance into the First World War.

The commencement of hostilities produced a substantial decline in espionage activities as the closing of the German embassy destroyed the Kaiser's spy network in America. Interestingly, the greatest anti-German hysteria did not hit the United States until after German intrigue had dwindled away to almost nothing. From 1917–18 all things German came to be viewed with suspicion and horror, and many German-Americans found themselves harassed by their anxious neighbors.

The memory of Germany's intrigues during the World War I era shaped the way government policymakers and the American public thought about the Nazi Fifth Column in the late thirties and early forties. It was widely anticipated that Adolf Hitler would prove even more willing to resort to clandestine assaults against the United States than had the Kaiser. Consequently, Americans viewed any sign of Nazi intrigue with a sense of déjà vu. Though German Fifth Column activity before World War II was limited in scope and rather ineffective, there were enough real cases to help set off a national panic. Thanks to the experience of World War I, Americans had come to see espionage, sabotage, and subversion as favored devices of the ruthless Huns.

The First World War experience also left Americans determined to avoid, as much as was possible, the outrageous violations of civil liberties which anti-Germanism had produced under Wilson's administration. The fear of internal enemies which struck America in the thirties and forties tended to be anti-Nazi rather than anti-German. Prior to World War II, the United States remained on the qui vive for Nazi agents, sympathizers, and dupes; this wariness, however, did not result in a repeat of the widespread victimization of German-Americans that had occurred during the First World War.

The two anti-German scares which hit America in this century, one during the Wilson administration and the other during Franklin Roosevelt's tenure, were produced by many of the same factors. In both cases the exposure of actual acts of intrigue reinforced the American public's sense of vulnerability to Fifth Column enemies. The media, the British, and various members of the American government also behaved in a way which exacerbated tensions. An examination of German intrigue in the United States during the First World War and the resulting spy mania thus provides a necessary prologue for any study of the nation's Nazi Fifth Column scare.

German Intrigue, 1914–17

The Central Powers used their American embassies and consuls as bases from which to supervise clandestine intrigue. Joachim von Bernstorff served as the German ambassador in Washington throughout the period of American neutrality. Bernstorff was aware of the campaign of secret warfare being run out of his embassy. However, he steered clear of personal involvement in daily operational matters. Heinrich Albert, the privy counselor and commercial attaché to the embassy, was the paymaster for much of the German intrigue run in America. Woodrow Wilson believed that this man was the most dangerous agent the Germans had in the United States.[2] Military attaché Captain Franz von Papen and naval attaché Captain Karl Boy-Ed initially maintained the closest control over espionage, sabotage, and subversion matters. On the West Coast, Franz Bopp, the German consul in San Francisco, took charge of secret operations. The Austrian embassy also became involved in various American intrigues, though to a lesser degree than its German counterpart.

Germany began its clandestine attacks against America in 1914. At the outset of the European war the British blockade trapped a large contingent of German military reservists in the United States. In an attempt to smuggle some of these men back to Europe, military attaché Papen and his assistant Wolf von Igel authorized the forgery of passports. Hans von Wedell, an American citizen and a German reserve officer, was placed in charge of the effort to acquire false identifying papers. Wedell enlisted longshoremen, seamen, and others to apply for passports. Once these documents were issued, the picture of the legitimate holder of the passport was replaced with that of a German reserve officer. These forgeries usually proved convincing enough to allow reservists to slip through the Allied blockade.

The Justice Department became aware of the German passport scheme and took action to close it down. Only a few months after beginning his operations, Wedell fled the country out of fear that government agents were preparing to arrest him. He was replaced by Carl Ruroede. However, Ruroede's tenure lasted less than a month. A Bureau of Investigation sting operation ended his illegal activities. Federal agent Albert Adams posed as a waterfront bum and promised to help Ruroede acquire false passports. Adams brought four passports to the German operative. The State Department had made out the documents and Ruroede gladly accepted them. After completely exposing the German passport mill, the bureau moved in and made their arrests. President Wilson decided to keep the passport issue quiet in hopes of reducing tensions with Berlin. Nonetheless, the discovery of Wedell and Ruroede's activities enlivened the White House's suspicions regarding the Germans.[3]

Passport forgery proved a far less bothersome violation of neutrality than sabotage. The Wilson administration repeatedly found Germany guilty of involvement in different acts of destruction. Some of the sabotage was directed against Canada but launched from the United States; other acts were actually performed inside the United States. German targets included canals, bridges, shipping, and defense plants.

In September 1914, German agent Horst von der Goltz traveled by train to Buffalo, New York. Goltz planned to cross the border into Canada and blow up the Welland canal, which connected Lake Ontario and Lake Erie. Several accomplices accompanied him. Upon reaching the border, however, Goltz and his men panicked and failed to follow through on their sabotage plot. In October 1915, the Germans recalled Goltz. On the way back to Europe he surrendered himself to Scotland Yard. He revealed his role in the abortive Welland conspiracy and he added that the entire plot had been overseen by the German military attaché Papen. After completing their interrogation, the British extradited Goltz to America where he was tried, convicted, and jailed.

Authorities uncovered another German attempt at sabotage in February 1915. Werner Horn, a German reserve officer, was asked to destroy the international bridge of the Canadian Pacific Railway located at Vanceboro, Maine. This sabotage, if successful, would have hindered the transport of American war materials to the city of Halifax. Horn prepared an explosive device and left it at the bridge. However, the bomb never detonated. American authorities arrested Horn shortly after his unsuccessful effort. The captured spy confessed to his own wrongdoing but did not implicate the German embassy in the act.

On the West Coast, the German consul in San Francisco, Franz Bopp, was linked to several acts of sabotage. In the spring of 1915, Bopp dispatched two agents to Tacoma, Washington. These operatives destroyed a barge loaded with gunpowder and bound for Russia. A few months later, one of the paid saboteurs, Louis Smith, turned himself in to the Justice Department. Smith detailed the consul's supervision of the Tacoma bombings. Eventually the government built an elaborate case against Bopp and other members of his office. He was tried for and found guilty of "conspiracies to interfere with the transportation of munitions of war by dynamiting and blowing up factories, railroad bridges and tunnels, trains, docks and steamships."[4]

In March of 1915, Captain Franz von Rintelen of the German navy arrived in New York City with a sum of $500,000. Rintelen intended to limit the shipment of United States defense goods to the Allies. In order to achieve this end he claimed that he would either "buy up or blow up" American munitions. The energetic spy quickly went about laying the groundwork for a campaign of undercover warfare. Military attaché Papen suggested that Rintelen contact Dr. Walter Scheele, a German industrial spy with a specialty in chemistry. After Rintelen explained his sabotage plans, Scheele developed a special incendiary device. This fire bomb consisted of two separate compartments divided by a metal disc; one chamber contained pyric acid and the other held sulphuric acid. Over time the two acids ate away the metal disc, mixed together, and generated a flame. These bombs were manufactured in New York harbor aboard the interned German vessel S.S. *Friedrich der Grosse*. Disgruntled stevedores, many of them Irish, planted the devices. After setting up his organization in New York City, Rintelen helped to establish similar operations in Baltimore and New Orleans.

Rintelen's acts of intrigue extended beyond arson. For example, he created a phony labor union entitled Labor's National Peace Council. This organization worked to encourage strikes along the waterfront. After some initial success the plot fell apart. Rintelen also entangled himself in conspiratorial scheming with the deposed Mexican dictator Victoriano Huerta. The two men met in New York City and discussed the possibility of Germany assisting Huerta in his efforts to regain power. The general suggested he might be willing to wage war against the United States, once he reestablished control over Mexico. American Secret Service agents who had been tailing Huerta monitored these discussions.

In August, Rintelen was recalled to Germany. Rintelen's departure relieved Papen and Boy-Ed; the two men had always viewed him as an interloper on their turf. Rintelen returned home aboard the Dutch ship *Noordam*. He traveled under a Swedish passport using the name E. V. Gauche. When the *Noordam* docked at Falmouth, England, British intelligence agents were waiting (thanks to their interception of German cable traffic). They arrested Rintelen and interrogated him. In May, 1917, the British extradited him to the United States where he served a four year prison term for his multifarious activities.[5]

Other German agents besides Rintelen sought to sabotage cargo bound for the allies. In October of 1915, Robert Fay, a German secret service agent, was arrested for his attempts to disrupt transatlantic shipping. While investigating Fay, American Secret Service agents searched the suspect's New Jersey apartment where they uncovered a variety of explosives, a map of New York Harbor, a suitcase full of disguises, and several pieces of correspondence with the Imperial Government. The German agent denied the involvement of higher-ups with his operations. Nonetheless, both the press and the United States government assumed that Fay had been assisted by Papen. In fact, three years after his arrest Fay admitted this to be the case.[6]

The extent of Germany's campaign against transatlantic shipping is hard to measure with precision. From 1915 to 1917 incendiary devices were discovered aboard 47 vessels bound for Allied countries.[7] Fires of mysterious origin disabled or sank a number of other ships. Insurance rates skyrocketed.

Disruptive fires and explosions also plagued defense factories and storage depots. Authorities found it difficult to determine whether a particular mishap was the result of sabotage or merely an accident. In many instances investigators uncovered strong circumstantial evidence of German involvement in acts of destruction, but lacked definitive proof. Press accounts reported that between 1914 and 1916 there were approximately 50 cases of unexplained fires occurring at munitions factories and storage centers.[8] Two of the more prominent cases involved disastrous fires at the munitions dump at Black Tom Island on July 30, 1916, and the Canadian Car and Foundry Company at Kingsland, New Jersey, on January 11, 1917.

Black Tom Island, transformed into a peninsula with landfill, sat in New York Harbor directly across from the Statue of Liberty. The site served as the terminal point for the Lehigh Valley Railroad Company and as an enormous powder and munitions depot. At Black Tom Island various war goods destined for shipment to the Allies were picked up by barges and transported to merchant vessels. Shortly after midnight on July 30, 1916, a fire began at Black Tom. The blaze spread quickly to railroad cars and barges packed full of munitions. An astonishing and dangerous fireworks spectacle illuminated the skies around New York City. The aftershocks of the explosions shattered plate glass windows in Manhattan and Brooklyn. The disaster resulted in hundreds of injuries, but luckily no one was mortally wounded. The fire at Black Tom devastated barges, railroad cars, piers, and warehouses and destroyed millions of dollars' worth of munitions. Damage estimates were set at approximately $20 million. Preliminary press reports passed off the disaster as an accident, as did an initial investigation by the Bureau of Investigation. It was not until after the war that serious efforts were made to show German culpability for the destruction.

Five months after the Black Tom affair a disaster of almost equal proportion struck the Canadian Car and Foundry Company at Kingsland, New Jersey. This Canadian owned business produced approximately 3,000,000 shells a year. The Germans sabotaged the plant by infiltrating agents among the factory's 1400 workers. A fire began at the workbench of a German agent and rapidly engulfed the plant. The blaze destroyed millions of shells and hundreds of thousands of fuses, cartridge cases, and detonators. Financial damages were estimated at $17 million. Unlike the Black Tom case, there was almost immediate suspicion of sabotage in the Kingsland disaster.

These cases eventually became the subject of lengthy litigation between the United States and Germany. In 1924 an Allied Mixed Claims Commission was convened, but a final decision was not reached until

1939. The umpire in the case, Supreme Court Justice Owen Roberts, ruled Germany responsible for the two disasters. Hitler's government refused to accept the commissioner's verdict. As a result, Germany did not finally pay off on its damages until 1954. The lingering nature of the Black Tom and Kingsland suits kept the whole issue of German espionage very much alive in the American press throughout the thirties. The case also helped bring John J. McCloy into a career of public service. As a lawyer for the firm of Cravath, deGersdorff, Swaine and Wood, McCloy served a vital role in investigating and prosecuting Germany for its sabotage at Black Tom and Kingsland. Largely because of his knowledge of past German intelligence operations, McCloy was asked to serve in Henry Stimson's War Department, where he became one of the Roosevelt administration experts on Trojan Horse activities.[9]

Even when it engaged in legal activities the German embassy found itself placed under fierce attack. On Saturday, July 24, 1915, German commercial attaché Heinrich Albert boarded a New York subway. Albert fell asleep during the ride and woke up just as the train reached his stop. In his haste he left behind his briefcase. Frank Burke, an American Secret Service agent who had been tailing Albert, immediately grabbed the portfolio. The contents of the briefcase were presented to Secretary of the Treasury, William G. McAdoo. The stolen documents showed German plans to buy up war supplies, divert American labor away from pro - Allied production, and influence American public opinion (through the possible purchase of newspapers and the funding of lectureships). These activities did not violate the law but they were widely perceived as improper meddling in American domestic affairs.[10]

Help from Great Britain

After the theft of the Albert papers, German and Austrian embassy officials sent reports to their respective governments wrongly blaming the British for the mishap. The Germans were not unjustified in drawing such conclusions, for Britain responded to German intrigue in America with a vigorous counterespionage campaign, and was in fact a more effective force in exposing subversive actions by the Central Powers than any of America's home front security services: the New York City Bomb Squad, the Secret Service, or the Bureau of Investigation.

Three factors help explain the remarkable success of British intelligence efforts in America. First, London intercepted a good deal of the German communications across the Atlantic. Such interceptions frequently proved past German indiscretions or else warned of future secret operations. Second, the British closely monitored the movements of suspected enemy agents in the U.S., with the cooperation of an independent Czech nationalist organization that had penetrated German and Austrian consulates in America. Third, London maintained excellent contacts with members of both the Wilson administration and the American press. These contacts allowed for the rapid unmasking of improper behavior by Britain's foes.

The Germans knew about the diverse activities of the British in the United States. In August of 1915, ambassador Bernstorff complained to Secretary of State Robert Lansing that he doubted whether "the world has ever witnessed a publicity campaign or a secret service bureau approaching the dimensions, influence and efficiency of what is maintained in this country by our enemies."[11]

On August 5, 1914, the British ship *Telconia* cut five of the German transatlantic cables running through the English channel. This action forced the Central Powers to utilize alternative means of communication with their foreign representatives. In an effort to maintain secure communications with Berlin and Vienna, the German and Austrian embassies in Washington occasionally attempted to slip documents through the British blockade. Such tactics often produced unfortunate results. For example, in the summer of 1915, British intelligence received a tip from sources inside the United States that J. F. J. Archibald, an American journalist, carried correspondence from the Austrian ambassador Constantin Dumba. The Royal Navy stopped the Dutch ship upon which Archibald traveled. After searching Archibald's papers the British found documents indicating that ambassador Dumba had proposed a scheme to "disorganize the manufacture of munitions of war" in the United States.[12] As part of this plan the Austrian ambassador suggested funding a number of foreign-language newspapers throughout America. These journals would encourage worker unrest in plants engaged with war production. Dumba primarily sought to influence laborers with attachments and sympathies to the Central Powers. Dumba's plan appeared to be a particularly sinister and dangerous attempt to take advantage of America's heterogeneous population. In response to this meddling in American internal affairs the Wilson administration requested that Dumba leave the country.

Shortly thereafter, the Royal Navy pulled off another intelligence coup which succeeded in further souring relations between Washington and the Central Powers. This incident involved military attaché Papen. In November of 1915, the Wilson Administration declared Papen persona non grata. The government acted because it suspected the German military attaché of fostering subversion in America. Papen had also been hurt by the Archibald affair. Among the documents captured by the British was a personal letter Papen had written to his wife in which he had made insulting comments about the Americans.[14] The State Department guaranteed Papen safe passage back to his homeland. This promise led the expelled attaché to assume that the documents he carried back to Germany would not be seized by the Allies. However, the British claimed that the safe passage guarantee applied only to Papen's person—

and not to his luggage—and they confiscated all the material he was carrying. Among Papen's holdings were check stubs which offered strong circumstantial evidence linking the German embassy to forgery and sabotage. The British found records of payments made out to saboteurs Werner Horn and Horst von der Goltz, as well as to passport forger Carl Ruroede.[15] Papen's angry complaints over the theft of his correspondence aroused little sympathy from the Americans.

Of course, the Central Powers had other means of communication that circumvented the Allies' blockade. However, these channels were also compromised. Room 40, the cryptographical section of British naval intelligence, achieved astonishing success in intercepting and deciphering German electronic and telegraphic communications. Under the leadership of William "Blinker" Hall, British naval intelligence acquired the German diplomatic and naval code books. The British succeeded in breaking the ciphers with which the enemy masked its communications. In a futile effort to protect transatlantic correspondence with its American embassy, Berlin employed a number of different routes for relaying messages. Material was transmitted over the wireless station at Nauen, or funneled through the Swedish diplomatic cable. The Germans also sought and were occasionally granted the use of the American cable. However, Room 40 knew of these routes and possessed the ability to tap into each one of them.[16]

One of the most stunning and significant intelligence coups of the entire war occurred in March 1917, with the successful exposure of the Zimmermann telegram. This communication revealed that the German foreign minister had sought an alliance with Mexico. The terms of the partnership called for the return of Arizona, New Mexico, and Texas, to the Mexican government as well as generous financial support from Berlin, in exchange for a joint war effort against the United States. The British passed this message on to the Americans. The Wilson administration's release of the telegram and Zimmermann's puzzling admission of the document's validity outraged American public opinion and helped to precipitate war with Germany.[17]

London's expert codebreaking was not the only reason for Germany's losses in the secret war in the United States. Thanks to close collaboration with Emmanuel Voska's Bohemian National Alliance, the British remained a step ahead of their adversaries. The Bohemian National Alliance was an organization of Czech nationalists who were dedicated to freeing their ancestral homeland from domination by the Austro-Hungarian empire. In 1915 Captain Guy Gaunt, the British naval attaché in Washington, established contact with Voska. Both men agreed to work together in order to thwart German and Austrian subversion in the U.S. Voska had established a small branch within his alliance (approximately 80 individuals) which functioned as a counterespionage unit. By utilizing this group of men and women, he planted operatives in the embassies and consulates of the Central Powers. Voska's spies also monitored popular German restaurants and clubs, eavesdropping on potentially revealing conversations. In the end, Gaunt received much valuable information from the Bohemian National Alliance, including tips which led to the capture of the Archibald papers.[18]

The British rapidly publicized and exposed the espionage they uncovered through the direct channels they maintained with the Wilson administration and the American media. In London, "Blinker" Hall carefully cultivated relations with the American embassy. Anglophile Ambassador Walter H. Page greatly admired Hall, calling him "one of the best and ablest servants that any Government has and a man who is as ardently American as any foreigner can be."[19] Room 40 also worked closely with Edward Bell, the secretary to the American legation. The British released many sensitive documents to Bell and Page, who were viewed as reliable friends of the Allies' war effort. Across the Atlantic, Guy Gaunt was on intimate terms with Colonel Edward House, Wilson's special adviser on foreign affairs. By the end of 1916, William Wiseman of MI6 developed an even closer relationship with House.[20]

The British sought to influence the American man on the street by providing friendly newspapers with the raw material for sensational exposés. In particular, Guy Gaunt worked with the Australian-born and English-educated editor of the *Providence Journal*, John Rathom. Rathom's colorful tales of sabotage, treachery, and betrayal brought angry and ineffectual protests from the German and Austrian embassies. Such anger was understandable given the national impact of Rathom's work. His articles were generally published simultaneously in the *Providence Journal* and the *New York Times*, and subsequently were picked up by other publications nationwide.[21]

The British produced a number of articles and books questioning the loyalty of Germans living in the United States. In April of 1915, the *Living Age* reprinted an article from the British *National Review* entitled "the Germanization of the United States." This essay claimed that Berlin planned to unduly influence the 1916 presidential election through the use of the German vote. In 1915, Frederic William Wile produced a book titled *The German-American Plot*. Wile accused German-Americans of lacking political independence and voting according to orders received from the Kaiser. In October of 1915, William Skaggs's *German-American Conspiracies in America* was published in London; this book also played up the Kaiser's alleged efforts to manipulate politics in the United States. On March 12, 1916, the *New York Times* printed a news item with a byline from the British suspense writer William Le Queux. The story claimed that a secret meeting had taken place in June of 1908, when the Kaiser had laid out plans for world conquest. Le Queux quoted William II bragging about his control of American political life:

Even now I rule supreme in the United States where almost one half of the population is either of German birth or of German descent, and where 3,000,000 voters do my bidding at the Presidential elections. No American administration could remain in power against the will of the German voters, who through that admirable organization, the German-American National League of the United States of America, control the destinies of the vast republic beyond the sea. If a man was ever worthy of a high decoration at my hands it was Herr Dr. Hexamer, the President of the League, who may be justly termed to be, by my grace, the acting ruler of all the Germans in the United States.

The Le Queux story almost certainly originated in Britain, as a piece of disinformation.[22]

Anti-German Hysteria

Germany's violations of American neutrality gradually helped to convince the nation that it was being attacked from within. Though Berlin's intrigue in the United States petered out with America's entry into the war, anti-German hysteria continued to rise. In 1918 the craze culminated with the lynching of Robert Prager, an alien unjustly accused of espionage. Many sources fueled the nation's anxiety. The German government's actions and the exposure of such actions in the press alarmed the public. Additionally, in the period 1914–17 many German-American institutions and organizations were so strident in their support of the Kaiser as to appear ambiguous in their loyalties. American political leaders and private preparedness organizations vocalized and exacerabated public concerns about German spies.

In 1910 there were 10 million Americans of German descent, of whom approximately 2.3 million were foreign-born. The size of the German minority was so great that any widespread disloyalty among this ethnic group appeared to be capable of disturbing the integrity of the nation. The Imperial Government exacerbated the public's fear of "hyphenated Americans" by recruiting German aliens and sometimes even German-American citizens for clandestine work in the United States. German Undersecretary Arthur Zimmermann compounded this problem by threatening to stir up domestic unrest in the U.S. in the event of war. In January of 1915, Zimmermann warned American ambassador James Gerard that there were "five hundred thousand trained Germans in America who would join the Irish and start a revolution." Gerard fired back that there were enough lampposts in America from which to hang all traitors.[23]

The U.S. government took the possibility of an insurrection by supporters of the Kaiser seriously. In August of 1915, Colonel House wrote of his concerns to the President:

> If our relations with Germany grow worse and if they finally come to a breaking point, are we sufficiently prepared for any outbreak which may occur within the United States?
>
> This is not looked for, but it may come and it seems to me it would be the part of wisdom to prepare in advance.

Wilson found the possibility of an armed uprising of German sympathizers "very slightly founded," but he admitted that such a prospect was not incredible.[24] No doubt Berlin's threat to spark civil war heightened pre-existing worries about the nation's German minority.

Historically, German-Americans had been viewed as prosperous, hard-working, civic-minded members of the republic. Suddenly and frighteningly they found themselves transformed from a model minority into a dangerous security threat. Unfortunately, many German-American organizations acted in ways that confirmed public prejudices.

Before America's entry into the war, the German-language press generally acted as cheerleaders for the Kaiser. These publications condemned Wilson for following biased policies and attacked the allies as the principle instigators of the war. Occasionally advertisements appeared in German language papers encouraging readers to purchase German war bonds. Space was also made available on editorial pages for official representatives of the Kaiser to lay out Berlin's viewpoint on issues relating to the war. Many Americans believed that the Central Powers subsidized the foreign language press. Hence these publications were widely seen as little more than official propaganda sheets. The revelation that the Germans funded George Viereck's national publication *Fatherland* reinforced these views.[25]

With America's entrance into the war, the German-language press came under fierce attack and microscopic scrutiny. Congress passed laws requiring that English translations of war stories be filed with the government. Some state defense councils called for an out-and-out ban on the German-language press. Advertising revenues dried up and readership levels declined. The net effect of these changes was that many German-language papers went out of business.[26]

German-Americans formed themselves into a wide range of social, charitable, and civic organizations. In 1914 the German-American Central Alliance was the largest of these organizations in the country. This group claimed a nationwide membership of over two million and was particularly strong in the Midwest. The alliance saw itself as an educational and patriotic body devoted to preserving German culture, protecting German immigrants, and bolstering the principles of democracy and civil rights. Working under the assumption that the American media and government were unduly biased toward the Allies, the alliance stoutly and often intemperately defended Germany. The organization helped to confirm charges of disloyalty made against it by ending many sessions with the playing of "Deutschland über Alles" or "Die Wacht am Rhein" and by hanging German flags in its meeting halls. Even more damning was the organization's support for German war relief and the German Red Cross. After the U.S. declared war, Congress attempted to pass legislation withdrawing the charter of the German-American Alliance. However, in July 1918, the organization preempted congressional action by dissolving itself.[27]

President Woodrow Wilson played an important part in augmenting America's fear of internal enemies. In the late summer and early fall of 1915 Wilson began to make passing comments on the dangers posed by disloyal minorities.[28] In his annual message to Congress on December 7, 1915, the President used rhetoric almost guaranteed to generate a public panic:

> There are citizens of the United States, I blush to admit, born under other flags but welcomed under our generous naturalization laws to the full freedom and opportunity of America, who have poured the poison of disloyalty into the very arteries of our national life; who have sought to bring the authority and good name of our Government into contempt, to destroy our industries wherever they thought it effective for their vindictive purposes to strike at them, and to debase our politics to the uses of foreign intrigue . . . such creatures of passion, disloyalty and anarchy must be crushed out. They are not many but they are infinitely malignant, and the hand of our power should close over them at once. They have formed plots to destroy property, they have entered into conspiracies against the neutrality of the Government, they have sought to pry into every confidential transaction of the Government in order to serve interests of their own.[29]

Following Wilson's lead, the Democratic party included a plank in its 1916 presidential platform excoriating hyphenated Americans. The President kept up his rhetorical offensive even after the United States had entered World War I. In June of 1917 he claimed that the Germans had "filled our unsuspecting communities with spies and conspirators, and sought to corrupt the opinion of our people, in their own behalf."[30]

Shortly after U.S. entry into World War I, President Woodrow Wilson issued an executive order establishing the Committee on Public Information (CPI).[31] This organization eventually played a key role in raising anti-German hysteria. Wilson appointed his longtime supporter George Creel to head the agency. The CPI and its leader quickly asserted tremendous influence over public opinion. Wilson authorized the committee to direct the release of government news at home and supervise the distribution of propaganda abroad. Domestically the CPI attempted to unify America behind the war effort. In pursuing this objective the committee issued pamphlets, news releases, advertisements, posters, and cartoons. The agency also enlisted 75,000 volunteer speakers ("Four-Minute Men") who delivered brief patriotic addresses in countless local communities. The Creel committee stressed simple themes. It demonized the enemy, defended the Allies, and promised a harmonious postwar world once the Hun was defeated.

In addition to its ability to generate stories, the committee subtly pressured the media into voluntary cooperation with the government's war program. Technically, the committee lacked the authority to censor; this power lay with the Justice Department and the Post Office. However, the CPI maintained close ties with both of these departments and shaped the way censorship policy was enforced. Moreover, as a member of the wartime censorship board, George Creel exerted considerable influence over such matters. Practically speaking, the committee could make life uncomfortable for any branch of the media which proved uncooperative.[32]

The Creel committee heightened support for the war by claiming that the Kaiser ultimately aimed at world domination. For example, a CPI pamphlet entitled *Why America Fights Germany* offered readers a frightening account of a German invasion of the United States. The fictionalized scenario described the advance of Prussian troops through New Jersey toward New York City. As the Huns advance they rob and pillage a typical American town. An old woman is hanged, while "some of the teachers in the two district schools meet a fate which make them envy her." At the end of this invasion yarn the government informed readers that the story was far from fanciful: "The general plan of campaign against America has been announced repeatedly by German military men. And every horrible detail is just what the German troops have done in Belgium and France. . . ." Other committee publications also stressed the unlimited objectives of the Kaiser. The CPI produced a map showing the United States (or New Prussia) after German conquest. The general point of these works was to let the public know that the Hun would head for America if he was not stopped in Europe.

The committee produced several pieces highlighting German intrigue in America. A pamphlet entitled *The German Whisper* held that propaganda agents for the Kaiser were active in "every community in the United States." Americans were asked to contact the Justice Department if they heard any suspicious rumors. Almost half a million copies of this pamphlet were produced. Another CPI publication, *The Kaiserite in America*, achieved circulation figures of 5.5 million and was directed principally towards traveling businessmen. The booklet warned that the Kaiser's agents ran whispering campaigns in the U.S. designed to damage home-front morale. The pamphlet credited the Germans with fabricating all kinds of lies, including a story that Woodrow Wilson's assistant Josephus Daniels had been executed as a spy. In July of 1918, a piece entitled *German Plots and Intrigues in the United States During the Period of Our Neutrality,* by Earl Sperry and Willis Mason West, detailed a range of hostile activities which Berlin had directed against America prior to Wilson's declaration of war.[33]

Anxiety over the state of America's home-front security led the Wilson administration to press for new protective legislation. On June 15, 1917, Congress passed the Espionage Act. This law made it illegal to interfere with the Selective Service Acts, to encourage U.S. servicemen to forsake their duties, or to spread rumors aimed at undermining America's war effort. The espionage bill dissatisfied Attorney General Thomas Gregory; he pushed Congress to amend the legislation. On May 16, 1918, Congress passed a stronger law, the Sedition Act. This bill banned a host of activities thought to be unpatriotic. It became an offense to speak or write any language which brought scorn or disrepute upon the United States government, the American flag, the uniform of the army or navy, or the Constitution of the United States. The bill also outlawed any actions which encouraged the cause of the Central Powers or discouraged the sale of war bonds.

Wild rumors questioning the loyalty of German-Americans raged across the country. Stories had it that the Kaiser's agents in America poisoned well water and placed ground glass in food and medical supplies sent to the front. German-American musicians were alleged to be passing along coded propaganda in the tunes they played. John Lord O'Brian, Assistant to the Attorney General, noted a number of the bizarre tales brought to the attention of the government: "submarine captains landed on our coasts went to the theatre and spread influenza germs; a new species of pigeon, thought to be German was shot in Michigan; mysterious aeroplanes floated over Kansas at night, etc."[34]

A national patriotic frenzy led to an effort to expunge all things German. Cities, streets, schools, businesses, and even foods bearing names of Germanic origin were rechristened (for example, Berlin, Ohio, was renamed Lincoln; German Street in Cinncinnati was called English Street; the Bismarck school of Chicago became the General Frederick Funston School; Germania hotels were called American hotels; sauerkraut became "liberty cabbage").[35] Schools curtailed the instruction of German and many churches halted the use of German-language services. Some localities banned the performance of German music and theater. Scattered cases were reported of the burning of German books.[36]

Anti-German hysteria resulted in the intimidation and harassment of many individuals. A private anti-spy organization, the American Protective League (APL), attracted over 260,000 volunteers. These amateur sleuths, with support from the Justice Department, conducted investigations into suspected cases of espionage, sedition, and disloyalty. The APL trumpeted the supposed spy threat through various publications.[37]

Throughout the country, citizens, whether members of the APL or not, took it upon themselves to monitor their German neighbors. Superpatriots saw tentative support for bond drives, public use of the German language, and open criticism of the government as evidence of disloyalty. Vigilante mobs occasionally beat up or tarred and feathered suspected traitors. Those deemed insufficiently patriotic were often forced to kiss the American flag or sing "The Star Spangled Banner."

The anti-German panic hit its high-water mark on April 5, 1918, when a mob of several hundred people lynched resident alien Robert Prager just outside the city limits of Collinsville, Illinois. Prior to the hanging, rumors of a planned effort to sabotage a local mine ran rife throughout the region. Suspicion focused on Prager, an irascible German-born drifter. The accusations of disloyalty leveled against him were groundless. In fact, shortly after Congress had declared war against Germany, Prager had taken out citizenship papers and had unsuccessfully applied to join the United States Navy. However, these facts proved of little consequence. At 9:30 p.m. on the evening of April 4, a mob appeared outside of Prager's door and ordered him outside. The group of approximately 75 men (mostly miners) marched the unfortunate German alien through the streets of Collinsville. An alert police officer saw what was happening and rushed to Prager's assistance; he pulled the suspected spy out of the crowd and brought him to the local police station for protection. Anxious to maintain order, the police closed the local taverns. This step proved disastrous as the initial gathering of miners soon found itself reinforced by the displaced patrons of Collinsville's drinking establishments. After some delay the crowd stormed into the local jail and spirited Prager away. Nervous police officers trailed behind the mob up to the Collinsville city limits. At this point the officers dispersed, reasoning that their jurisdiction ended at the city's frontiers. Prager repeatedly avowed his innocence, but to no avail. One of his last requests prior to his hanging was that he be buried wrapped in the American flag.

The lynching temporarily shocked the nation. The President held a cabinet meeting immediately after the episode. Several months later Woodrow Wilson released a statement opposing vigilantism. However, these comments received little fanfare and did not lead to any protective legislation. An investigation and trial of suspected ringleaders in the Collinsville mob produced no convictions. Prager's murder went unpunished.[38]

With America's victory in World War I, domestic fears regarding German spying disappeared. However, the coming of peace saw a new hysteria strike the nation. Bolshevik Russia came to be perceived as possessing many of the same traits as Wilhemine Germany: a hostility to democracy, an expansive foreign policy, and a willingness to use all sorts of treacherous means to attain any end.[39] In 1919 America's citizenry became convinced that Communist agents constituted a threat to internal security similar to the one which German spies had seemingly posed only a few years earlier. The Great Red Scare ended within a year. However, in the thirties and forties the apparent successes of authoritarian regimes in Italy, Japan, the USSR, and especially Germany helped once again to revitalize the nation's sense of its vulnerability to internal enemies. Once more Americans feared that their experiment in democracy was being challenged by insidious foes.

From 1914 to 1917, Germany conducted secret operations in America. Retrospectively, this resort to intrigue can be seen as folly. Berlin's violations of American neutrality had only a marginal impact on the war, yet such acts helped to alienate both the public and the Wilson administration. The German government, the Roosevelt administration, and the American public all drew lessons from these historical events.

As the Second World War approached, Hitler tried to avoid the appearance of meddling in internal American affairs. The Reich offered little support to the German-American Bund, cutting off relations with the organization in 1938. Nonetheless, attempts by the Nazis to distance themselves from the Bund proved futile, as the organization continued to act as though it took orders from Berlin. Ultimately, many Americans came to see the Bund as a treasonous Fifth Column organization. Another sign of the Reich's desire to avoid arousing American spy mania was Foreign Minister Ribbentrop's insistence that the Abwehr (German military intelligence) refrain from committing acts of sabotage in the United States. Admiral Wilhelm Canaris, chief of the Abwehr, agreed to this restriction. Though the Nazis continued espionage operations in the U.S., they did not attempt any acts of sabotage until after Hitler had declared war against America.[40]

From 1939 to 1941, the German chargé d'affaires Hans Thomsen repeatedly cautioned Berlin against initiating too vigorous a program of clandestine warfare in America. Thomsen warned his superiors that prior to World War I German intrigue had contributed nearly as much to America's decision to enter the war as had the termination of the *Sussex* pledge.[41] Arguing along similar lines the German military attaché Friedrich von Botticher and embassy counselor Karl Resenberg reported that "the United States would never have entered the war in 1917 had not German espionage and sabotage engendered mistrust and hatred among the American people."[42] Strangely, the embassy failed to heed its own advice and became involved in secretly funding pro-German propaganda. The Americans eventually discovered this activity (at least in part) and publicized it widely. In general, the Nazis took a more cautious approach to clandestine operations in America than had the Imperial Government. Nonetheless, the Reich remained involved in enough real Fifth Column activities to help spark and sustain a national panic.

The acute personal concern which President Franklin Roosevelt developed regarding the German Trojan Horse grew out of his World War I experiences. Throughout the Great War he had served as Woodrow Wilson's Assistant Secretary of the Navy. This position had allowed him to see the extent of German intrigue in America and made him aware of the nation's vulnerability to foreign penetration (historian Arthur Schlesinger, Jr., notes that Roosevelt carried a revolver with him for a brief time in 1917 after he was informed by the Secret Service of possible German designs on his life).[43] He fully expected Hitler to direct secret operations against America. Thus, FDR repeatedly warned the American public that it must be alive to the dangers posed by internal enemies, and he kept actively involved in the nation's counterespionage efforts. While Roosevelt feared the German Fifth Column, he wished to avoid the gross excesses of hysteria that had transpired between 1917 and 1918. One way he sought to keep a lid on popular passions was by placing the job of spybusting securely in the hands of the federal government. Roosevelt entrusted the task of domestic counterespionage to J. Edgar Hoover and the Federal Bureau of Investigation. The President saw to it that Hoover was given the authority, the men, and the money needed to overcome internal enemies. As the Second World War approached, FDR also remembered the many services which Britain had provided the Wilson administration in fighting German intrigue in America. Consequently he allowed British intelligence remarkable freedom to engage in operations on American soil.

The public did not soon forget the Kaiser's violations of American neutrality. Throughout the twenties and thirties a steady stream of popular literature appeared detailing past German spy operations in the United States. Book-length monographs, magazine articles, and newspaper features all kept Berlin's misdeeds of the 1914–17 era fresh in the public's mind. Some of this material was authored by participants in the espionage struggles of World War I. Other pieces were produced by the intelligence experts of the day. All in all, such writings reinforced widely held feelings that Germany was a treacherous foe—ready and willing to rely on Fifth Column tactics in order to achieve its objectives.

TWO

——∽∾∽——

Dangerous Demagogues,
Men on Horseback,
and Native Fascists

Fifth Column invasions depended, in part, upon a hostile outside power finding individuals and organizations ready to sell out their own nation. The United States never felt itself immune to home-grown traitors. In fact, as the thirties progressed, concern about domestic disloyalty mounted.

Shortly after Hitler's rise to power, the possibility of fascism in the United States became a matter of considerable public discussion.[1] *Harper's*, the *New Republic*, the *Nation*, *Christian Century*, and *Commonweal* ran pieces on the subject.[2] A number of monographs also addressed the matter: *Shirts*, compiled by Travis Hoke for the American Civil Liberties Union (1934); *Do We Want Fascism*, by Carmen Haider (1934); *The Choice Before Us*, by Norman Thomas (1934); and *The Forerunners of American Fascism*, by Raymond Gram Swing (1935).[3] Most of these articles and books stopped short of prophesying doom for American democracy. Instead, they tended to point out dangerous trends which suggested that the United States was more vulnerable to fascism than many cared to admit. Liberals and radicals were particularly troubled by the possibility that America might go the way of Germany and Italy. However, such fears also afflicted conservatives who detected signs of incipient fascism as well as Communism in the New Deal.

Several authors offered fictional explorations of the fascist menace. In 1934, writer Rex Stout anonymously published a hair-raising suspense thriller entitled *The President Vanishes*. This story tells of an antidemocratic conspiracy among Wall Street financiers, munitions makers, and a paramilitary group known as the Gray Shirts. In Stout's novel the

President stages his own disappearance in order to alert the public to the threat posed by his reactionary opponents. In December, Paramount studios released a cinematic rendering of *The President Vanishes* into movie theaters across America.[4]

Even more alarmist than *The President Vanishes* was Sinclair Lewis's novel *It Can't Happen Here*. This cautionary tale first appeared in bookstores across America in the autumn of 1935. The novel centers on Doremus Jessup, a liberal-spirited Vermont newspaper editor, and follows his response to the rise of totalitarianism in America.

In Lewis's story the nation's democratic system is undermined by a demagogic senator from the West, Berzelius "Buzz" Windrip. After winning the Democratic nomination for the presidency, Windrip pledges to redistribute the nation's wealth and panders to America's racial and religious prejudices. His campaign is assisted by a canny publicity agent named Lee Sarason and a radio minister named Bishop Prang. Unscrupulous Wall Street moneymen provide Windrip with financial backing and an organization known as the Minutemen gives him the muscle to intimidate opponents. In the general election Windrip defeats Republican candidate Walt Trowbridge and "Jefferson" party candidate Franklin Roosevelt.

Upon gaining the White House, the new President takes responsibility for all powers of governance. Dissenting congressmen and Supreme Court Justices are jailed. Shortly after the election, Windrip's publicity agent Lee Sarason seizes control of the government. Sarason, in turn, is ousted from power by the Secretary of War, Colonel Dewey Haik. Haik militarizes the nation, initiating an expansionist war with Mexico. His regime quashes all civil liberties, transforming America into a "corporative" state. An American S.S., known as the "Corpo's," terrorizes the citizenry. The government interns suspected enemies in concentration camps.

In the face of such developments, the novel's hero joins an underground resistance movement aimed at overthrowing the government. The resistance has some reason to cheer when a democratic rebellion flares up in the western part of the United States. However, this insurgency bogs down. Lewis makes it clear that a number of Americans are firmly devoted to the "Corpo" state. His character Shad Ledue epitomizes the sort of disgruntled lower-middle-class figures who find satisfaction in serving the new fascist regime. At the novel's conclusion most of America is still under Corpo control. In spite of this, Lewis finishes his story with the hopeful, if hokey, message that "a Doremus Jessup can never die."[5]

In February 1936, Metro-Goldwyn-Mayer generated a national sensation when it backed out of plans to produce a cinematic rendering of *It Can't Happen Here*. While Lewis's story was still in the manuscript stage, MGM purchased the film rights and began initial production work. The studio assigned Pulitzer prize-winning dramatist Sidney Howard to craft a screenplay and slated actor Lionel Barrymore to play the film's leading role. However, Joseph Breen of the Production Code Administration warned Louis B. Mayer that *It Can't Happen Here* was likely to cause considerable controversy overseas. Breen called the proposed feature "inflammatory" and "dangerous."[6] Fearing the loss of foreign revenues, the studio put the film on the shelf. This act brought huzzahs from Germany and Italy.[7] However, author Sinclair Lewis was outraged by MGM's decision, which he called "a fantastic exhibition of folly and cowardice."[8]

In the wake of the Lewis-MGM brouhaha, book sales for *It Can't Happen Here* doubled.[9] The novel soared to fifth place on the bestseller list for 1936.[10] Denied access to the silver screen, Lewis turned to the stage, offering an adaptation of his novel to the WPA Federal Theatre Project. In the fall of 1936, a theatrical version of *It Can't Happen Here* opened in eighteen different cities across America.[11] The story's "worst case" scenario of the fascist menace thus gained an unusual popularity nationwide.

Most reviewers of *It Can't Happen Here* doubted the plausibility of the events described in its pages. *Newsweek* noted that Lewis had "taken the bit in his teeth and galloped off to never-never land."[12] *Time* added that the book presented a kind of dictatorship "too weird to be convincing or alarming."[13] The *New York Times* averred that Lewis's novel transported the horrors of German and Soviet totalitarianism "too completely" to America.[14] Benjamin Stolberg, reviewer for the *New York Herald Tribune*, scoffed at the possibility of a fascist takeover in America:

> As yet we have no effective revolutionary movement against which European fascism is a crazed reaction. And we have no part of a medieval barbarism, toward which fascism is a psychopathic reversion, the only past we have are the two American revolutions, the Revolutionary and the Civil wars, whose conceptions of political democracy and middle class economy have been plowed under the American mind a thousand times.[15]

There were some critics who felt differently. For example, Clifton Fadiman of the *New Yorker* warned: "It can happen here. Read Lewis's book and find out how." Fadiman went so far as to claim that it was "a public duty" to read Lewis's novel.[16] Nonetheless, such views were rare. Lewis himself expressed considerable confidence in America's resilience to fascism. He told reporters that as long as the spirit of free inquiry remained alive, "it won't happen here."[17]

It Can't Happen Here was rightly seen as an overdrawn and hysterical tale. Still, part of the story's appeal lay in its ability to play on the twinge of concern which many Americans, not just those on the left, felt about native fascism. This subdued anxiety was grounded in historical realities. Throughout the pre-World War II period, demagogues, potential men on horseback, and native fascists increasingly captured the public's attention.

The thirties witnessed the emergence of several charismatic political insurgents such as Huey Long, Charles Coughlin, Francis Townsend, Gerald L. K. Smith, and Gerald Winrod. These individuals won over mass followings by identifying ready scapegoats for the nation's difficulties and by promising simple solutions to America's many problems. The popularity of such men and their ability to profit from the despair caused by the Depression was widely interpreted as a symptom of the weakened state of American democracy. Some observers feared that a fickle public might turn to a "strong" leader who was little concerned with the niceties of constitutional government.

The Depression decade gave rise to numerous rumors of armed conspiracies against American democracy. In 1930, a paramilitary group known as the Khaki Shirts threatened a Mussolini-style march on Washington. In 1934, retired Marine General Smedley Butler told Congress that he had been asked by Wall Street interests to lead a veterans' army 500,000 strong against the government. In 1939, Congress unraveled an apparent attempt to unify several native fascist groups behind retired Army General George Van Horn Moseley. None of these military "plots" ever amounted to much and none of them caused an all-out national panic. Yet the existence of such stories reveals the lingering, if controlled, anxiety which permeated the country.

The proliferation of anti-semitic, pro-fascist organizations proved an even more worrisome development during the thirties. In fact, these extremist groups lacked the power to threaten the government. Still, they did win enough of a following and enough media coverage to generate considerable public suspicion. The activities of the German-American Bund were particularly distressing because of the Bund's apparent submission to the orders of a foreign principal. The notion of enemy states offering aid, comfort, and direction to domestic radicals quite understandably troubled many citizens.

In retrospect, it is clear that during the thirties totalitarianism had little chance of succeeding in America. Yet for those living through the tumultuous decade, this fact was not so obvious. Overseas, one nation after another turned to dictatorial governments. At home, there were enough danger signs to at least justify a modicum of concern that Nazi Germany—and other totalitarian states—might find in America enough raw material to create a dangerous, anti-democratic Trojan Horse.

Demagogues

In a decade full of demagogues there was none greater than Huey Long. Long earned a national reputation as a cunning, charismatic, and ruthless political operator. His boundless ambition and authoritarian style led many contemporary critics to conclude that he had all the makings of an American dictactor.[18]

In 1928, Long won the governorship of Louisiana. Over the next four years he established hegemony over the state legislature, state courts, and government bureaucracy. Long used his power to push through extensive public improvements: he built highways, bridges, hospitals, and schools. His programs were funded through a combination of higher corporate taxes and increased public borrowing. The Kingfish—a nickname attached to Long after a character on the "Amos 'n' Andy" radio show—won the adulation and political support of the poor and the near-poor. Members of this constituency proved his most steadfast allies.

In 1932, Long won election to the United States Senate. After this victory, he maintained and even strengthened his iron grip over Louisiana politics. The Kingfish handpicked his successor to the governorship, a servile yes-man named Oscar K. ("O.K.") Allen. He regularly shuttled back and forth between Washington and Baton Rouge, keeping a keen eye on his political fiefdom. Long's control over his state was so complete that the press exaggerated only slightly when it described him as "the dictator of Louisiana."[19]

Long was viewed with considerable skepticism and some fear by Washington insiders. He soon alienated his Senate colleagues as well as President Roosevelt. Long's perceived neglect of his congressional duties, his political grandstanding, and his willingness to insult fellow legislators made him a despised figure on Capitol Hill. The situation was no better with the White House. In 1932, FDR allegedly identified Long, along with General Douglas MacArthur, as one of the two most dangerous men in America. Despite his personal feelings, Roosevelt tried to work with the Louisiana senator. However, by June 1933, Long's jibes at the administration led to a termination of the rapprochement. Roosevelt began selecting the Kingfish's political opponents for federal patronage jobs in Louisiana. From that point until Long's death in 1935, relations with the administration went downhill.[20]

Long's isolation from other Democrats did not lead to his political demise. Instead, he carved out an independent power base. His quotability and flamboyant style allowed him to make effective use of the media. Through the radio and press he offered Americans an alternative to the New Deal. The Kingfish argued that poverty could be ended by distributing national wealth more equitably. In 1933 he called upon the Senate to outlaw both inheritances greater than $5 million and annual personal income exceeding $1 million. All revenues generated from this program of confiscatory government taxation were to go to the needy. Long's attempt at soaking the rich made no headway in Congress.

In 1934, the Kingfish introduced the "Share Our Wealth" plan, a more sweeping effort to redistribute America's economic resources. This proposal offered a little something for everyone. All families in America were to be guaranteed a homestead—including car, radio, and residence—worth $5000, and an annual income of $2000 to $2500. Long's plan promised pensions to those over sixty, college scholarships for talented but impoverished young people, bonuses to World War I veterans, protected wages and limited hours for workers, and government purchases of surplus agricultural products for farmers. The scheme was pure fantasy. The country did not have enough millionaires to provide adequate funding for Long's program. Moreover, much of the nation's concentrated wealth was difficult to break down into liquid assets which could be divvied up among the poor.

In spite of these problems, Long's "Share Our Wealth" plan had a powerful populist appeal. The Kingfish skillfully promoted his scheme, urging supporters across America to form "Share Our Wealth" clubs. Such organizations began to spring up nationwide. Long soon claimed that his movement numbered seven million strong. While this figure was exaggerated, the Kingfish clearly attracted a mass following and was especially strong in the South.

Long had ambitions for national power. He spent much of 1935 attacking "Prince Franklin" and his advisors. He accused Postmaster General James Farley of corruption, described Secretary of Agriculture Henry Wallace as "the ignoramus of Iowa," and referred to Secretary of Interior Harold Ickes as the "chinch bug of Chicago."[21] Long also stepped up his criticism of Roosevelt administration policies. He opposed the World Court, decried the Wagner Act as inadequate, and denounced the National Recovery Act as a form of government despotism. Long's actions suggest that he was mulling over a presidential run, if not in 1936 then in 1940. In fact, he publicly admitted that a try for the White House was a possibility. How far his political career might have gone will never be known, because in September 1935 he was assassinated.

If Huey Long was the most notorious of the thirties demagogues then Father Charles Coughlin ran a close second. Using the new medium of radio Coughlin turned himself into a national political power. He originally preached much the same message as Long, attacking the monied interests and calling for a broader distribution of wealth. By the time of the Pearl Harbor attack his rhetoric had taken a disquieting turn toward anti-semitism, and he was widely viewed as a pro-German propagandist. Only the protection afforded by his priestly status shielded him from a Justice Department prosecution for seditious activity.[22]

In October 1926, Coughlin gave his first radio sermon over station

WJR in Detroit. He hoped to use the airwaves in order to spread the gospel and to raise funds for his newly established parish in Royal Oak, Michigan. The young priest possessed a pleasing voice and became an instant hit with Detroit-area listeners. Leo Fitzpatrick, the station manager at WJR, made Coughlin's talks a regular Sunday feature. The cleric's popularity grew and within a year his homilies were heard throughout Michigan. In the autumn of 1930 Coughlin went national. CBS signed the priest to a contract which allowed him to reach an estimated audience of 40 million Americans in 23 different states.[23]

At first, Coughlin's talks focused on religious matters. However, after 1930 he increasingly spoke out on secular affairs, attacking communism, prohibition, and birth control. As the Depression worsened Coughlin heaped scorn upon the nation's bankers and financiers. He lost patience with Herbert Hoover and harshly condemned the government's tight money policies. CBS grew uncomfortable with the political tone of Coughlin's talks and—despite the priest's indisputable popularity—dropped his contract in 1931. NBC also shied away from the controversial cleric. Undaunted, Coughlin purchased air time on radio stations throughout the country, thus assuring himself access to a national audience.

During the 1932 election campaign Father Coughlin savaged Herbert Hoover, denouncing the embattled incumbent as a tool of concentrated wealth. Though the radio priest did not explictly endorse any candidate, he was clearly delighted with Roosevelt's landslide victory. Coughlin presumed that he had played a major part in the election's outcome and expected that the new President would turn to him for advice. In the early days of FDR's presidency Coughlin's sermons fulsomely praised the administration, pronouncing the New Deal "Christ's Deal" and telling listeners that it was either "Roosevelt or ruin."[24]

From 1934 to 1935 Coughlin gradually grew disenchanted with FDR. The White House's monetary policies helped create a rift with Roosevelt, for the radio priest believed in an inflated currency under the supervision of the federal government. Coughlin insisted upon the coinage of silver. He also proposed abolishing the Federal Reserve Bank and replacing it with a government bank. This central bank was to be run by democratically elected representatives and would supposedly keep Wall Street plutocrats from controlling the nation's economy. Roosevelt balked at such measures. Coughlin saw the President's hesitancy as a sell-out to financial and banking interests. Yet more than issues alone were responsible for Coughlin's feud with the White House. Roosevelt's unwillingness to admit Coughlin into his inner circle rankled the cleric and made him more willing to criticize the President.

In November 1934, Coughlin founded the National Union for Social Justice (NUSJ). He argued that this organization would lobby for the interests of ordinary people of all races and religious persuasions. The

NUSJ took its inspiration from Pope Leo XIII's encyclical letter *Rerum Novarum* (1891) and Pope Pius XI's follow-up encyclical *Quadragiesmo Anno* (1931). Both papal documents decried the evils of unregulated capitalism and insisted upon the need to respect the dignity of laborers. Coughlin laid out a series of sixteen principles for his National Union. These principles endorsed the private ownership of property, but also backed a more equitable distribution of wealth. Coughlin believed that Communism and laissez-faire capitalism both suffered from the problem of concentrating ownership in the hands of a few. As the radio priest grew dissatisfied with the New Deal he increasingly moved to use the NUSJ as a foundation for nationwide political action.[25]

Coughlin's disappointment with the White House led him to intensify his participation in the political process. In March 1936, he started up *Social Justice*, a weekly publication which mirrored his views on a range of public issues. One month later Coughlin mobilized the NUSJ for involvement in upcoming primary elections in Pennsylvania and Ohio. NUSJ-backed candidates performed indifferently, winning only 12 of 24 elections in Pennsylvania and only 12 of 32 races in Ohio.[26] Nonetheless, Coughlin boasted that his National Union had become a political force that could not be ignored. When neither the Republican nor Democratic parties sought his support, the priest moved to create a third party. In June he met with Republican William Lemke, a populist congressman from North Dakota. Shortly thereafter the Union party was created and Lemke announced his candidacy for the presidency.[27]

Coughlin was the key agent behind the creation of the Union party. However, Lemke also depended on backing from Dr. Francis Townsend. Townsend was the leader of a national drive for government-sponsored old-age pensions: each individual over sixty years of age was to be guaranteed a monthly pension of $200. Recipients were required to spend this money within 30 days and to give up all forms of employment. Funding for the pensions was to be derived from a 2 percent transaction tax which would be applied every time a commodity changed hands. Townsend backers saw the pensions as a way to protect the elderly, open up jobs, and stimulate the economy. In fact, the plan was a chimera which would have bankrupted the country for the benefit of one group. Historian Arthur Schlesinger, Jr., notes that the proposal would have meant transferring one half of the nation's income to one-eleventh of its population. Moreover, the 2 percent transaction tax was regressive and favored big business. Despite the Townsend plan's obvious shortcomings, many Americans rallied around it. In 1936, the movement claimed three and a half million supporters.[28]

Dr. Townsend shared Coughlin's contempt for FDR. The physician was angry at the White House's refusal to accept his pension plan and resented the rough treatment he had received in congressional hearings from New Deal supporters. Townsend thus succumbed to Coughlin and Lemke's call for a third party run for the presidency.

Dr. Townsend lacked the flair and speaking power of Father Coughlin. However, Townsend's lieutenant Gerald L. K. Smith was an oratorical match for the radio priest. Smith, a former supporter of Huey Long's Share Our Wealth movement, latched on to the old-age pension movement in 1936. Together with Coughlin he stumped for the Lemke campaign through the summer and early fall. The two men indulged in over-the-top campaign rhetoric. Coughlin called FDR a "communist," "liar," and "doublecrosser." Smith accused the President of planning to create a dictactorship.[29] Such bitter invective backfired, discrediting Coughlin and Smith far more than it did FDR.

Smith proved a liability for the Union party. In October, while the presidential campaign was nearing an end, he announced the creation of an independent anti-Communist organization. Smith vowed that this new group, the Committee of One Million, would seize control of the government. For this action he was repudiated by the Lemke campaign and the Townsend movement. Townsend assured his followers that he had no sympathy for fascism.[30]

The Union party failed miserably in the November elections, for many reasons. Lemke was a bland, uninspiring candidate who was consistently overshadowed by his more charismatic backers. The coalition among Coughlinites and Townsendites was the product of pure pragmatism and the two movements did not work well together. The party lacked organizational structure at the local level and failed to make it on the ballot in many states. Consequently, Lemke gained less than a million votes in November. This was a humbling experience for Coughlin, who had vowed that he would give up his broadcast career if the Union party did not take in at least nine million votes (Despite his promise, the radio priest returned to the air within a few months. He claimed that this was the dying wish of Archbishop Michael Gallagher, his longtime friend and superior.)[31]

By 1938 Father Coughlin's popularity had declined, but it was still estimated that 10 percent of those who owned radios listened to him.[32] Unfortunately, Coughlin's sermons veered off toward anti-semitism. He increasingly identified his personal bogeymen—Communists, bankers, and financiers—with Jews. *Social Justice* reflected the same bigotry, printing the *Protocols of the Learned Elders of Zion*, a tsarist forgery purporting to expose an international Jewish conspiracy to destroy Christianity.

Coughlin's activities encouraged anti-semites to commit acts of thuggery. In May-July 1938 the radio priest urged the creation of a Christian Front in order to combat Communism. Christian Front groups sprang up in Boston, New Haven, Hartford, and New York. These organizations were marked by intense anti-semitism. Working- and lower-middle-class Catholics made up the bulk of the group's rank and file membership; better-educated professionals manned the front's leadership positions. Coughlin exerted little control over these groups once they were organized. Christian Front activity was most intense in New York City where Fronters organized boycotts of Jewish merchants and helped incite street fights with Jews.[33]

In January 1940, the Federal Bureau of Investigation arrested a group of eighteen individuals, most of whom were connected with New York City's Christian Front, and charged them with plotting to overthrow the United States government. None of the accused was convicted. However, a highly publicized trial revealed the Christian Fronters to be a group of unbalanced cranks and successfully discredited the entire movement.

In 1939 a small ultra-reactionary group splintered off from the Christian Front and formed the Christian Mobilizers. This break occurred because the Mobilizers favored increased violence against Jews and Communists; they also backed open cooperation with the German-American Bund. These extreme anti-semites were led by Joseph McWilliams, a man whom radio commentator Walter Winchell dubbed "Joe McNazi."[34]

McWilliams grabbed headlines when he launched a bid for election to the House of Representatives in New York's 18th Congressional District. He created the American Destiny party and endorsed an anti-semitic, pro-dictatorship platform. McWilliams appeared at speaking engagements in a covered wagon—symbol of America's pioneer spirit. His speeches consisted of far right ravings: "Adolf Hitler is the greatest leader in the history of the world . . . Herbert Hoover is mentally deficient and Roosevelt is an amateur Englishman, a Jew, and the leader of the Fifth Column in this country."[35] When President Roosevelt heard of McWilliams's political activities, he ordered the Justice Department to investigate.[36] The American Destiny party demonstrated little popular appeal, winning barely 1000 votes in the general election. Father Coughlin disclaimed any attachment to the Christian Mobilizers, publicly rejecting a donation from McWilliams to the NUSJ.

Despite the radio priest's shunning of McWilliams, many interventionists were convinced that Coughlin was a Nazi Fifth Columnist. They pointed to his overt anti-semitism, generous interpretation of Nazi actions, and endless attacks on Britain. In the wake of the *Kristallnacht* (a pogram directed by the Nazis against Germany's Jewish population), Coughlin defended National Socialism as a reasonable response to Communism and downplayed the actual violence which had been directed against German Jews. After the invasion of Poland, he claimed that Britain had gone to war with Germany for purely economic reasons. He applauded the Nazi attack on Stalin's Soviet Union as an important blow against Communism. Coughlin repeatedly urged America to pursue a noninterventionist "Fortress America" foreign policy.[37]

In 1939 the National Association of Broadcasters designed a code aimed at removing Coughlin from the airwaves. The NAB placed severe limits on the sale of radio time to those speaking out on controversial political issues. New rules allowed for discussion of such matters only during free time. Additionally, each radio station reserved the right to examine the content of all prospective broadcasts on public issues. These steps pushed Coughlin off the air in the fall of 1940.[38] Removed from broadcasting, he focused most of his energies on *Social Justice*. The government acted to shut down this publication after America's formal entry into the war. In the spring of 1942, emissaries from the Roosevelt administration warned Bishop Edward Mooney of Detroit that the Justice Department was considering filing charges against Coughlin unless he withdrew from all political activities. Mooney ordered his subordinate to retire from public life or face defrockment. Coughlin complied with this ultimatum and quietly lived the rest of his days out of the public eye.

Father Coughlin was not the only clerical figure linked to domestic fascism. Gerald K. Winrod, an evangelical minister based in Kansas, was also suspected of anti-democratic leanings.[39] In 1925 Winrod founded the Defenders of the Christian Faith. This group attacked liberal theology, evolution, and the nation's alleged decline in morality. Thanks to Winrod's organizational and preaching skills, membership in the Defenders of the Christian Faith soared. By 1934 the group's principal publication, *The Defender*, had 60,000 subscribers; four years later circulation was up to 110,000.[40]

Over time Winrod's preaching took on an increasingly anti-semitic tone. He expressed belief in the validity of *The Protocols of the Learned Elders of Zion*, publishing it in the *Defender*. By 1934 Winrod overcame his initial skepticism of Nazism and began expressing growing sympathy for the Third Reich. He lauded Germany as a bulwark against Communism and displayed little outrage over Hitler's harsh treatment of Germany's Jews. Winrod's liberal opponents soon were characterizing him as "the Jayhawk Nazi."

In 1938, Winrod entered the Republican primary for Senate in Kansas. Newspaper editor William Allen White nervously informed the White House that Winrod—"a Fascist, raw and unashamed"—had a good shot at electoral victory. L. M. Birkhead, a Unitarian minister in Kansas and the executive director of Friends of Democracy, organized an effective campaign against Winrod. Birkhead suggested that Berlin was supplying the fundamentalist preacher with funds and ideas. Such tactics put Winrod on the defensive. He used several of his radio addresses to deny any affection for either Nazism or fascism, and he claimed allegiance only to Americanism. Winrod ultimately placed third in the Republican primary, winning approximately 50,000 votes.[41] After the election he continued to be accused of ties to Berlin. In May 1939, the *Saturday Evening Post* named Winrod as a Fifth Columnist.[42] The minister's estranged wife lent credence to such charges when she claimed that her husband planned on taking over the country after it had experienced a revolution (Mrs. Winrod recanted these accusations after she had reconciled with her husband).[43] The federal government remained suspicious of Winrod. In 1942 the Justice Department included his name in a suit filed against 33 of the country's suspected seditionists. These charges were eventually dismissed.

Demagogues such as Long, Coughlin, and Winrod were feared because of their ability to cloud the public's judgment and perhaps seize power through the democratic process. A less prominent but recurring worry during the thirties was the possibility of a military coup. An individual with control over armed men might imitate Benito Mussolini and forcibly take over the reins of government. For Americans living through the Depression this possibility was not entirely incredible.

In 1932 a paramilitary organization known as the Khaki Shirts was formed. A flim-flam man named Art Smith gained control of the group and located his national headquarters in Philadelphia, Pennsylvania. Smith appointed his wife as treasurer of the organization and set membership fees at $2. He boasted that the Khaki Shirts had 10 million members (however, when forced to testify under oath he claimed only 10,000 followers). Smith also said his adherents possessed rifles, machine guns, tanks, and artillery. The Khaki Shirts backed a hodgepodge of policies, which included: the establishment of a thirty-hour work week; the inflation of America's currency; the strengthening of the army; and the deportation of radicals.

The organization aroused fierce opposition from the left. In July 1933, anti-fascist radicals interrupted a Khaki Shirt rally in Astoria, New York. A scuffle ensued, shots were fired, and one of the protestors was killed. Smith accused one of the radicals of having committed the crime. This charge was false and eventually landed the Khaki Shirt leader in jail. In April 1934, he was convicted of perjury.

In the middle of 1933, Smith announced plans to organize a march on Washington. The stated goal of this venture was to make Franklin Roosevelt dictator of the United States. Smith boasted that he would inundate the capital with 1.5 million Khaki Shirters. The march was set to take place on Columbus Day. On October 11, a group of approximately 1000 men gathered in Philadelphia. Though the men had been promised transportation to Washington, Art Smith had made no arrangements for buses. As the day wore on and the crowd grew more restive, Smith decided a strategic getaway was in order. He slipped out one of the windows of Khaki Shirt headquarters. Shortly after Smith's escape, the Philadelphia police raided the organization's headquarters. Law enforcement officers uncovered a small number of rifles and handguns. They arrested 27 Khaki Shirters on charges of firearms violations.

Despite Smith's absence, the March on Washington did take place, though turnout proved to be considerably less than 1.5 million. On October 12, 1933, some 44 Khaki Shirters from Baltimore, Maryland, and Camden, New Jersey, descended on the nation's capital. A police escort met the tiny caravan, made up of three automobiles and two battered trucks, at the Washington D.C., city line. The group, which included six "generals" and four "colonels," was conveyed to a local precinct station and told to go home. With this inglorious end the Khaki Shirts disappeared from history.[44]

In November 1934, retired marine general and two-time Congressional Medal of Honor winner Smedley Butler lent credence to the possibility of a military takeover of the government. In an appearance before the McCormack-Dickstein committee, Butler claimed to have headed off a coup attempt by Wall Street interests. The general testified that Gerald C. MacGuire, a bond salesman for Grayson M. P. Murphy, had asked him to organize a veteran's army of half a million men. This force was to be used to seize control of the government and ease FDR out of power. Paul Comly French, a reporter for the *New York Evening Post* and *Philadelphia Record,* supported Butler's claim. French testified that he had met with Maguire and that the bond salesman had said:

We need a fascist government in this country to save the Nation from the Communists who want to tear it down and wreck all that we have built in America. The only men who have the patriotism to do it are the soldiers and Smedley Butler is the ideal leader. He could organize one million men over night.

When asked about these matters, Maguire denied any involvement in a coup plot.[45] After Butler and French's testimony no additional evidence of a conspiracy was made public. The story thus quickly disappeared from the nation's headlines.

If Butler had proven himself a democrat, other military men seemed less reliable. In September 1938, George Van Horn Moseley, a retired general in the United States Army, issued a stinging attack on Franklin Roosevelt and the New Deal. In the ensuing months Moseley made several violently anti-semitic and anti-Communist speeches. He also maintained contact with a number of right-wing extremist groups. Later in the year George Deatherage of the Knights of the White Camelia went to Atlanta to visit Moseley. Over the course of several weeks Deatherage outlined to the general a plan to bring many anti-communist groups (including groups with fascist leanings) together in one organization under Moseley's leadership. Though Moseley backed the objective of a broad front against left-wing subversion, he balked at Deatherage's proposal.[46]

In the spring of 1939, House Un-American Activities Committee investigators exposed this intrigue. James Campbell (a captain in the Army Reserve), George Deatherage, and George Van Horn Moseley were asked to testify before Congress. HUAC revealed to the public several documents which seemed to implicate the three men in a fascist conspiracy against the government. On December 14, 1938, Deatherage wrote to Campbell: "I believe as you do that it will take military action to get this gang out and the organization must be built around a fighting force. That's the idea of the boss [Moseley] also, but must be kept on the Q.T."[47] Moseley flatly, and apparently truthfully, denied having accepted Deatherage's schemes. Nonetheless, the general's testimony was troubling. Moseley excused Nazism and fascism as necessary antitoxins to the disease of Communism: "They [pro-Nazi groups] are trying to sustain our democracy and the other fellows [Communists] are trying to destroy it. . . ."[48] Moseley defended the Bund's Madison Square Garden rally as a patriotic gathering. The general did not back down from past anti-semitic statements, which included charges that those who favored war with the Axis powers were working for "Jewish hegemony throughout the world."[49] Several periodicals put forward Moseley as America's most likely man on horseback.[50] For a time the general came to symbolize the threat which reactionary elements of the military posed to democracy.[51]

A number of radical right-wing organizations were formed during the thirties. The most controversial of these groups was the German-American Bund. In May 1933, Rudolf Hess authorized Heinz Spanknobel to establish a new American Nazi organization.[52] The German consul in New York and various leaders of preexisting fascist groups helped Spanknobel create the Friends of the New Germany (FONG). FONG openly proclaimed its desire to spread National Socialism throughout America. The organization was divided into three administrative departments: East Coast, Midwest, and West Coast. Spanknobel centered his own activities in New York City. (Prior to World War II, Gotham remained the headquarters for American Nazi activities.)

Spanknobel proved a vigorous leader of the Friends. However, his activities gained widespread notoriety and helped lead to press and governmental investigations of American Nazism. Spanknobel tried to gain a position of influence over New York City's entire German-American community. In 1933 he stormed into the offices of the German-language paper *New Yorker Staats-Zeitung* and insisted that the editors publish stories supportive of the Third Reich. The paper refused Spanknobel's demand and made public his effort to influence editorial policy. Spanknobel also endeavored to infiltrate the United German Societies, an organization composed of hundreds of New York City's various German-American groups. Mayor Fiorello La Guardia and congressman Samuel Dickstein (D, New York) both voiced concern over Spanknobel's activities. In fact, Dickstein urged that the FONG leader be deported. In October 1933, a federal grand jury indicted Spanknobel for failing to register as a foreign agent. Faced with government prosecution, he left America and returned to Germany.[53]

The Friends of New Germany continued to function after Spanknobel's departure. From 1933 to 1935, FONG maintained 5000 to 10,000 members.[54] The most important posts in the organization tended to be occupied by German citizens who belonged to the National Socialist party. The Friends' rank-and-file membership was principally composed of German citizens who had initiated the naturalization process and German émigrés who had only recently received American citizenship.

The Friends of New Germany attacked Jews, Communism, and the Versailles treaty. Until 1935, the Third Reich was quite supportive of FONG. Berlin hoped that the group might consolidate German-Americans behind National Socialism and tilt American public opinion toward a more favorable view of the Reich. Several agencies of the German government maintained close contact with the Friends, offering the American group both advice and money. Berlin also used FONG in order to disseminate propaganda in America.

FONG was widely viewed as part of a "Nazi-intern." In March 1934, the House of Representatives established a committee to examine subversive propaganda in the United States with a special focus on "the extent, character, and objects of Nazi propaganda." John McCormack chaired the committee, and Samuel Dickstein served as vice-chair. McCormack performed his job in a cautious and responsible fashion. He avoided sensational public accusations and held most of the committee's hearings in closed executive sessions. Throughout the course of the investigation, Congressman Dickstein behaved in a less restrained manner. He repeatedly voiced alarm at the extent of Nazi activities in the U.S. Dickstein placed FONG membership at ten times its actual number and publicly accused Berlin of smuggling weapons to Nazi sympathizers in the United States.[55] In February 1935, the committee released a report of its findings, noting that home-front Nazis had targeted "20-odd-million Americans of German birth or descent." The report also said that evidence existed that the Friends received orders and cash from the German government.[56]

The Reich soon saw that its support for the Friends of New Germany irritated the general American public and failed to win over German-Americans to Nazism. In December 1935, Rudolf Hess ordered that all German citizens leave FONG. Berlin's order proved fatal to the Friends, since Reich nationals made up 60 percent of the organization's membership.[57] Germany helped further destroy the Friends by recalling to the Fatherland many of the group's leaders.

In March 1936, the formation of the German-American Bund (Amerikadeutscher Volksbund, or AV) filled the vacuum left by FONG's collapse. An AV convention in Buffalo, New York, selected Fritz Kuhn, a

former member of the Friends, as *Bundesleiter*. The Bund was not supposed to accept German citizens among its members. Nonetheless, the
AV eluded compliance with this request. Kuhn proved an able leader.
He curtailed intra-bund squabbling, expanded AV membership, and
made his organization a profit-making venture.[58]

The Bund backed the concept of pan-Germanism, praised Hitler's
achievements, and warned of a worldwide Jewish/Bolshevik conspiracy.
Bundists lashed out against Franklin Roosevelt, opposing him in both
the 1936 and 1940 elections. The AV newspaper claimed that Roosevelt
was under the influence of a Jewish clique which allegedly included Bernard Baruch, Henry Morgenthau, Felix Frankfurter, Frances Perkins,
and Adolf Berle (although the latter two were Protestant). The Bund
proved strongly isolationist and after Hitler's invasion of Poland counseled America to practice neutrality.

The Bund left little doubt of its attitude toward Nazism. The organization's rallies featured swastikas, Nazi salutes, German songs, and pae-
ans to Hitler's Third Reich. The AV set up an American version of the
Hitler youth, in which children were instructed in German language,
German history, and National Socialist philosophy. The Bund also established a number of recreational camps throughout the country. The
most notorious were Camp Nordland in Andover, New Jersey, and
Camp Siegfried in Yaphank, Long Island. Bund camps acted as recreational magnets for thousands of vacationers.

The Reich distrusted Fritz Kuhn's organization. Kuhn, on the other
hand, falsely boasted of close ties with the leaders of Germany. In 1936
a Bund contingent visited Berlin and met with Hitler. Photographs were
taken of Kuhn and the Fuehrer together. The AV leader used his courtesy
visit as proof of Hitler's support. At the urging of the German Foreign
Office, Hitler made his discontent with the Bund unambiguous. On
March 1, 1938, Berlin barred German citizens from membership in the
AV and outlawed the use of German emblems by the organization. Historian Sander Diamond has concluded that Germany's "relationship
with the Bund was of no consequence after March 1, 1938."[59] Despite
this objective reality, the perception lingered in the media, the government, and the public that a close alliance existed between the AV and
Hitler. In October of 1939, *Look* magazine ran a picture of a Bund
camp with the headline "Hitler speaks, the Bund obeys."[60]

The government launched a number of investigations into the AV. In
the summer of 1937, Attorney General Homer Cummings announced
an FBI probe of the Bund. However, a few months later the Bureau
reported that it had been unable to uncover the violation of any federal
laws. In May 1938, Samuel Dickstein persuaded Congress of the need
to conduct yet another examination of subversive doings in the United
States. Martin Dies of Texas was selected to head the House Un-
American Activities Committee. The Bund and Fritz Kuhn, along with

suspected Communist and Communist-front groups, became major targets of the Dies committee.[61]

In February 1939, the Bund held a "Pro-American" rally at Madison Square Garden in honor of George Washington's birthday. Fritz Kuhn addressed a crowd of 22,000. Kuhn favorably compared Hitler to Washington, ferociously attacked FDR, and boasted that his organization would have over a million members by 1940. Kuhn delivered his address while standing in front of a thirty-foot portrait of George Washington. Mayor Fiorello La Guardia dispatched 2000 New York City policemen to insure order at the gathering. Kuhn also had 3000 members of the fighting arm of the Bund, the Ordnungs-Dienst (OD), present at the rally. The police and stormtroopers lent a martial air to the gathering. This feeling grew as fistfights sporadically broke out between the O.D. and various hecklers in the audience. The bizarre meeting gained international press coverage and helped to unnerve the American public.[62]

After the Madison Square Garden rally, the Bund's fortune took a turn for the worse. New York District Attorney Thomas Dewey successfully prosecuted Fritz Kuhn for larceny and forgery. With Kuhn in prison the AV suffered internal divisions and financial difficulties. Moreover, historian Leland Bell has noted that due to a number of repressive measures taken at the federal and state level "the Bund was harassed out of existence."[63] Congress prohibited Bundists from participating in WPA work. HUAC and the FBI conducted extensive investigations into the AV's operations. At the state level, California began an inquiry into Bund activities and New Jersey officials closed down Camp Nordland. Faced with massive organizational problems and intense public disapproval, the Bund dissolved itself on December 8, 1941, the day after the Pearl Harbor attack. The federal government took control of the AV's records a few days later and confined several of the group's leaders.[64]

The Bund's apparent subservience to foreign interests made it the most despised of the radical right groups in pre-World War II America. No other Nazi Fifth Column group received as much attention from the public. Nonetheless, other extremist organizations in the United States shared many of the Bund's principles.

The rise of Adolf Hitler to the chancellorship of Germany inspired William Dudley Pelley to found an organization modeled after the Nazi S.S.[65] This group, the Silver Shirts, was based in Asheville, North Carolina. Members posed as protectors of Christianity against "Judeo-Bolsheviks." Pelley spoke of the need for an American Hitler, praised the Third Reich's accomplishments, worked with the German-American Bund, and established contact with various Nazi propaganda agencies in Germany. The Silver Shirts were structured along military lines with a hierarchy of titles and ranks. Members wore a uniform of blue pants, a silver shirt, and hat. Dues were $2 per person.

By 1934, the group had penetrated twelve states and reached a peak membership of 15,000. Pelley was repeatedly subjected to congressional investigation, appearing before House committees in 1934 and 1940. He also faced constant legal trouble. In 1934, a North Carolina court convicted him of stock fraud. After paying a fine he was released on parole. Pelley's many difficulties led to a decline in the Silver Shirts. By 1938 membership had dropped to only 5000; three years later the group was dissolved, yet the Justice Department continued to pursue Pelley.[66] In 1942, the government convicted him on charges of violating the espionage act and sent him to prison for the duration of World War II.

The Silver Shirts were only one of a host of organizations believed to sympathize with Hitler's Germany. The racial component of National Socialism appealed to some American nativists. On August 18, 1940, hundreds of Ku Klux Klansmen met with Bundsmen at Camp Nordland in a show of solidarity. The Imperial Wizard attacked the meeting, and the Klan's national newspaper, *The Fiery Cross*, expressed discontent with the Bund.[67] Nonetheless, many of the xenophobic individuals drawn to the Klan in the twenties would form radical-right splinter groups in the thirties.

In the Midwest ex-Klansmen helped organize a group known as the Black Legion. The Legion denounced blacks, Jews, and Catholics. The group included members from both the working and middle classes. The Black Legion organized itself along military lines and demanded complete obedience from all members. General V. F. Effinger, leader of the Black Legion, called his group "a guerilla army designed to fight the Republican and Democratic parties."[68] Such a description was no exaggeration. The Black Legion engaged in violent reprisals against its enemies. These attacks ranged from beatings to murders. Unfavorable publicity and harsh legal action helped to crush the secret society. In 1936 and 1937 two feature films appeared denouncing the group: *Legion of Terror,* starring Bruce Cabot, and *Black Legion*, starring Humphrey Bogart. In 1937 13 members of the Black Legion were given life sentences for murder and 37 others were jailed for less severe violent crimes. These convictions broke the back of the terror group once and for all.

Apostates from the Klan formed right-wing hate groups nationwide. For example, George Deatherage organized the Knights of the White Camelia. The Knights claimed membership of 10,000 and based their operations in West Virginia. Deatherage accepted the swastika as his organization's emblem and openly attacked democracy. He maintained contact with the Nazi propaganda agency, World Service, and with members of the German Foreign Office.[69] George W. Christians, another ex-Klansman, formed the Crusader White Knights. His extremist group was based in Tennessee and emphasized anti-semitic and anti-Communist themes. Christians was a disturbed man. The FBI noted that he wrote "railing, incoherent, and rambling letters" to such diverse figures as Stalin, Mussolini, and Churchill. In a chummy note to Hitler, Christians commented: "Dear Adolpf: It seems to me the time has come to think about how we are going to divide up the British Empire." He ended this correspondence: "Yours for an exciting New Year." Though cited by the *Saturday Evening Post* as an important native fascist group, the Crusader White Knights never gathered much support; an FBI report written in 1941 noted that "at the present time, Christians appears to be the only member."[70]

During the thirties America teemed with extremist groups espousing anti-Jewish, anti-Communist, and anti-democratic beliefs. A number of individuals (including Robert Edmondson, Eugene Sanctuary, and James True) produced and disseminated radical right-wing literature.[71] However, these organizations and individuals never posed any real danger to the republic. American fascists were in large measure a motley collection of cranks, con men, malcontents, and lunatics. In a September 1940 piece for the *Saturday Review of Literature*, Harold Lavine wrote that with three or four exceptions the nation's radical right was made up of semi-literates, the kind of people who spelled "please" p-l-e-e-z.[72] Though perhaps hundreds of fascist groups existed throughout the United States, these organizations never attracted mass followings. For example, the Bund and the Silver Shirts were two of the most feared right-wing groups. Yet the former never exceeded 25,000 members and the latter attracted no more than 15,000 followers.

Throughout the Great Depression Americans demonstrated antipathy toward both right-wing and left-wing radicalism. Faced with the greatest national emergency since the Civil War, the public turned to pragmatist Franklin Roosevelt for answers. Roosevelt was no revolutionary. His New Deal reforms aimed at preserving democratic government and liberal capitalism. FDR's programs helped many Americans, but they ultimately failed to end the Depression, and hard times lingered on until the Second World War sparked recovery. Yet in spite of America's lengthy and cataclysmic economic crisis, fascism and Communism remained fringe movements. The vast majority of the nation's populace viewed these radical ideologies with fear and disdain. Most Americans believed that home-grown extremists had little chance to succeed without outside assistance.

THREE

~*~

The Opening Alarm

The Rumrich Spy Case

In 1938 the Federal Bureau of Investigation uncovered an extensive Nazi spy ring centered in New York City. A shocked public learned that Germany had planted agents within America's armed forces and defense industries. The FBI presented conclusive evidence linking German government officials to the espionage network. Though the situation caused grave concern, it did not set off a national panic in and of itself. Experts informed the public that the ring had acquired little intelligence of real value and that the captured Nazi spies had operated in a reassuringly clumsy manner. Nonetheless, the case recalled the years immediately before United States entry into World War I, when agents for the Kaiser had engaged in hostile operations against America. *The Chicago Tribune* noted that the indictment of eighteen individuals for espionage was the "greatest exposé of spy activities since the world war."[1] *Newsweek* similarly observed that "not since the World War has there been such feverish activity in rooting out alleged German spies."[2] It was clear that the quiet days of the interwar era were over. Now America had become a target for the Nazis. The New York spy case was key to the emergence of a Fifth Column scare. The elaborate web of intrigue which the government unmasked in 1938 seemed to prove Hitler's commitment to offensive action against the United States.

The New York case became one of the hottest news stories of 1938. From the initial roundup of the hostile agents in February to their convictions on espionage charges eleven months later, the affair repeatedly garnered front-page headlines from the national press. The media attention was so extensive that it would have been difficult for any citizen to have avoided hearing about the case.

The saturation coverage continued even after the German agents were sentenced to prison terms. Leon G. Turrou, the FBI agent principally responsible for investigating the New York espionage ring, helped keep the story alive. He resigned from the Bureau and signed lucrative contracts with the *New York Post*, Random House, and Warner Brothers Motion Pictures, promising to detail his involvement in the fight against German espionage in America. He supplemented these accounts with radio appearances and a national lecture tour. Turrou's various renderings of his adventures stressed the sensational and lurid elements of the case. The ex-G-man warned America that the spy ring he had helped to break comprised only one small part of a large-scale Nazi conspiracy against the United States.

The bizarre and intriguing facts surrounding the case largely explain the media's enthusiastic response to the story. *New York Times* journalist Hanson Baldwin described the affair as "A Spy Thriller—in Real Life." Baldwin noted that the whole story was straight out of a dime novel:

> The dramatis personae in this first major American spy case include clerks and soldiers, beautiful women, British Secret Service men, army and navy intelligence officers (who conducted the early investigations and developed the case until the Federal Bureau of Investigation took over), G-men, State Department agents, newspaper reporters, German seamen, Yorkville residents, etc.[3]

The clandestine German intelligence network which the FBI cracked in 1938 made up part of an organization which had been developing over many years.[4] In 1927, the Abwehr, Germany's secret service, sent William Lonkowski to the United States. Lonkowski arrived in New York City with orders to acquire American military secrets. The German spy gained employment at the Ireland aircraft corporation in Long Island, New York. Lonkowski, code-named "Sex" (after one of his many aliases, William Sexton), soon set about recruiting agents. Two of his earliest and most productive operatives were Otto Voss and Werner Gudenberg, for whom "Sex" won jobs at the Ireland corporation. Eventually both men moved on to positions at other defense plants. Voss found employment at a Baltimore company that performed defense work for the United States Navy; he later took a post at the Seversky plant in Farmingdale, Long Island. The Curtiss Aircraft plant in Buffalo, New York, hired Gudenberg. Both men used their positions in order to acquire the blueprints of various military devices produced by their employers.

Lonkowski eventually left Ireland aircraft and hired on as a correspondent for the German aviation journal *Luftreise*. This job was a convenient cover for his intelligence work. "Sex" forwarded a range of
material to Berlin, yet throughout the early thirties he received little encouragement. The Abwehr continued to pay him his monthly salary but
otherwise appeared to have lost complete interest in spying on the Americans.

In addition to Lonkowski's ring, the Nazis also received intelligence
from an organization run by a German-American named Ignatz Griebl.
Griebl was a prosperous physician in Manhattan's German colony of
Yorkville. He was born in Bavaria in 1899, and served as an artillery
officer in the German Army during World War I. He attended medical
school at the University of Munich, emigrating to the United States in
1925. Shortly after his arrival, Griebl became an American citizen, and
he eventually joined the United States Army medical reserve. Griebl also
became active in pro-German organizations. In 1933 he was selected
president of the Friends of New Germany. One year later, the doctor
wrote a note to Joseph Goebbels proffering his services for intelligence
work.

Griebl's offer to spy for the Reich was forwarded to Gestapo head-
quarters and eventually reached Paul Kraus. Kraus headed the Gestapo's
Maritime Bureau and was responsible for smuggling intelligence between
Germany and the United States. He placed agents aboard liners of the
North German Lloyd and Hamburg shipping lines. These individuals
served as couriers for the Nazis. Kraus forwarded intelligence collected
by his men to Lieut. Commander Erich Pheiffer of the Abwehr post at
Wilhelmshaven.

Pheiffer was a key player in Germany's revitalized intelligence efforts
in the United States. German espionage in England, North America, and
South America was supervised from Ast X of the Abwehr at Hamburg.
Pheiffer was stationed at Wilhelmshaven, a sub-branch of Ast X. From
this post he actively encouraged the espionage work of Lonkowski and
Griebl (who had merged their operations late in 1934). The intelligence
which Pheiffer received from his two operatives in the United States
included the specifications of various army and navy aircraft.[5]

On September 25, 1935, the Americans finally stumbled onto Germany's spy operation. A customs guard stopped Lonkowski when he
attempted to board the liner *Europa*. The guard discovered film strips
and letters concealed within a violin case which Lonkowski was carrying. Customs called in military intelligence for assistance. After an un-
productive round of questioning by the authorities, Major Joseph Dalton
of G-2 released Lonkowski. Dalton asked him to return at 10 a.m. the
next day for further interrogation. Upon his release, Lonkowski removed
all his money from the bank, borrowed a car from Ignatz Griebl, and

headed for Canada. From there he obtained transit to Germany. The Americans let the case drop without uncovering the broader ring which "Sex" had established.[6]

After Lonkowski's forced departure from America, Griebl continued to spy for the Abwehr. He received $300 monthly, with bonus payments for the acquisition of particularly useful information.[7] In 1937, he returned to Europe for another meeting with German intelligence officers. The philandering doctor left his wife behind in America, and instead traveled with his mistress Kate Moog. Erich Pheiffer greeted Griebl and Moog upon their arrival at Bremen. The couple were brought to Berlin to see Captain Hermann Menzel, head of the navy intelligence section, and his deputy commander Udo von Bonin. Griebl and Moog were also introduced to the chief of the Abwehr, Admiral Wilhelm Canaris, and the head of Amstgruppe I, Colonel Hans Piekenbrock. During these meetings the Abwehr expressed gratitude to Griebl for his espionage activities and promised to reward him for his services. This trip was to have serious consequences for the Germans. When the FBI finally captured Griebl, he revealed the direct role which Abwehr officers had played in spying on the United States.

During discussions with Menzel and Bonin it was suggested that Griebl's attractive companion Kate Moog set up a salon in Washington funded by German money. According to Turrou's memoir, the Germans asked Moog to explain the Nazi viewpoint on issues to Americans. She was asked to focus attention on "underpaid Navy and Army officers," and to introduce servicemen to "pretty women . . . good food . . . good drink." Ultimately, Moog refused the offer, and the Germans did not press the issue. Nonetheless, after Griebl's capture and confession, the United States press widely publicized Germany's effort to ensnare vulnerable soldiers. News accounts invariably described Moog as a "beauteous" and "alluring" siren.[9] The "femme fatale" angle of the story suggested to the public that the amoral Germans continued to rely on Mata Hari types just as fiction said they had during the First World War.

Griebl's spy network was finally undone thanks to the colossal incompetence of a Nazi agent named Guenther Gustav Rumrich. Rumrich was born in Chicago in 1911. He grew up in Europe, and returned to the United States at the age of eighteen. In January of 1930, Rumrich enlisted in the United States Army. He went AWOL shortly after signing up. For this offense he was courtmartialed and served a six-month prison term. Surprisingly, Rumrich opted to reenlist after his release from prison. He was stationed in the Canal Zone and later was posted to Fort Missoula in Montana. Financially strapped, the ne'er-do-well G.I. embezzled company funds and went AWOL for a second time. He headed for New York City, where he took odd jobs as a dishwasher and a Berlitz language instructor. After reading a book by Colonel Walter Nicolai, chief of German intelligence during World War I, Rumrich volunteered to spy for the Nazis. In March 1936, he wrote a letter to Nicolai enclosed in an envelope to the Nazi party newspaper *Voelkischer Beobachter*. Rumrich claimed to have been a lieutenant (false) in the air corps who had served in Panama (true) and Hawaii (false). He wrote that if the German war office was interested in his services, a message addressed to Theodore Koerner should be placed in the public notice column of the *New York Times*.

Astonishingly, the Germans took up Rumrich's proposal. Two to three weeks after writing to Nicolai, Rumrich came across a notice in the *Times* instructing him to contact a man named "Sanders" at P.O. Box 629, Hamburg, Germany. "Sanders" was in fact Captain Ernst Mueller of the Abwehr. In order to test their new recruit the Germans asked for information on American forces in Panama. Having spent time in the Canal Zone, the ex-G.I. gladly supplied "Sanders" with reliable data. When the Panama intelligence checked out, the Abwehr added Rumrich to their list of American agents, giving him the codename "Crown."

"Crown" worked hard to generate information for his controllers, and he won a few minor espionage victories. Rumrich managed to acquire information on the rate of venereal disease in the United States Army. He called Fort Hamilton, an army post guarding New York harbor, and posed as a major in the medical corps. Rumrich claimed to be giving a classified lecture on V.D. and asked that information on the subject be assembled and dropped off to him at a telephone booth on a Brooklyn street corner. A clerk at Fort Hamilton complied with this unusual request. Yet in spite of his occasional successes in acquiring such data, Rumrich was simply not in a position to collect important information. He needed help from people with access to real intelligence.

"Crown" did manage to persuade an old army buddy, Private Erich Glaser, to assist him in his activities. Glaser served in the 18th Reconnaissance Squadron of the Army Air Corps and was stationed at Mitchell Field, Long Island. From this post he collected intelligence for Rumrich. Most of Glaser's data was innocuous. For example, he gave his friend copies of *The Army and Navy Register* and *The Ordnance Journal*, declassified publications freely available to the public. Somewhat more significant was Glaser's theft of an air force code. However, by and large, Rumrich supplied the Germans with chicken feed. The paltry recompense which he received from his Abwehr controllers underscored the triviality of his contributions to German intelligence: For example, "Crown" was paid only $70 for the Air Corps code which Glaser had obtained.[10]

The Germans maintained contact with Rumrich through Karl Schlueter. Schlueter was a steward aboard the vessel *Europa* and a member of the Gestapo's Maritime Bureau. In this capacity he functioned as a courier for German intelligence. On New Year's Eve, 1938, Schlueter arranged to meet "Crown" at a popular night spot for New York's German colony, the Café Hindenburg. At this meeting Rumrich was informed of a number of specific pieces of intelligence desired by the Nazis. Such material included the blueprints to the Navy's new aircraft carriers *Yorktown* and *Lexington* and the United States Army's defense mobilization plans for the East Coast. Schlueter also asked for 50 blank passport forms. (The Reich sought these documents largely in order to penetrate the Soviet Union with agents disguised as American seamen.)[11] The Germans considered these items quite important. They demonstrated their particular interest in this material by promising "Crown" $1000 for the carrier designs and $300 for the passports.[12]

One of Rumrich's contacts suggested a fantastic scheme aimed at acquiring blueprints for the Navy carriers *Yorktown* and *Lexington*. The plan called for the drafting of a letter on forged White House stationery to the construction chief of the navy. The Germans hoped to dupe the navy into giving away carrier designs through the issuance of bogus instructions. Though Rumrich claimed he did not agree with this idea, he admitted that he requested that his contacts in Germany provide him with stationery. He never received this material. Rumrich later tried to get the blueprints by directly asking an engineer aboard the *Saratoga* to provide the material in exchange for money. This approach proved fruitless.[13]

Rumrich developed an even more outlandish plan to acquire the army's mobililization plans for the East Coast. He hoped to steal the documents from Colonel Henry W. T. Eglin, commander of the 62nd Coast Artillery at Fort Totten, New York. "Crown's" proposal called for Eglin to be lured to the Hotel McAlpin in downtown Manhattan. Here he was to be overpowered and stripped of whatever classified materials he was carrying. (In interviews with the FBI, Rumrich claimed that gas hidden in a fountain pen would be used to disable Eglin.) Originally a woman was to be used to draw the American officer to the hotel. However, since this approach would not ensure that Eglin brought the desired documents along with him, Rumrich devised new tactics. He suggested that forged orders be drawn up directing the American officer to attend a top secret meeting at the hotel. After Eglin had been robbed of the documents he was carrying, efforts would be made to blame the affair on the Communists.

The Germans showed no interest in this plan and Rumrich later told the FBI that he had also dismissed it as unworkable. Any effort to have implemented the scheme would have failed as British intelligence had penetrated "Crown's" pipeline to the Abwehr and was aware of some of the spy's proposed operations, including the Eglin kidnapping scheme.[14]

In addition to his periodic meetings with Schlueter, Rumrich stayed in touch with German intelligence through the mails. The Germans instructed "Crown" to forward correspondence to Mrs. Jessie Wallace Jordan in Dundee, Scotland, a relay station for the Abwehr. Thanks to a suspicious postman, MI5 was alerted to the unusual volume and geographic range of the mail being received by Mrs. Jordan. The security conscious British began to steam open her correspondence. In this way MI5 intercepted evidence indicating Rumrich's plot to acquire the blueprints for the *Yorktown* and the *Lexington*, and his proposal to steal defense plans from Colonel Eglin. The British notified the Americans of the details of the Eglin plot, and a trap was prepared for "Crown." However, because the Abwehr had terminated the operation, Rumrich eluded authorities. Nevertheless, American officials were grateful to British intelligence for its assistance and were impressed by its efficiency.

"Crown" was finally captured after he bungled an attempt to gain blank American passport forms for the Germans. On February 14, 1938, Rumrich called Ira Hoyt of the New York Passport Division. He claimed to be Secretary of State Cordell Hull on a top-secret visit to New York.[15] "Crown" brusquely ordered Hoyt to deliver 35 passport blanks to the Hotel Taft in the name of Edward Weston. Hoyt found the request strange and called in the Alien Squad of the New York Police. The police prepared a dummy package for "Mr. Weston" and delivered it to the Taft. A special detail of officers maintained surveillance over the package. After making his call, Rumrich became uneasy. Fearing that something had gone wrong he initiated an elaborate series of steps to make sure the package he ordered was not being trailed by the police. Rumrich called the Western Union office in Grand Central Station and asked that a messenger go to the Hotel Taft and pick up an item for Mr. Weston. Later in the day he telephoned Western Union and requested that his package be sent to the company's Varick Street office. Rumrich instructed this office to deliver the package to a nearby tavern. He convinced a woman in the bar to sign for the item. Even at this point Rumrich remained uneasy. He left the tavern, walked across the street, and asked a young boy to retrieve his package for him. The boy complied with "Crown's" request. Just as Rumrich received his package two detectives moved in and asked him to accompany them to police headquarters.[16]

Major Dalton of G-2 interrogated Rumrich. The captured spy admitted his ties to the plot against Colonel Eglin. Dalton sensed that the government had stumbled onto a major espionage network. Feeling his resources inadequate for the investigation he requested that the FBI take over the case. J. Edgar Hoover agreed, placing Agent Leon G. Turrou in charge of the investigation.

The captured spy fully cooperated with Turrou in hope that he would receive lenient treatment from the government. "Crown" revealed that his main contacts with German intelligence were Karl Schlueter, a steward aboard the *Europa*, and Jennie Hofmann, a hairdresser on the same vessel. He added that Schlueter was expected back in America in only a few days. When the *Europa* arrived in New York on February 24, it was greeted by agents from the FBI. Unfortunately for Turrou, Schlueter had not made the transatlantic crossing. Despite this disappointment, the FBI was able to bring in Johanna Hofmann for questioning. When confronted by Rumrich, the young hairdresser admitted her guilt, though at first she refused to reveal everything she knew. Hofmann confessed that she was transporting a number of packages for Schlueter and she unwisely agreed to allow Turrou's men to search her cabin for these items. FBI agents found five letters. One was addressed to Kate Moog; another to Ignatz Griebl; a third to Rumrich (this letter contained $70 for the code which "Crown" had received from Griebl); a fourth to Johann Steuer, an employee of the Sperry Gyroscope Company; and a fifth to Otto Voss.[17] Much of this correspondence was in code, but Bureau agents found the key to the code among Hofmann's personal affects. This discovery prompted the hairdresser to decode voluntarily the letters for Turrou.

After winning a full confession from Hofmann, the Bureau broadened the scope of its investigations. Turrou called in Dr. Ignatz Griebl for questioning, and much to the investigator's delight the Nazi spy "sang like a canary."[18] Griebl betrayed many of his operatives in the United States, including Otto Voss and Werner Gudenberg. He also confessed to the role which German government officials played in supervising the espionage ring.

The FBI decided against arresting Griebl, believing that the greatest degree of cooperation could be won by treating the Nazi spy in a cordial fashion. This proved to be an unfortunate decision. On May 11, 1938, Dr. Griebl stowed away aboard the German liner *Bremen* and slipped out of the country. Werner Gudenberg, one of Lonkowski's early recruits, also fled the United States in the same way.

Lamar Hardy, the federal district attorney for the Southern District of New York, used the evidence which Turrou had gathered to prepare a major espionage case. On June 20, 1938, a federal grand jury indicted 18 individuals for conspiring to steal military secrets. Only four of those indicted were actually in government custody: Voss, Rumrich, Hofmann, and Glaser. The other defendants were almost all in Germany, safely outside the reach of American law enforcement (Mrs. Jennie Jordan was the one exception, and she was already serving a four-year prison term in Britain). District Attorney Hardy went ahead and indicted individuals whom he had no intention of prosecuting because he wanted to awaken the public to the dangers of foreign espionage. He noted that "the American public must be made aware of this spy plot and impressed with its dangers."[19]

The press turned Turrou into a media hero. Stories noted that the G-man had been involved with almost every important case handled by the Bureau and that he was rated as one of the organization's preeminent agents. Turrou loved the spotlight and played the part of ace G-man to the hilt. He sagely told reporters that an FBI agent was born, not made: "The investigator has to have certain personal qualities . . . psychology is the main thing. Secondly, intuition is necessary—the ability to distinguish between guilt and innocence. Then there's human judgment. You've got to judge whether people are telling you the truth or a lie."[20]

Turrou submitted his resignation to the FBI after the grand jury issued indictments in the case. He claimed his decision was based on ill health and a desire to pursue new career opportunities in writing. Yet immediately upon leaving the Bureau the ex-G-man negotiated an informal deal with J. David Stern, the publisher of the *New York Post* and *Philadelphia Record*. News accounts indicated that Stern had promised from $25,000 to $40,000 for the stories. (In fact, the ex-agent was offered only a guaranteed payment of $10,000 and his official contract was not drawn up until mid-July.)[21] On June 22, 1938, the *Post* publicized Turrou's upcoming series with a full two page spread. Readers were promised "the most astounding revelation ever published by any newspaper." The *Post* claimed that Americans would "learn the authentic story of the German conspiracy to debauch, paralyze, and undermine the military forces of the United States." Turrou pledged to give readers a complete picture of the secret war Germany was waging against America: "a swirling, gigantic, insidious maze of plots and counterplots in the maddest and most vicious and insane spy syndicate in modern history." The ex-G-man warned that our military intelligence had been virtually "stripped of every important naval and military secret it possessed." He claimed a recent meeting between President Roosevelt and an important ship-builder was "known in detail in Nazi spy headquarters in Germany within a few hours!" The *Post* ad finished with a patriotic flourish from Turrou: "The bitter hate and enmity that seem to have motivated this spy plot, the potential danger to my country, have shaken me so that I have come to the conclusion that it is my patriotic duty to inform the American public."[22] Turrou made no mention of his anticipated stipend from the *Post*.

J. Edgar Hoover was infuriated when he learned of Turrou's plan to write a newspaper series on the spy case. On June 24 Hoover wrote to Joseph Keenan, the assistant to the Attorney General, and recommended that Turrou's letter of resignation be refused and "this employee be dropped from the rolls of the Federal Bureau of Investigation with prejudice."[23] In short, the Bureau told their ex-agent that he could not quit because he was already fired. The FBI's explanation for this punitive step was that Turrou had violated the "G-man oath." By taking this oath, Bureau agents pledged not to divulge information of a confidential character uncovered in the course of performing their duties. In fact, Turrou had signed and broken just such an agreement.[24]

The ex-agent's failure to honor his promise of secrecy made him the target of unfavorable press comment. *Time* magazine dismissed Turrou's claim that he had resigned from the Bureau for reasons of ill health, sarcastically observing that the "tired" Mr. Turrou was going to turn out enough articles to run for several weeks.[25] *Time* added that Turrou had struck a bargain with the *Post* only fifteen minutes after tendering his resignation to the Bureau.[26] Turrou's public image as a brilliant, hard-working detective was badly tarnished. Now the press, with prompting from the FBI, painted the ex-agent as a cynical opportunist who failed to keep his word.

Turrou refused to accept FBI criticism meekly. He lashed out against J. Edgar Hoover, proclaiming that the director "is just sore because he didn't get a chance to write the stuff." Turrou cavalierly dismissed the G-man oath. "If I signed it, it was not when I joined the FBI but in 1935, with a lot of other papers, which I supposed were routine." Turrou observed that Hoover derived a "huge income" from writings based on his access to confidential FBI files. He wondered why the oath of secrecy only applied to agents and not to the director.[27] Turrou's charges led reporters to investigate the annual income which the Bureau's director received as a result of his personal writings. The figures were startling; the *New York World Telegram* reported that the director's earnings in 1938 from his writings approached $100,000.[28] Neither Hoover nor Turrou emerged unscathed from this cockfight. The papers assiduously reported their petty squabbling, which could not help but undermine the credibility of America's counterespionage efforts.

The sensational ads promoting Turrou's newspaper series generated concern not only within the FBI but also in prosecutor Lamar Hardy's office. John Burke, an assistant attorney on Hardy's staff, moved to win an injunction prohibiting the publication of the *Post* articles. Burke claimed that Turrou's stories jeopardized future government prosecutions. A judge agreed with the D.A. and issued an injunction blocking publication.[29]

The government's action angered publisher J. David Stern. Stern claimed that the D.A. was preventing his paper from "publishing the news." With a touch of hyperbole he added that the injunction "was an attempt to erase the freedom of the press from the Constitution."[30] Stern shot off a telegram to the White House, which argued that Turrou's stories were a public service, "a means of bringing before the American people the gravity of this [espionage] situation."[31]

Stern was badly mistaken if he expected a sympathetic hearing from the White House. In a June 24 press conference the President rebuked Turrou and Stern, publicly questioning both men's patriotism:

The former Justice Department investigator, having obtained all the details on which the presentation to the Grand Jury would be based and before the trial on its indictments had begun, resigned from the government service and within fifteen minutes signed a specific contract, it was stated. The result was to jeopardize a criminal prosecution by the federal government.

There was no question here of the legality of either the agent or the syndicate publisher. The matter was entirely one of patriotism and ethics. But for an ex-government agent or a newspaper publisher to undertake to disseminate information of a kind involved in the Federal Investigation was to invite official concern as well as question the motive.[32]

The solemnity with which the President made these comments indicated to all the reporters present how seriously he viewed the situation. In all likelihood, J. Edgar Hoover had urged the President to speak out on the subject. Faced with open criticism from the White House, the *Post* agreed to withhold Turrou's articles until the New York spy trial was concluded. After the *Post* made this announcement Roosevelt sent a brief telegram to publisher Stern which simply stated "very glad to hear your decision."[33]

The trial of the accused Nazi spies received tremendous media coverage from the opening arguments in October until the final sentencing in early December. The government's case principally rested on the work of Leon G. Turrou and the confessions which he had wrung from Guenther Rumrich, Otto Voss, Ignatz Griebl, and Johanna Hofmann. The defense tried to discredit these confessions and ultimately challenged both the honesty and sanity of Leon Turrou. The ex-G-Man's dismissal from the Bureau and the controversy surrounding the attempted publication of his articles made him particularly vulnerable to such attacks.

Turrou was well aware that defense counsel would challenge his testimony on the grounds that he was a discredited agent of the Justice Department. He thus made considerable efforts to have the "prejudice" removed from his resignation. Through FBI intermediaries he extended an olive branch to Hoover, claiming that "newspaper reporters had placed words in his mouth designed to 'vilify' the Bureau and the Director." Turrou protested that he had turned down many opportunities to attack the FBI and that all his writings were intended only to "glorify the Bureau." He mixed such servility with more forceful persuasive techniques. J. Edgar Hoover was informed that "Turrou stated that if the defense began attacking him as a witness he would place the blame on the shoulders of the Director of the Bureau."[34] Turrou also turned to his friend Senator Robert Wagner of New York for assistance. Wagner launched an intense lobbying effort to have the ex-G-man rehabilitated. Joseph Keenan, the assistant to the Attorney General, told the Bureau that "much pressure is being brought to bear upon the Department for the purpose of having the prejudice removed from Turrou's resignation." Keenan wondered whether these "feverish efforts" might not have softened Hoover's resolve.[35] In the face of such pressure the director remained unforgiving, and refused Turrou's request.

As was expected, the defense attempted to place Leon G. Turrou on trial. It was argued that Turrou had coerced witnesses into signing false statements. Johanna Hofmann testified that the FBI had refused to let her go home until she had signed an incriminating confession.[36] Otto Voss claimed that the G-men had warned him that they "had ways" of making him talk. Voss added that the Bureau simply twisted his denials into affirmations.[37] John Dix, Johanna Hofmann's lawyer, charged Turrou with intentionally allowing Ignatz Griebl to escape in exchange for "framed" testimony against "small fry" defendants.[38] Griebl, safe in Germany, was happy to support this fantastic charge. He swore out a deposition claiming that Turrou had "coached" him on testimony and had "hinted" he should leave the country.[39] Guenther Rumrich had agreed to act as a friendly witness for the prosecution and stood by his confession. Nonetheless, defense lawyers had little trouble undermining the credibility of Rumrich's testimony. John Dix told jurors that Rumrich was a chronic liar and a self-admitted narcotics user.[40]

The defense's efforts to portray Turrou in an unflattering light went so far as to question the ex-G-man's sanity.[41] Mike Yacobehik testified that Turrou had let a room from him twenty years earlier under the name of Leon Petrov. Yacobehik claimed that "Petrov" had tried to kill himself and was taken to a hospital "for crazy people." Turrou pronounced the charge "a damnable lie," but lawyer Dix shot back that it was the ex-FBI agent who was lying.[42] Yacobehik's testimony heightened the carnival atmosphere surrounding the trial; his startling accusations against Turrou and his difficulties with the English language kept the courtroom convulsed with hysterical laughter.[43]

Dix's charges drew blood. The director was informed that testimony concerning Turrou's sanity "is creating a very unfavorable reaction in the minds of the newspaper reporters in respect of the Bureau." An FBI agent observing the trial warned headquarters that journalists were astonished that Hoover would select a man "who has no degree and is not anything like the quality of personnel that the Bureau is supposed to demand." A worried Hoover told his subordinate to "contact friendly reporters in a casual, sub rosa manner [and] apprise them of the fact that Turrou was appointed before the present standards of selection were raised."[44]

Turrou was unnerved and angered by Dix's efforts to smear him. He begged Hoover to appear on the stand as a character witness for him, but the director remained unmoved: "Absolutely no. What does he think I am. He was dismissed with prejudice and has disgraced the FBI and himself. If I appeared it would be just too bad for him."[45] Turrou did receive some help from the presiding judge, who repeatedly cautioned Dix against his scattershot accusations. (For example, Dix charged Turrou with accepting a bribe in an arson case.)[46] Tremendous personal animosity developed between Dix and Turrou. Dix described the ex-G-man as "a low illegal offspring of canine ancestry"[47] in front of a group of reporters. Turrou would later depict his chief tormentor as a vicious distorter of the truth. Ultimately, the defense's efforts to discredit the government failed. Still, such tactics kept the case in the newspapers, proving tremendously entertaining to the public, and providing little reassurance about the efficacy of America's counterespionage effort.

A federal grand jury eventually found Rumrich, Hofmann, Voss, and Glaser guilty of espionage. Judge John Knox issued stiff sentences to the defendants: Voss received a six-year prison term, Hofmann four years, Glaser two years, and Rumrich two years. Knox saw the case as a warning to America. The judge expressed relief at the apparent failure of Germany's intelligence efforts, noting that just as in the days of Boy-Ed and Von Papen "the chief accomplishment of these espionage agents . . . has been the creation of ill-will and resentment" between America's citizenry and the German government. However, the escapes of Wilhelm Lonkowski and Ignatz Griebl gravely concerned Knox. He pointedly blamed their getaways on "the ineptitude of our own protective agencies," and called for greater cooperation among these organizations.[48]

As a result of the New York spy case, District Attorney Lamar Hardy became a celebrity expert on the problem of foreign intrigue. Hardy met with President Roosevelt on October 8 and discussed the spy situation in America. After the meeting, FDR told the press that there had been "a considerable increase" in foreign espionage throughout the country.[49] Roosevelt called for greater intelligence coordination and more federal funds to deal with the problem. The President met once again with Hardy on December 9, 1938. After this session Roosevelt announced a new offensive against espionage. He warned that the spy menace was "a situation in which the roots went deep."[50] FDR's words strongly echoed Hardy's own post-trial observations. The D.A. had indicated that the convictions of Voss, Hofmann, Glaser, and Rumrich only "scratched the surface" of America's espionage problem: "We have no counterespionage in this country, and as long as that is so, the United States is an open field to foreign spies."[51]

The uncovering of a spy ring in New York City prompted warnings from a range of individuals thought to be well acquainted with espionage matters. Tom Tracy, an ex-FBI agent, told *Time* that America's "moral aloofness to the great international pastime of snoop-look-and-listen" had turned the country into "one vast peek-easy."[52] Albert Grzesinski, a former Prussian Minister of the Interior during the Weimar period, observed that German intelligence organizations "exceed everything that ever existed in the history of spying."[53] Franz von Rintelen, one of Germany's most notorious secret agents in America during the World War I era, warned the democracies against being "misled by the farci-tragical methods coming out in the course of the spy trial in America." From London, the ex-patriate von Rintelen warned that German spying was more clever and subtle than ever.[54]

Once the trial verdicts were in, J. David Stern ran Turrou's long-awaited series of newspaper articles on German espionage in the United States. These stories were syndicated nationwide. Random House simultaneously released a three-hundred-page book by Turrou entitled *The Nazi Spy Conspiracy in America*. The ex-FBI agent's colorful accounts of his investigations were intentionally alarmist. Turrou quoted the leaders of German intelligence boasting about their espionage network in America:

> In every strategic point in your United States we have an operative. In every armament factory in America we have a spy. In every shipyard we have an agent; in every key position. Your country cannot plan a warship, design a fighting plane, develop a new instrument or device, that we do not know of it at once!

Turrou concluded that the nation needed an improved counterespionage service because "for every spy we exposed, dozens more lurk hidden here."[55] The ex-G-man depicted the German-American Bund as the most important front organization for the Nazi Fifth Column in the United States. Despite all his alarmism, Turrou did not paint an entirely bleak picture. He described the typical Nazi spy as cowardly, immoral, and bungling, arguing that German espionage could be overcome as soon as the public and the government dealt with the problem.

Hollywood took an early interest in the New York spy case. In June of 1938, Jacob Wilk, Warner Brothers' story editor in New York, sent word back to California about Turrou's proposed articles in the *New York Post*. Jack Warner authorized Wilk "to inspect Mr. Turrou's material with a view to making a motion picture."[56] In September of 1938 the studio sent screenwriter Milton Krims to New York City to observe the proceedings of the espionage trial. Once guilty verdicts were reached in the case, Warner's feverishly began work on a feature-length film. The studio hired Leon Turrou as a technical adviser for the picture, offering him $25,000.[57] In fashioning their film's screenplay Krims and John Wexley relied heavily on the ex-G-man's version of events. Thus, when Warner's released *Confessions of a Nazi Spy* in April of 1939, the movie reflected the same sense of urgency which underlay Turrou's writings.

Confessions of a Nazi Spy marked a turning point in Hollywood. It was the first film to specifically identify and attack Hitler's regime. Previously, espionage thrillers had consciously avoided identifying the countries for whom villainous secret agents worked. This caution was the result of many factors. The Production Code Administration of the Hays office required that all features deal fairly with foreign nations. If Joseph Breen, chief of the PCA, refused his unit's seal of approval to a film, it lost the possibility of mass distribution. Hence, the major studios sought to avoid disagreements with Breen. Beyond its concerns about Hays office censorship, Hollywood also wanted to protect its overseas markets and avoid offending potential customers.

It is not surprising that Warner Brothers was the first studio to openly challenge the Nazis. During the thirties most of the big studios specialized in escapist motion pictures. However, Jack and Harry Warner took special pride in making "message" films on controversial subjects. In 1932, *I Am a Fugitive from a Chain Gang* dealt with brutality in southern prisons; in 1937 *The Life of Emile Zola* addressed anti-semitism. Throughout Hollywood Warner's was known as the "Roosevelt studio." Jack and Harry both worked actively for FDR's election in 1932. After the Democratic victory Jack Warner claimed that Roosevelt had offered him an appointment to a diplomatic post. The studio chief allegedly replied, "I'm very flattered, Mr. President . . . But I think I can do better for your foreign relations with a good picture about America now and then."[58]

Warner's treated foreign policy issues in many of its films. In the late twenties and early thirties the studio's features reflected the widely held revisionist view toward World War I. Pictures such as *Dawn Patrol*, *The Last Flight*, and *Captured* portrayed war as pointless. These films rendered sympathetic portraits of "good" Germans, who were just as much victims of the war as their Allied counterparts. Film historian John Davies notes that Warner's isolationism penetrated works which seemed to have little bearing on foreign policy. In *Robin Hood,* the famous outlaw of Sherwood Forest (Errol Flynn) blames England's domestic troubles on the crown's adventuresome foreign policy in the Holy Land: "I blame King Richard, whose job was here at home protecting his people instead of deserting them to fight in foreign lands."[59]

However, as the threat of Nazism began to manifest itself more clearly, Warner Brothers took an increasingly hostile stance toward Hitler's government. It was the first major studio to shut down operations in Germany. This step occurred in 1936 after Joe Kaufmann, a studio representative, was murdered in Berlin by a gang of Nazi thugs.[60] In 1938 the studio heads decided it was time to alert Americans to the Nazi menace. The revelations of a German spy network in New York City seemed to offer wonderful raw material for a motion picture which would issue just such a patriotic warning. Of course, Warner Brothers never believed there was a conflict between civic-mindedness and making money. They expected that a topical exposé on Nazi espionage would be a big box-office winner. (Such hopes were not unrealistic. A 1918 wartime propaganda feature entitled *My Four Years in Germany* earned $1,300,000 for the studio, and in 1941 the ardently interventionist *Sergeant York* proved to be the year's biggest money earner.)

The creative artists involved in making *Confessions of a Nazi Spy* felt a strong antipathy for Hitler's regime. Anatole Litvak, the director of the film, was a member of Hollywood's Anti-Nazi League, as was the picture's star Edward G. Robinson. Jewish actor Robinson specifically requested to be placed in the anti-Nazi film, telling producer Hal Wallis, "I want to do that for my people."[61] He was well cast as FBI agent Renard, a character modeled on Leon Turrou. Other cast members included Francis Lederer as the Rumrich figure; Paul Lukas the Griebl counterpart; George Sanders as the Kurt Schneider character; and Ona Lyn as the Kate Moog figure.[62]

In making *Confessions of a Nazi Spy* Warner Brothers consciously imitated the style of a documentary feature, interspersing actual newsreel footage throughout the picture. Just as in the *March of Time* series, a commentator narrated much of the story to viewers. (The studio unsuccessfully attempted to hire Westbrook Vorhees, voice of the *March of Time* features, to narrate the film.)[63] Much to the chagrin of the studio's legal department, Warner's refused to open their picture with a disclaimer indicating that the characters and events portrayed in the film were fictitious. The only compromise which director Litvack and producer Wallis made was the elimination of the actual names of participants in the spy case.[64] Nonetheless, the characters in the movie were unmistakably based on real life counterparts. Any filmgoer who had followed the newspapers in 1938 would have recognized this.[65]

The screenplay for *Confessions of a Nazi Spy* retold the details of the German espionage ring. However, Warner's refused to allow the facts of the case to get in the way of a good story, and at points the film invented dialogue and events for dramatic purposes. The movie made three principal points: Germany was seeking to destroy America; the German-American Bund was the Reich's most dangerous front organization in the United States; and it was time for citizens to wake up to the danger of the Nazi Fifth Column.

Confessions of a Nazi Spy stressed Germany's global objectives. The film's commentator informed viewers that "Germany is on the march . . . and its favorite music is the Horst Wessel song that ends with . . . tomorrow the world is ours." Toward the end of the picture a character intended to represent Nazi Propaganda Minister Joseph Goebbels stands in front of a map of the world, pointer in hand. He outlines Hitler's triumphs in Europe and then informs a gathering of German officers of the next stage in the Reich's advance:

Our power increases from day to day. All of Europe is at our mercy, on its knees, begging us not to destroy it. Austria is part of Greater

Germany. Czechoslovakia is through. Italy is with us and safeguards Jugoslavia. Japan is our ally. Our agents are succeeding in Rumania, Poland and Lithuania. Franco will soon have all Spain. France will be isolated from all sides.

[MOVES POINTER TO U.S.]

But now since our glorious victory at Munich, all our efforts must be directed at the strongest remaining democracy—the United States. Here we must repair the few petty mistakes that have recently been made . . .

Filmgoers were left in no doubt that the German government directly supervised Fifth Column activity in America. One scene in the film portrays a meeting between a Goebbels figure and Dr. Kassel (Ignatz Griebl). At this session Kassel is ordered to pursue a "divide and conquer" strategy in America: "Racial and religious hatreds must be fostered on the basis of American Aryanism. Class hatreds must be encouraged in such a way that labor and the middle class will become confused and antagonistic. *In the ensuing chaos, we will be able to take over control*" (my emphasis). Goebbels then promises to double his propaganda output so that Nazi material might reach "every city, town, village in the U.S." After this scene the film showed montage shots of grocery clerks sneaking pamphlets into shopping bags; men sliding propaganda under the doors of work lockers; an airplane dropping leaflets from the sky over a city; and a man throwing pamphlets into the street. The film's commentator noted that the stream of Nazi propaganda attempted to penetrate "every nerve and fibre of American life, inciting racial prejudice and ridiculing democracy."[66]

Warner's film attempted to goad the public into a more vigilant approach toward foreign espionage. *Confessions of a Nazi Spy* depicted smug and arrogant Germans who were amused by American stupidity. In one sequence of the film, von Eichen, a German intelligence officer, questions his subordinate, Straubel, on the wisdom of hiring a dull-witted man for espionage work. Straubel confidently notes that the Americans are "a very simple-minded people and one doesn't need a wolf where a weasel will do." Later in the film Nazi intelligence officers are shown seeking to persuade the Kate Moog character to act as a Mata Hari in the United States. She expresses concern over the possible dangers involved in espionage, but is reassured by her lover Dr. Kassel, who claims that the "fools" in America "are all asleep." A grinning German agent adds that "by the time they wake up . . . it may be rather too late to stop us."[67]

Confessions of a Nazi Spy identified the German-American Bund (AV) as the principal arm of Hitler's Fifth Column. The film depicted the AV as a front organization for Nazi espionage and propaganda and suggested that the Bundists were in fact a secret army preparing to take

up arms against the American government. These accusations enraged
Fritz Kuhn, the leader of the Bund. He filed a $5 million lawsuit against
Warner Brothers on behalf of his organization and its members. The
government eventually dismissed the suit after Kuhn was found guilty
of embezzling Bund funds. Nonetheless, Kuhn's protests were not entirely frivolous, as the charges *Confessions of a Nazi Spy* made against
the Bund were exaggerated.

When Warner Brothers released *Confessions of a Nazi Spy* in April
1939, the AV was very much on the minds of the public. Only two
months earlier the Bund had held a pro-American rally at Madison
Square Garden honoring Washington's birthday. *Confessions of a Nazi
Spy* included sequences reminiscent of that rally. In the film Dr. Kassel
repeatedly addresses crowds of cheering Bundists. In one speech before
a packed hall Kassel denounces the Constitution and the Bill of Rights,
claiming that these documents are at the heart of the United States' problems. A group of American Legionnaires in attendance at the Bund rally
challenges Kassel's speech. One Legionnaire notes that "we don't want
any isms in this country except Americanism." Another adds that America is a free country and "I got a right to speak up. . . ." A third man
disgustedly notes that the Bundists are "worse than gangsters." While
the Legionnaires patriotically speak their minds, they are descended
upon by a pack of stormtroopers, who beat them into silence.[68]

Warner's ended their film by reminding audiences that hostile German
activities could no longer be met with indifference. The final scene of
Confessions of a Nazi Spy takes place in an ordinary diner. After successfully prosecuting the German spy ring, the District Attorney and the
FBI agent ponder the potential menace of future Nazi subversion. The
D.A. expresses faith in the public: "It's true we're a careless, easy-going
optimistic nation. . . . But when our basic liberties are threatened—we
wake up." Happily this sentiment is vindicated by a conversation which
they overhear in the diner. A counterman tells two customers of his
anger at the recent espionage activities of the Germans. He fumes at "the
nerve of those Nazis . . . trying to stir up the kind of trouble here they're
making in Europe." The first customer agrees, noting that everybody "is
pretty sore about the whole thing." A second customer concludes the
conversation by adding that if Germany's behavior does not change,
"we'll fight and how we'll fight." Reassured, the D.A. exclaims, "The
voice of the people." The agent responds with quiet reverence, "And
thank God for such a people," and on this optimistic note the film
ends.[69]

Confessions of a Nazi Spy was a paean to the Federal Bureau of
Investigation. The film dutifully paid homage to many of J. Edgar Hoover's favorite themes. Bureau agents were portrayed as law enforcement
professionals who solved cases through clever interrogation and not "the
third degree." The film underscored the public's ultimate responsibility

for combating espionage and glossed over Bureau mistakes in the real espionage case. (For example, the escapes of the Griebl and Gudenberg were blamed on America's overly lenient system of justice, rather than on FBI carelessness.)

In spite of Warner's "kid glove" treatment of the G-men, Hoover was not happy with *Confessions of a Nazi Spy*. Even before the film's release he was suspicious, noting that the studio indulged in "all kinds of ballyhoo and publicity in making the picture, even making statements that spies were trying to commit acts of sabotage on the lot while the picture was being made." The director predicted that "the trouble with the picture is that it will probably create a good deal of public hysteria about spies which is a bad thing because the spy situation is not one-tenth as bad as the yellow journals present."[70]

Hoover's anxieties regarding the film proved prophetic. Warner Brothers engaged in a vigorous, often outrageous public relations campaign. The Bureau "confidentially secured a copy of the press book" issued by Warner Brothers and quickly realized that "startling methods" were being employed to sell the picture. The studio encouraged theater owners to create widespread talk about the showing of *Confessions of a Nazi Spy* through individual telephone calls and personal letters. Local support for the film was also to be won by contacting newspapers, schools, and civic groups. The hoped-for capstone of the public relations campaign was to be the creation of "Americanism week." L. B. Nichols, the head of public relations for the Bureau, piously expressed shock over the exploitation of "Americanism" for the sole purpose of attracting film audiences.[71]

In some localities theater owners engaged in wildly irresponsible promotional campaigns. In Texas and New Mexico, Special Agent R. J. Untreiner noted the following advertising strategy for *Confessions of a Nazi Spy*:

> The first step . . . is to distribute a small pink card bearing a Swastika and across the top the words "Heil Hitler!" The next step is to distribute identical cards, except that they are a different color . . . and on the reverse side of the card is the full title of the picture, together with other information relating to the place and date the picture is to be shown, etc. Following the distribution of the last mentioned card there are usually distributed some handbills advertising the picture.[72]

In the state of Washington the Bureau received a handbill ostensibly produced by American Bundists. The text claimed that *Confessions of a Nazi Spy* was a fake which tried to discredit "the good workers of Hitler." Potential viewers were warned that "Hitler and the Third Reich will take serious reprisals against you if you see this picture when Adolf

Hitler realizes his inevitable destiny over America!" The dodger turned out to be a publicity gag produced by the Mercy theater chain.[73]

Such cases of outright dishonesty were uncommon. Yet even the film's more conventional publicity went beyond the bounds of good sense. Advertisements were absurdly provocative. One poster asked "What do you know about the man next door?"; another warned that "Enemy Eyes Are on You!" In Los Angeles the film's promoters set up billboards with large swastikas on them and the signs included a message advising citizens to "Keep the Fifth Column Out of America."[74]

Confessions of a Nazi Spy thoroughly dissatisfied J. Edgar Hoover. He complained that the film misrepresented Bureau methods and procedures and tricked the public into thinking that the spy picture had been officially sanctioned by the FBI. In early June, Hoover spoke to Will Hays of the Motion Picture Production and Code Administration. The director contended that *Confessions of a Nazi Spy* had violated the law by featuring reproductions of Bureau badges without authorization. Hoover also revealed his anger at Warner Brothers for hiring Leon Turrou as a technical adviser to the film. The director told Hays that the Bureau had promised free assistance from actual agents but the studio had opted to rely "on a man who had been discharged by us."[75] When the German-American Bund sued Warner Brothers for libel, the studio's lawyer, Fulton Brylawski, asked for permission to look at Bureau files relevant to the spy case. After being informed of Brylawski's request Hoover wrote Clyde Tolson: "Let Turrou help him out. He got him into the mess."[76]

The Bureau attempted to use the fallout surrounding *Confessions of a Nazi Spy* in order to gain a tighter rein over Hollywood's various fictionalized depictions of the FBI. L. B. Nichols of the Bureau drafted a letter to Will Hays under the signature of Attorney General Frank Murphy. Murphy's letter held that "whenever the motion picture industry desires to portray upon the screen an alleged factual situation wherein governmental bureaus are concerned, it would be highly desireable to secure the prior consent of the governmental agency involved." In particular, Murphy cited *Confessions of a Nazi Spy* as a film which conveyed to the public the false impression that "it was made with specific approval and cooperation of the Federal Bureau of Investigation." The Attorney General concluded that prior government approval of film projects would insure accuracy and avoid "a misportrayal of the actual methods of operation of the agency involved."[77]

In response to complaints from the Attorney General, the Hays office issued a lawyerly "Statement of Purpose." This document indicated the film industry's desire to "avoid any misrepresentation of, or any matter derogatory to the establishment, the personnel or the activities of the Department of Justice and all other governmental departments, in motion pictures."[78] These guidelines represented an effort to placate Hoover without sacrificing the studios' creative control over stories involving the Bureau. The film industry pledged only to "advise" with the proper authorities. This vague promise left Hollywood free to make movies about the FBI or any other federal agency without formal approval from the government. Understandably, the Bureau was dissatisfied as it obsessively sought to manage its public image. L. B. Nichols noted that "the statement sounds well" but "it does not mean an awful lot." An FBI legal review of the guidelines concluded that the MPPA had "weasled."[79]

Confessions of a Nazi Spy attracted considerable attention from Hitler's government. Before the film's release the German consul in Los Angeles sent a letter to Joseph Breen of the Production Code Administration complaining about the picture.[80] Hans Thomsen, the chargé d'affaires in Washington, told Secretary of State Cordell Hull that he believed Warner's picture might cause unnecessary resentment between Germany and America. Thomsen observed that the film "could easily convey the false impression of the intentions of his government."[81] In July of 1939, the German consul in San Francisco contacted state secretary Weizsacker to inform him of the harmful effect which *Confessions of a Nazi Spy* was having on the Reich's image in America.[82]

Internationally, Warner's feature stirred up controversy. Eighteen countries banned the film (including Denmark, Norway, Holland, Sweden, and Hungary). Poland did exhibit the feature; however, after the Nazi occupation of that country, unverified news stories reported that several Polish theater owners had been hanged for showing it. Postwar interviews by the OSS indicate that the Abwehr was indeed very interested in *Confessions of a Nazi Spy*. After invading Poland, the Germans confiscated a print of Warner's film and had it screened for Admiral Canaris and other German intelligence figures.[83]

In America, *Confessions of a Nazi Spy* opened to generally positive critical notices. The *New York Daily News* rated the picture good to excellent, claiming it "combined the genuine thrill of a detective and spy story." The *Chicago Tribune* described the film as "a brilliantly revealing exposé of the spy system of the Third Reich." The *Los Angeles Times* praised the picture's script, direction, and acting. There were some bad reviews. *New York Times* critic Frank Nugent thought the picture did little more than "make faces at Hitler." He expressed doubt that "Nazi propaganda ministers let their mouths twitch evilly whenever they mention our constitution or Bill of Rights."[84]

The exuberant critical response toward *Confessions of a Nazi Spy* largely reflected admiration for Warner's bold attack on Hitler. Most reviews, even negative ones, explicitly praised the studio's courage in making the film. *Variety* saw the picture as one of groundbreaking significance:

For the sheer theme, its treatment and its bearing on German-American relations make the social implications far more important than the immediate question of how much money the release makes for the theaters or for Warner Brothers. . . . Decades from now what's happening may be seen in perspective. And the historians will almost certainly take note of this daringly frank broadside from a picture company.[85]

Despite all the publicity surrounding the film and the kindly critical notices garnered from reviewers, *Confessions of a Nazi Spy* never became a box-office hit. Warner's was disappointed by the picture's modest financial success and rereleased the feature in May of 1940. Studio executives speculated that in 1939 the film had been one step ahead of the public; they hoped that with intervening events it might find a larger audience. The 1940 release included clips of the Nazi's latest triumphs in Europe along with a brief treatment of the Fifth Column's alleged whispering campaign against President Roosevelt. Still, the picture failed to draw large audiences and remained only a slightly profitable business venture.

The heads of Warner Brothers believed that they had performed a patriotic act in making *Confessions of a Nazi Spy*, regardless of its box office performance. After the film's premiere, Jack Warner fired off a telegram to President Roosevelt which described his movie as a "Great American Document of Civilization."[86] Warner invited FDR to screen the film, an offer which the President seems to have politely refused. When isolationists in Congress conducted an investigation of the film industry in 1941, they attacked *Confessions of a Nazi Spy* as undisguised propaganda. In testifying before this committee Harry Warner stoutly defended the film:

> I cannot conceive how any patriotic citizen could object to a picture accurately recording a danger already existing within our country. Certainly it is not in the public interest for the average citizen to shut his eye—ostrichlike—to the attempts of Hitler to undermine the unity of those he seeks to conquer. The experience of Norway and its Quislings, and the sad fate of too many other countries is too recent not to be in our memories. And we certainly have no apology for producing *Confessions of a Nazi Spy*.[87]

The pride which Warner's studio took in their picture was largely justified. Its release marked a significant milepost in Hollywood's movement toward an explicitly interventionist position. As Warner's publicity men boasted, the picture was indeed the first "to call a swastika a swastika."

The spy film eventually became the preferred genre for attacks on the

Axis. After *Confessions of a Nazi Spy* all of the studios began churning out pictures dealing with the Fifth Column. Between 1939 and 1941 Hollywood released 24 features which dealt with the problem of espionage. In 1942 alone the studios produced over 70 pictures stressing spies, sabotage, and subversion.[88] The Fifth Column provided a way for Americans to feel involved in the fight against fascism, before American G.I.s were actually engaged in battle with the Wehrmacht. Hollywood was eager to help Americans feel as though they constituted an important part of the Allied crusade against Hitlerism.

The unmasking of the Griebl spy network did not reveal the loss of vital national secrets nor did it set off an immediate nationwide panic. Nevertheless, the affair marked a clean break with the interwar era and reminded citizens of the nation's vulnerability to foreign subversion. As a news story the spy case provoked concerned comments from the President and various experts on intelligence matters. The unusual facts and personalities surrounding the Griebl ring kept the public interested in the drama. The unraveling of the New York spy network left Americans with the unsettling possibility that this episode exposed only the tip of a Fifth Column iceberg.

The New York spy case offers an interesting example of the way in which the media often acts as a gigantic echo chamber. The same story was told over and over again in a variety of different forms. As the events of the case grew more distant, distortion increased. Leon Turrou and Warner Brothers both saw a didactic purpose in their renderings of the affair. Hence, they interpreted events in a fashion designed to heighten popular alarm, believing America could be aroused only by an unambiguous warning. Turrou and Warner's also must have seen that a lurid spy story was more likely to sell newspapers, books, and movie tickets than a staid, undramatic account. Patriotism thus combined with self-interest to produce a sensational interpretation of the Nazi Fifth Column menace.

FOUR

~~~

Other Fifth Columns

Italy, the Soviet Union, and Japan

On the evening of October 30, 1938, Orson Welles's Mercury Theatre of the Air presented a radio dramatization of *The War of the Worlds*. The program, aired on the Columbia Broadcasting System, was structured in the form of a series of news reports. Only loosely adapted from H. G. Wells's original story, it vividly described a Martian invasion of Grovers Mills, New Jersey. At four separate points in the broadcast CBS announced that "the entire story and all its incidents were fictitious." Local stations also interrupted the show with similar disclaimers. Nonetheless, the day after Welles's broadcast aired, newspaper accounts described "a tidal wave of terror" which had "swept the nation." Reports told of terrified citizens who had fled their homes, weeping college students who had made farewell telephone calls to loved ones, and stouthearted individuals who had volunteered to battle the hostile extraterrestrials. A study by social scientist Hadley Cantril concluded that over one million Americans had been frightened by the *War of the Worlds* broadcast. Welles issued a public apology for the panic sparked by his program, and the chairman of the Federal Communications Commission pronounced the whole affair "regrettable."[1]

How had a farfetched piece of radio entertainment created such hysteria? One wag cracked that "as good an explanation as any for the panic is that all intelligent people were listening to Charlie McCarthy." (The Edgar Bergen show was playing on another network at the same time.) On a more serious note, a poll of 250 social scientists concluded that the Sudeten crisis had spooked the American public, thus leaving the nation susceptible to Welles's dramatization. Newspaper editorialists concurred. The *New York Times* blasted CBS for forgetting that "our people are just recovering from a psychosis brought on by fear of a war." The *New York World Telegram* averred that "nerves made jittery by actual though almost incredible threats of war and disaster had predisposed a good many radio listeners to believe the completely incredible." Columnist Heywood Broun thought that the response to the Welles broadcast confirmed the fact that "Jitters have come home to roost."[2]

The Munich crisis alarmed observers in the United States. Throughout the Depression, America focused principally on its own domestic difficulties. However, by the autumn of 1938, the increasingly fragile state of the international order turned the nation's eyes toward foreign policy issues. Authoritarian regimes in Germany, Italy, Japan, and the Soviet Union all seemed to be mounting a challenge against the world's democracies. As these dictatorial states successfully played the game of power politics, many Americans began to wonder whether the future was on the side of totalitarianism. The disquieting rise of hostile and aggressive regimes in Berlin, Rome, Moscow, and Tokyo left much of the public predisposed to accept fanciful tales of invasion—even tales of a Martian attack.

The War of the Worlds broadcast caused a national panic by describing an external invasion of the United States. However, prior to Pearl Harbor, few Americans believed that the United States was really in imminent danger of a conventional military attack from its earthly rivals. Instead, the public feared that foreign adversaries—Germany, Italy, the USSR, and Japan—were mounting a more subtle and a more insidious invasion of the United States, an attack which relied upon a hidden army of Fifth Columnists.

For different lengths of time, and in varying degrees, press reports identified Italy, Japan, and the Soviet Union as Trojan Horse accomplices of the Third Reich. In the spring of 1940, the *New Orleans States* summarized the commonly held notion that the world's dictators worked together to subvert the United States:

> This nation harbors plenty of rats ready to spring their dark deeds of destruction and treachery at the opportune moment. All of them are active in behalf of an axis that offers the only obstacle in the world to American peace, the Axis that turns on Rome, Berlin, Moscow, and Tokyo. No other country would have any reason to infiltrate their fifth columns in this republic.[3]

The Fifth Column was thus viewed as as a tool which the world's totalitarian regimes used in order to undermine their democratic rivals. The overall panic which gripped the United States between 1938 and 1942 cannot be understood merely by examining popular fears of the

Nazi Trojan Horse. One needs to also assess America's concerns regarding Italian, Soviet, and Japanese Fifth Column activity.

The Italian Fifth Column

Neither the American public nor the federal government ever became overly agitated by the threat of an Italian Fifth Column. This relative calm largely reflected the realities of international power. Mussolini's Italy constituted a far less threatening foe than Hitler's Germany. Il Duce was widely viewed as a comic figure who was incapable of doing much harm if left to himself. When pollsters asked Americans in June 1940 to identify the nation exerting the worst influence in Europe, 53 percent named Germany, 34.2 percent the Soviet Union, 1.8 percent Great Britain, and only 1.2 percent chose Italy.[4]

The media did produce occasional exposés on Mussolini's alleged Fifth Column intrigue in America. A June 1940 article in *Fortune* magazine contained one of the most alarming assessments of the Italian menace. This piece argued that Mussolini had 25,000 operatives in the United States, who in the event of war "would act as enemy soldiers with all the duties of soldiers." The story claimed that the Fascist International almost exactly replicated the Nazi International, except for the fact that the former was numerically stronger than the latter. *Fortune* added that the OVRA (Opera Voluntaria Repressione Antifascista, or Bureau for the Suppression of Anti-Fascism) was very active in the United States, coercing recent immigrants into working for Mussolini. For all its attempts to build up the Italian Fifth Column, the *Fortune* article began by describing Mussolini's agents as "Hitler's Helpers," thus asserting the primacy of the Nazi threat.[5] Not all publications expressed the same fear of an Italian Fifth Column as did *Fortune*. In July 1940, *Colliers* concluded that if America's Italian population was "the only menace we had to worry about, we could all live lives 99.9% free of care."[6]

Neither Congress nor the White House lost much sleep over the Italian menace. Martin Dies, the chairman of the House Un-American Activities Committee, investigated possible Italian subversion in America. In his book *The Trojan Horse in America*, Dies noted that throughout America over 100,000 people of Italian descent had attended meetings of various fascist organizations. He added that the OVRA was active in America.[7] Yet despite such comments, HUAC expended little of its energy examining the Italian Fifth Column. Dies's committee chose to focus instead on Nazi and Communist intrigue. President Roosevelt was even more doubtful of Rome's ability to organize an effective subversive force in the U.S. FDR told Attorney General Francis Biddle that on matters of subversion the Italians were "a lot of opera singers," whereas "the Germans are different, they may be dangerous."[8]

After Pearl Harbor the White House did take a few steps to contain possible Italian Fifth Column activity. In January 1942, the government reclassified unnaturalized Italians as enemy aliens. However, this move was only a precautionary measure. The FBI remained confident about the loyalty of Italians. A Bureau report noted that "the Italian colonies throughout the United States in general remain patriotic to this country."[9] In the first three days after Pearl Harbor, the FBI arrested only 147 Italians, compared with 857 Germans; only 228 Italians were interned for the entire course of the war, compared with 1,891 Germans. On October 12, 1942 (Columbus Day), President Roosevelt, acting on a recommendation of the Justice Department, removed Italians from the category of enemy aliens. Historian John Diggins notes that Roosevelt's action was the result of many factors. FDR hoped to win political points with Italian-American voters, as well as to raise the morale of Italian-American soldiers. However, Diggins concludes that the best explanation for the President's decision was "the awareness of the abiding loyalty of Italian Americans."[10]

The Communist Fifth Column

Starting in the mid-thirties, many commentators began noting parallels between the dictatorships of Joseph Stalin and Adolf Hitler.[11] For example, newspaper columnists Walter Lippmann, Dorothy Thompson, Herbert Agar, and Raymond Clapper, historians Charles Beard and Louis Fischer, poet Archibald Macleish, and playwright Robert Sherwood all suggested a growing convergence between the USSR and Germany. This trend occurred in spite of the two states' avowed enmity for one another and their apparent antipodal positions on the political spectrum. The rejection of free speech, the submergence of individual rights, the apotheosis of a single leader, and the government's control over all institutions within the state were only a few of the alarming similarities which were detected between the regimes in Berlin and Moscow.[12]

As Les Adler and Thomas Paterson have noted, the Nazi-Soviet pact accelerated the tendency of Americans to view Nazism and Communism as essentially one and the same thing. In 1939, the press coined the word "Communazi" to describe the perceived identity between Hitler's and Stalin's political philosophies. Columnist Eugene Lyons expressed a widely shared view when he argued that the Ribbentrop-Molotov deal (securing an alliance between Germany and the USSR) revealed Hitler's Brown Bolshevism and Stalin's Red Fascism as "aspects of the same totalitarian idea."[13] A similarity between the Soviet Union and Nazi Germany that did not escape the attention of the American public was each state's highly developed intelligence apparatus and devotion to intrigue. For almost two years Soviet espionage, sabotage, and subversion seemed nearly as threatening to America as Hitler's Trojan Horse. In fact, Hitler and Stalin were thought to have combined forces so as to initiate a common Fifth Column offensive against the United States.

Popular dread of Communism is easy to document. In July 1940, a Roper poll found that 38 percent of Americans wanted to deport or jail all Communist sympathizers; another 33 percent wanted to prohibit Communists from organizing or agitating.[14] Numerous incidents of mob action against Communist party organizers underscored the public's fear of "Red" subversion.[15] Moscow's involvement in Fifth Column activity was highlighted by the revelations of several prominent Communist defectors, by the investigations of the House Un-American Activities Committee, and by the outbreak of several strikes in America's defense industries.

Shortly after the conclusion of the Ribbentrop-Molotov pact, two Communist defectors, Walter Krivitsky (Samuel Ginsberg) and Jan Valtin (Richard Krebs), gained celebrity status in the United States. Both men wrote memoir accounts which exposed extensive Soviet intelligence operations in the United States. In their widely distributed writings and in appearances before congressional investigating committees, Krivitsky and Valtin warned of the susceptibility of democratic regimes to foreign penetration.

Walter Krivitsky was one of the earliest and most important Soviet defectors to the West. From 1935 to 1937 Krivitsky served as the chief of Soviet Military Intelligence (GRU) for Western Europe. Dread of Stalin's purges led Krivitisky to quit the GRU and seek refuge in the West. In the spring of 1939, Krivitsky wrote a sensational series of articles for the *Saturday Evening Post* which exposed Soviet intrigue in Europe and America. He later assembled material from these pieces into a book entitled *In Stalin's Secret Service*.[16] Krivitsky described OGPU murders outside the Soviet Union, Comintern plots in Germany, and attempts by Stalinist agents to pass counterfeit bills in the United States. The ex-GRU officer wrote that the Communist party in the United States was "more closely connected than any other . . . with our OGPU and Intelligence Service."[17] He added that many members of the CPUSA engaged in espionage for the Soviet Union.

The United States government moved to take advantage of the ex-GRU man's knowledge. Krivitsky met with officials from the State Department and the FBI. He later appeared publicly before the House Un-American Activities Committee. His dramatic testimony, delivered in October 1939, made the front page of the nation's major newspapers. Krivitisky claimed that the OGPU had penetrated the American armed forces, government, and major defense industries. He repeated his charge that the United States Communist party received its orders and funding direct from Moscow. Krivitsky's testimony specifically identified the individuals who had most recently run the OGPU and Soviet military intelligence in the United States.[18]

After his appearance before the Dies committee, Walter Krivitsky did not make news again until February 1941, when he was discovered shot dead in a hotel room in Washington, D.C. Police found three suicide notes: one to Krivitsky's wife; another to his attorney, Louis Waldham; and a third to his editor, Suzanne LaFollette. Local law enforcement ruled the death a suicide, but controversy immediately enveloped the case. Krivitsky's associates claimed foul play. The general's wife suggested that OGPU agents had forced her husband into shooting himself. According to this scenario Soviet killers had agreed to spare Krivitsky's family as long as the general did himself in. Louis Waldman told the public that Krivitsky had claimed to have seen known OGPU killers in New York shortly before his death. Waldman suggested that one of these hit men had most likely murdered his former client. In Congress, Martin Dies ominously observed that "what happened to Krivitsky may happen to a lot of others." Mississippi congressman John Rankin called the general's death "homicide." J. Parnell Thomas, an investigator for the Dies committee, recalled Krivitisky telling him, "If they ever try to prove I took my own life don't believe it." Krivitsky's demise left the country to face the shocking possiblity that even in the United States one could not escape Stalin's reach. Given the recent murder of Leon Trotsky in Mexico, few doubted the Soviet Union's capacity for committing foreign assassinations.[19]

Another ex-Communist who temporarily stepped into the national spotlight was Jan Valtin. Valtin, a German, was at one time a member of the Comintern. In 1937 he turned his back on world revolution and sought refuge in the western democracies. Free from party control, Valtin penned a horrifying memoir of his life as a Communist. His book, *Out of the Night*, proved a national best-seller in America, winning a spot as the Book of the Month Club special selection for February 1941. Those who did not have the endurance to read all 752 pages of Valtin's autobiography could turn to condensed renderings in *Reader's Digest* and *Life*.[20] Valtin's memoir combines melodrama and suspense. He notes the tragic death of his wife in a German concentration camp and the disappearance of his son. Valtin describes his capture, interrogation, and torture by the Nazis, and his work as a double-agent for the Germans. *Out of the Night* ends with Valtin fleeing the secret police of both Germany and the Soviet Union, a finale which underscored the popular notion that Stalinism and Hitlerism were two sides of the same coin.

Reviewers at *Time* magazine noted that Valtin's book "painted a savage picture of the depravity of the Comintern, OGPU agents, the world's Communist parties," and showed that "the Russian Fifth Column is coterminus with the globe."[21] *Out of the Night* principally discussed Valtin's subversive work in Germany. Nevertheless, the book also showed that the United States was not impervious to enemy penetration. Valtin described his illegal entry into America and his efforts to convert

U.S. seamen to the Communist creed. He also admitted that while in Los Angeles he had committed a felonious assault upon a Communist party turncoat. Valtin claimed that he performed this crime, for which he was sent to San Quentin prison, under direct orders from his Communist party superiors.[22]

Valtin appeared before the Dies committee in the spring of 1941. In his testimony he denounced alleged acts of subversion by both Germany and the Soviet Union. Valtin claimed that the Nazis sought to generate a civil war in the United States. He further argued that Communists in America's maritime trade unions were trying to reduce the amount of lend-lease aid shipped to Great Britain.[23]

In Congress, the anti-Communist standard was taken up most prominently by Representative Martin Dies. In 1938, Dies gained bipartisan support for the creation of the House Un-American Activities Committee (HUAC). HUAC devoted significant energy to the investigation of right-wing groups, but ended up focusing principally on the Communist menace. Dies sought to publicize dramatically the activities of Communists and leftist fellow-travelers. His committee held hearings, issued reports, and zestfully pursued press coverage. The Texas congressman displayed special interest in examining Red penetration of the federal government and organized labor. Such work proved gratifying to Dies, because it allowed the conservative southerner to attack the Roosevelt administration.[24]

In 1939, Dies asserted that over 2,850 known Communists held government positions. The HUAC chairman made it clear that he believed that the White House coddled Communists. In particular, Dies charged Secretary of Labor Frances Perkins with indifference toward the Red menace. This accusation was largely founded on Perkins's failure to deport Harry Bridges, the radical Australian-born leader of the West Coast Longshoreman's Union. Perkins held that Bridge's membership in the Communist party was not proven. In addition to attacking prominent Roosevelt advisers, Dies pursued specific New Deal programs which he thought displayed left-wing bias. For example, HUAC attacks helped bring about a cut in funding to the Federal Theater and Writers' Projects, WPA programs in which Communists were involved.[25]

Congress as a whole was worried by both Communist and Nazi Fifth Columns and produced several important pieces of legislation aimed at safeguarding domestic security. In June 1940, the Senate and House passed the Alien Registration Act, or Smith Act. The legislation called for the registration of all aliens and authorized the deportation of noncitizens belonging to revolutionary groups. Additionally, the law made it a crime to "advocate, abet, advise, or teach the duty, necessity, desirability or propriety of destroying any government in the United States by force or violence. . . ." The Alien Registration Act made membership in a revolutionary group a punishible offense, thus preventing the government from having to prove individual violations of the law. In September 1940, FDR approved the Voorhis Registration Act. This act attempted to uncover enemy Trojan Horses by mandating that all organizations under foreign control register with the Justice Department.[26]

The Communist menace also disturbed the Roosevelt administration. In particular, members of FDR's cabinet were anxious about a combination of Soviet and Nazi Fifth Column operations. In April 1941, Assistant Secretary of War John McCloy and Undersecretary of War Robert Paterson approached President Roosevelt to complain of the threat sabotage and subversion posed to war production. McCloy and Paterson argued that a no-holds-barred approach was needed to fight Communist and Nazi Fifth Column work. The two advisers specifically recommended the formation of an extra-legal "suicide squad" within the FBI. FDR gave the proposal preliminary approval, but he asked the War Department to broach the matter with Attorney General Robert Jackson. Jackson was outraged by the suggestion. He wrote an indignant letter to the President complaining that McCloy and Paterson "believe that normal methods should be abandoned and that investigators should be unrestrained in wire tapping, in stealing of evidence, breaking in to obtain evidence, in conducting unlimited search and seizures, use of dictaphones, etc. etc." The Attorney General said that such a policy would "rapidly demoralize" the Justice Department, "lead to the early and permanent discrediting of the Federal Bureau of Investigation, and destroy the reputation of the Roosevelt Administration."[27] Jackson wrote a blistering letter to McCloy which outlined the dangers of operating outside the boundaries of the law: "The man who will today rifle your desk for me tomorrow will rifle mine for someone else. I just don't want that type of fellow in my outfit." The Attorney General added that the FBI men had been "carefully schooled against these methods" and would not participate in violations of the law. McCloy responded to Jackson by claiming that "the machinations of German agents" would not be uncovered "without applying abnormal and, no doubt in some cases, quite distasteful means."[28] However, in the end Jackson blocked the establishment of an FBI "suicide squad."

The War Department continued to press for greater government protection of America's defense industries. Late in May 1941, Secretary of War Stimson and Secretary of the Navy Frank Knox sent a joint memorandum to the White House which proposed several steps to thwart Fifth Column activities. Knox and Stimson expressed less concern about possible acts of sabotage than about enemy-inspired strikes and work slowdowns. The two cabinet officers noted that their uneasiness was based on intelligence reports from the Office of Naval Intelligence and military intelligence, which reported that labor difficulties were "in many cases instigated by Communist and other subversive elements acting in the interest of foreign enemies." Knox and Stimson asked the President to take action which would prevent strikes and expand the FBI's responsibility "in the fields of subversive labor control."[29] FDR speculated that subversive elements were probably behind some of America's labor disputes, and he passed along the Knox/Stimson proposals to the Attorney General.[30]

Knox and Stimson's concerns were a product of the tremendous labor difficulties which slowed America's war production in 1940 and 1941. Communist party members encouraged many of the work stoppages in the nation's various defense industries. For example, Communist Harold Christoffel led a strike at the Allis-Chalmers plant in Milwaukee, Wisconsin. This plant was responsible for manufacturing turbines and generators for United States Navy vessels. In November 1940, a work stoppage at the Vultee aircraft plant in Los Angeles was encouraged by UAW organizer and C.P. member Wyndham Mortimer. In June 1941, Mortimer led workers at the North American Aviation plant out on strike. This plant was responsible for the production of nearly 25 percent of the United States fighter aircraft. The national UAW refused to sanction the strike at North American Aviation and urged laborers to return to work. The local union ignored these pleas. Finally, President Roosevelt called on the army to break through the picket lines and restore production at the plant.[31]

The role of Communists in defense strikes was well known and the cause of considerable public concern. A *Reader's Digest* article claimed that Red Fifth Columnists (subservient to both Hitler and Stalin) burrowed within the labor movement and jeopardized the entire preparedness program: "An invading Communist army—shielded by an uninformed public and coddled by the authorities—has moved into positions from which on orders from Moscow or Berlin, it can jam the wheels of American production and paralyze our national defense."[32] During the period of the Nazi-Soviet pact, the Communist party in the United States was fervently isolationist. Britain's struggle with Germany was described by the party as a clash between two rival imperialisms. The *Daily Worker* savagely attacked Roosevelt, arguing that the President's renewal of the Selective Service Act and his support for Lend-Lease were dictatorial. Communist party Chief Earl Browder ineffectually argued that his organization was loyal to America. He claimed that it was not the Communists who were the traitors but rather America's main-line political parties: "Who are the 'fifth column' in the United States? . . . Martin Dies . . . The Roosevelt Administration . . . The Republican Party leadership."[33]

Fear of a Soviet Fifth Column in America subsided almost immediately after the Germans launched Operation Barbarossa. Hitler's invasion of the Soviet Union transformed American Communists into diehard supporters of the Roosevelt administration. C.P. members no longer encouraged strikes but stressed the need to keep production high in order to vanquish Germany. Stalin shrewdly sought to curry favor in the West by dissolving the Third Communist International. This step, taken in 1943, led an exultant Martin Dies to note that his congressional committee appeared to have lost its raison d'être. The common fight against Hitler quickly dispelled the public's fears that Soviet agents threatened domestic stability. Despite the wartime alliance, many Americans remained suspicious of Stalin. Conservative writers such as Max Eastman offered a critical assessment of the Soviet dictator: "Stalin is the weaker of two gangster-tyrants, and common sense demands that we support his resistance to Hitler. But common sense also warns against the added strength this gives his American agents with their own more subtle plots against our way of life."[34] Important government officials such as J. Edgar Hoover shared Eastman's hostile attitude toward Moscow. However, after the German invasion of the Soviet Union, it would not be until the destruction of Hitler that a new fear of Communist subversion again swept America.

The Japanese Fifth Column[35]

Prior to the Pearl Harbor attack, Americans displayed little concern over the danger posed by Japan's Fifth Column. In fact, Japanese espionage was generally viewed with bemused contempt. In March 1939, a *Reader's Digest* article entitled "So Sorry for You: Japanese Espionage Used To Be Funny—But No More" tried to convince the public that Tokyo had improved its Trojan Horse operations, especially in Asia. The author, Hallett Abend, criticized the American public's view of Japanese espionage as "a national joke." Even though Abend's piece aimed at increasing popular awareness of Tokyo's alleged Fifth Column prowess, his article conceded that "the Japanese spy, even in the Orient, does have his comic as well as his highly exasperating aspects."[36]

The initial confidence which Americans felt about their ability to withstand Japanese Fifth Column activities was grounded in a number of hard facts. The Japanese population in the United States was small (approximately 127,000 in 1940) and was concentrated along the nation's West Coast. Berlin, Rome, and Moscow all drew from a larger and a more geographically dispersed pool of likely sympathizers than did Tokyo. Moreover, white Fifth Columnists were in a better position to avoid arousing suspicion in America than were Asian Fifth Columnists. Before Pearl Harbor set off a mini-"Yellow Peril" scare along the West Coast, most Americans thought that the primary menace which Japan posed to domestic security had to do with possible naval and military espionage. Yet even this danger never seemed overly threatening, since in the years prior to the Pearl Harbor attack the Office of Naval Intelligence and the Federal Bureau of Investigation handily smashed several Japanese espionage rings. The skill of American investigators and the apparent ineptness of Tokyo's operatives proved reassuring to the public.

In 1936, Harry Thompson, a former yeoman in the U.S. Navy, was arrested for selling secret materials to the Japanese. Thompson frequented the docks in San Diego and San Pedro, sneaking aboard ships and gathering data on the movements, personnel, and equipment of various American naval vessels. He passed this information on to Toshio Miyazaki, a Japanese naval officer, who posed as an English-language student at Stanford University. Thompson made a poor spy. He drank heavily and had a loose tongue. Thompson foolishly revealed his espionage work to his roommate Willard Turntine. Turntine conveyed this information to naval authorities. Shortly thereafter, Thompson was arrested, tried, and sentenced to fifteen years in prison.

Later in 1936, the FBI discovered that John Semer Farnsworth, another ex-U.S. service man, was in the employ of Tokyo. Farnsworth, a former lieutenant commander in the United States Navy, had been court-martialed in 1927 after seeking a loan from an enlisted man. Bitter and bankrupt, he offered his services to Russia, Italy, Peru, China, and Japan. Tokyo accepted his proposal. The FBI concluded that over a period of several years Farnsworth obtained "documents, writings, code books, signal books, sketches, photographs, photographic negatives, blueprints, plans, maps, models, notes, instruments, appliances and other information relating to national defense."[37] Farnsworth passed this intelligence to his foreign controllers in exchange for $20,000.[38] The FBI placed him under surveillance after discovering that he had borrowed a confidential naval report from a friend on active duty. This surveillance eventually allowed the Bureau to uncover his treason.

The arrests of Thompson and Farnsworth sparked a brief flurry of interest in domestic security matters. The *Literary Digest* nervously noted that Tokyo was spending an alleged $12 million on intelligence operations, while only a paltry $200,000 was allotted to America's naval and military intelligence units.[39] *Newsweek* claimed that the Thompson and Farnsworth cases had produced the biggest spy scare since World War I.[40] In spite of such worries, discussion of Japanese secret operations quickly faded from the headlines. The botched espionage activities of both Thompson and Farnsworth suggested that government had Japanese intrigue under control.

In the spring of 1941, the ONI and FBI broke into Japan's Los Angeles consulate and photographed a large number of secret documents. These materials compromised Tokyo's entire West Coast spy network and led to the apprehension of Itaru Tachibana and Toraichi Kono. Tachibana, a Japanese naval officer, oversaw secret operations on the West Coast. He entered the United States posing as an English language student at Stanford University. Toraichi Kono was a subordinate of Tachibana's and a former butler for comedian Charles Chaplin. Kono hired Al Blake, a retired naval officer, and asked him to gather intelligence on war production, defense installations, and ship movements. Blake immediately reported to United States naval authorities, who told him to play along with the Japanese. In June, the government arrested Tachibana and Kono, charging them with espionage. Secretary of State Hull, seeking to avoid upsetting diplomatic relations with Japan, kept the affair quiet. Tachibana was spared prosecution and simply deported. Still, the episode proved highly significant for America's counterintelligence efforts. On the basis of information acquired during the burglary of Japan's Los Angeles consulate, Lieut. Commander Kenneth Ringle, chief of ONI in southern California, determined that Tokyo's espionage activities did not threaten national security. The FBI agreed with Ringle. The Tachibana case also reinforced the FBI and Ringle's belief that Tokyo preferred to use occidental agents for its American intrigue rather than ethnic Japanese.[41]

By 1941, America's intelligence experts were confident in the loyalty of the Nisei (the first-generation Japanese born in the United States), and believed that the Issei (immigrant Japanese), while possibly retaining sympathy for Japan, would generally tend to remain loyal to the United States. Of course, the FBI and ONI kept a close watch on America's Japanese community. They recruited informants from among the Nisei, and compiled lists of suspect organizations and individuals. Primary responsibility for identifying subversive elements in the Japanese population fell to the FBI.

Before the outset of the war, the Bureau developed a three-tiered system for categorizing members of potentially disloyal groups (e.g. German, Japanese, Italian). Group A included those considered "dangerous"; Group B comprised individuals thought "potentially dangerous"; while Group C was left for those thought to be on the fringes of disloyalty.[42] By early 1941, the government listed over 2000 Japanese in Group A, B, or C. Initial Bureau plans called for the internment only of Group A suspects. However, when the war began, the FBI arrested individuals from all three groups: three days after Pearl Harbor, 1,291 Japanese were in custody; by the middle of February the figure was up to 2,192. Those arrested were primarily Japanese-born (Issei), and included businessmen, Japanese-language instructors, leaders of civic and cultural organizations, and religious figures.[43] Some were quite understandably suspect, such as leaders of the militant nationalist organization the Black Dragon Society; others were simple fishermen whose links to Japanese military and intelligence operations were nonexistent. The FBI believed that its early roundup had completely ended the threat of any Japanese Fifth Column. Indeed, historian Bob Kumamoto has persuasively argued that the Bureau's enemy list wrongly identified as disloyal many individuals simply interested in preserving Japanese culture.[44] While the FBI's steps were excessive, J. Edgar Hoover proved far more level-headed than almost any other public figure of his day. After his initial precautionary steps, Hoover consistently argued against mass internment, forcefully contending that such a program was unnecessary and legally dubious. The director reached such a sane position because of the remarkable job of counterespionage which the Bureau had performed in the years leading up to Pearl Harbor.

Other sources besides the FBI and ONI viewed the Japanese as generally trustworthy. In 1941, President Roosevelt set up a small intelligence gathering apparatus under the supervision of journalist John Franklin Carter. The Carter organization received its operating budget from the President's special emergency fund and served FDR as an independent source of information. In October, Carter received from his subordinate C. B. Munson the first of several reports which detailed the Japanese situation on the West Coast and Hawaii. Carter wrote FDR that Munson saw "no evidence which would indicate that there is danger of widespread anti-American activities. . . ." Rather, "it was more likely that the Japanese were in danger from whites . . . than the other way around."[45] Munson's other studies reached the same conclusion: namely, that the Japanese were loyal Americans. When the federal government began to move toward a policy of mass internment, Munson fired off an angry letter to FDR's secretary, Grace Tully, warning that ". . . we are drifting into a treatment of the Japanese corresponding to Hitler's treatment of the Jews."[46]

In the immediate aftermath of Japan's attack on Pearl Harbor, rumors of betrayal and treachery overwhelmed Hawaii and the West Coast. The Japanese Fifth Column, which had once been viewed with a smile, now was contemplated with dread. Innumerable stories told of Tokyo's alleged efforts to contaminate America's food and water supply, to sabotage defense plants, dams, and other strategic locations, and to prepare the way for an invasion of the United States mainland. The FBI worked double-time to quell such fantasies. On December 12, 1941, Hoover assured the White House that stories of arrow-shaped fires set by Fifth Columnists to guide bombers to Seattle were unfounded. A Bureau investigation revealed that a local farmer had been burning brush, and that his fires did not point in any particular direction. Hoover also debunked an alleged sabotage plot against the Bonneville Dam; the director noted that power lines at the site had been damaged by cattle rather than by enemy spies.[47] All of these efforts at rumor control proved futile as government officials and the popular media churned out one tale after another of Japanese treason.

Secretary of the Navy Frank Knox helped to enflame popular passions when he announced on December 15, 1941, that Japan's attack on Hawaii was "the most effective Fifth Column work of the entire war . . . with the possible exception of Norway." Knox's comments made front-page headlines, despite the fact that what he said was pure hogwash.[48]

Attorney General Biddle informed the President that the Navy Secretary's statements ran directly counter to FBI findings. At a December 19, 1941, cabinet meeting, Knox told the President that there was significant Fifth Column activity in Hawaii and called for the President to "take all of the aliens out of Hawaii and send them to another island." Biddle again denounced the Navy Secretary's assertions as spurious. The Attorney General insisted on the overall loyalty of the Japanese in Hawaii.[49]

The chief of the Army's Western Defense Command, Lieut. General John L. DeWitt, encouraged the Japanese spy scare. Shortly after December 7, DeWitt began releasing a series of terrifying reports. He claimed that numerous acts of enemy sabotage were being carried out along the West Coast. Moreover, in spite of contrary evidence from the Federal Communications Commission, DeWitt announced that Japanese submarines were receiving radio transmissions from American agents; these secret shortwave communications allegedly betrayed U.S. shipping schedules. In fact, the sinking of several U.S. merchant ships off the coast of California helped to lend credibility to this rumor. DeWitt's headquarters released a warning on December 7 of an impending air raid on San Francisco, and on December 11 the Army issued an alert which warned of a Japanese fleet approaching the Bay City. The general's alarmist posture disturbed FBI chief Hoover, who expressed concern that the army "was getting a bit hysterical."[50]

After Pearl Harbor, the Western Defense Command began making an escalating series of demands for a government counterattack on Japanese intrigue. DeWitt called for FBI raids on the homes of all aliens along the coast. The Bureau eventually did conduct several searches of alien homes and businesses. The press and General DeWitt emphasized the fact that the dynamite, ammunition, guns, radio receivers, and other contraband confiscated in FBI raids proved the reality of Japanese Fifth Column plotting. However, the Department of Justice reached a different conclusion: "We have not found a single machine gun nor have we found any gun in any circumstances indicating that it was helpful to our enemies. We have not found a camera which we have reason to believe was for use in espionage."[51]

DeWitt took several steps designed to transfer responsibility for West Coast security from the Justice Department to the War Department. Starting in early January, DeWitt began initiating policies which would eventually lead to the mass evacuation of the Japanese from the West Coast and their internment in inland detention camps. (Interestingly, the government never interned the Japanese population living in Hawaii, despite the greater vulnerability of these islands to hostile attack.) The Justice Department wanted to limit security areas within narrow geographical confines. However, beginning in February the Western Defense Command began to pressure Washington for the internment and evacuation of all Japanese from the West Coast. DeWitt repeatedly expressed the view that the Japanese were "an enemy race" and, as such, could never be fully trusted.

The Justice Department was outraged. Biddle, as well as his principal advisers, found the WDC proposals to be absurd. On February 7, Biddle told FDR that the Justice Department "believed mass evacuation at this time inadvisable, that the F.B.I. was not staffed to perform it; that this was an army job not, in our opinion, advisable; that there were no reasons for mass evacuation. . . ."[52] Hoover shared Biddle's viewpoint; the director viewed wholesale internment as a foolish response to public and political pressure.[53] However, the weight of the media, West Coast politicians, and various patriotic, civic, and economic organizations, combined with the insistence of General DeWitt proved too much for President Roosevelt and the War Department.

In January, John Hughes of the Mutual Broadcasting Network ran a series of radio broadcasts on the danger which Tokyo's agents posed to domestic security. He offered America's radio listeners a chilling picture of the situation on the West Coast:

> . . . thousands of Japanese fifth columnists are wandering around at will—or perhaps "wandering" is not the word—they know what they're doing, and what they intend to do. . . . It is all very well to be nice to our enemies, at least to the point of recognizing that they are human beings, and worthy of humane treatment, but to give them a sort of preferred status that permits them to continue their operations against us, seems a little thick.[54]

On February 12, syndicated columnist Walter Lippmann warned that the West Coast was "in imminent danger of a combined attack from within and without." Lippmann called for the establishment of a security zone along the West Coast which excluded all persons, citizens and aliens alike, whom the military authorities viewed as a security threat.[55] Columnist Westbrook Pegler also chimed in with vigorous support for an internment of the Japanese: "the Japanese in California should be under guard to the last man and woman right now and to hell with habeas corpus until the danger is over." Hearst columnist Henry McClemore contended that the Japanese were not entitled to any constitutional protections: "Herd 'em up, pack 'em off, and give 'em the inside room of the badlands. Let 'em be pinched, hurt, hungry and dead up against it. . . ."[56] By late January and early February the editorial pages of most West Coast papers were demanding evacuation of the Japanese.[57]

In Washington, calls went up from the nation's West Coast congressmen for tough action against the Japanese. Leland Ford of Los Angeles was the first to urge mass evacuation. When the Justice Department attempted to block tough security measures, Ford lashed out with fury. He warned Biddle to "stop f - - - - - g around" or else he would clean out the Attorney General's "god d - - - - d office in one sweep."[58] On February 13, representative Clarence Lea sent a letter to FDR on behalf of all West Coast legislators. Lea urged the wholesale evacuation of the Japanese from all sensitive areas. The President passed this note on to the Secretary of War. Though most agitation for anti-Japanese measures came from California, Washington, and Oregon legislators, a few other congressmen also voiced their worries. Martin Dies declaimed that Pearl Harbor was the result of "a maudlin attitude toward fifth columnists" and that unless the government became more vigilant the West Coast was likely to be the next target of Tokyo's treachery. John Rankin of Mississippi and Senator Tom Stewart of Tennessee expressed doubt that anyone of Japanese ancestry could be trusted.[59]

On the West Coast, state and local politicians, economic assocations hostile to the Japanese, and various civic and patriotic groups agitated for evacuation. In California, Governor Culbert Olson, Attorney General Earl Warren, and Los Angeles mayor Fletcher Bowron all backed Japanese internment as the most practicable way to counteract sabotage and other Fifth Column activities. The governor of Oregon as well as the mayor of Portland also favored a mass evacuation policy. While Washington governor Arthur Langlie steered clear of hysteria, the state's attorney general, Smith Troy, and the mayor of Seattle endorsed evacuation. In addition to genuine fears about domestic security, many of these officials were following a politically expedient course, which protected them against charges of indifference to the Fifth Column.[60]

Several special-interest groups helped push for internment. Organizations such as the Western Growers Protective Association, the Grower-Shipper Vegetable Association, the California Farm Bureau Federation, and the Los Angeles Chamber of Commerce all had economic motives for removing the Japanese. Xenophobic organizations such as the Native Sons of the Golden West and the California Joint Immigration Committee saw evacuation as the only safe way to deal with a perfidious un-American race. Patriotic groups such as the American Legion urged internment of the Japanese as a necessary wartime precaution.[61]

On February 17, Secretary Stimson asked General Guillon to draft an executive order authorizing the implementation of an evacuation program. Stimson's action was spurred on by General DeWitt, who warned of indications that the enemy was "organized and ready for concerted action at a favorable opportunity." On February 18, Stimson met with Justice Department officials to discuss the newly minted executive order. Biddle remained adamant in his opposition to the proposed policy, but admitted its constitutionality. On February 19, 1942, President Roosevelt signed Executive Order 9066. This order allowed the War Department to restrict access to certain military areas. While the Japanese were not specifically mentioned in the order, the presidential document was clearly aimed at them. In March, Congress initiated a bill allowing enforcement of the executive order; the legislation was approved without opposition.[62]

By June 1942, over 97,000 Japanese had been placed in relocation centers; as of October the figure rose to 111,999 out of a total of approximately 127,000.[63] Just when internment reached its peak, the hysteria which had inspired Japanese evacuation began to die down. No doubt this was partly a response to the harsh government action against the Nisei and Issei. Other factors helped end the panic. The American victory at Midway in June 1942 made talk of any enemy invasion of the West Coast transparently absurd. The complete failure of any Fifth Column activities to unfold in America quieted the nation's jittery nerves.

After 1942, most Americans lost interest in Japan's Trojan Horse weapon. An occasional book or film appeared on the subject (for example, Alan Hynd's *Betrayal from the East* was released in 1944 and turned into a feature film in 1945), but these pieces were rare compared with the flood of anti-Japanese material which surfaced in the winter, spring, and summer of 1942. Strangely, though fears of Japanese espionage, sabotage, and subversion sharply declined after the first twelve months of the war, the government did not end its internment program until December 1944. As early as the spring of 1943, Secretary Stimson, Assistant Secretary McCloy, and Chief of Staff Marshall all agreed that military necessity no longer justified the evacuation program. However, General DeWitt insisted on maintaining internment, and until he was replaced as chief of the WDC in the autumn of 1943 little progress was made on the matter. In May 1944, Stimson formally told the President that the detention of the Japanese was no longer defensible on military grounds. However, with one eye clearly on the upcoming presidential election, FDR refused to act until after he had gained a fourth term in the White House. Finally, on December 17, 1944, the government ended the exclusion of all Japanese from sensitive areas of the West Coast.[64] In contrast to the case of the Nazi Fifth Column, there is little evidence that Roosevelt felt grave concern at the menace posed by a Trojan Horse directed from Tokyo. After all, he never insisted on internment of the Japanese population residing in the Hawaiian islands. FDR's willingness to accept the harsh treatment of Japanese residing on the West Coast reflects a pragmatic and shameful concession to political realities. Japanese Americans lacked any electoral clout; public opinion in California, Oregon, and Washington backed stern security measures against a potential enemy; and opposition to the desires of the army and War Department opened up the President to charges of failing to protect the home front.

For a few months following the Pearl Harbor attack, the fear of a

Japanese Fifth Column hit fever pitch. On the West Coast especially, such hysteria briefly surpassed worries about Hitler's Fifth Column, though of course the German and Japanese Fifth Columns were always thought to be working in concert. Both the media and the government stressed the gravity of Tokyo's Trojan Horse menace. In April 1942, Mark Gayn of *Reader's Digest* went so far as to claim that "the success of the German Fifth Column in Norway, France and the Lowlands did not compare in scope or thoroughness to the Japanese Fifth Column in the Philippines, Hawaii, and British Malaya."[65] The spasm of panic which convulsed the West Coast caused the government to take security steps against the Japanese far harsher than those initated against any other group. Tokyo's alleged Fifth Column offered a convenient pretext for various groups to endorse internment. Morton Grodzins, the most thorough examiner of the West Coast Japanese spy scare, has noted that "The War provided the unique situation whereby patriotism . . . could become parallel with economic, racial, and political considerations."[66] In sum, fear of the Japanese Fifth Column was a momentarily convulsive phenomenon. Though brief in duration, the panic's intensity greatly agitated the public and made possible the tragedy of internment.

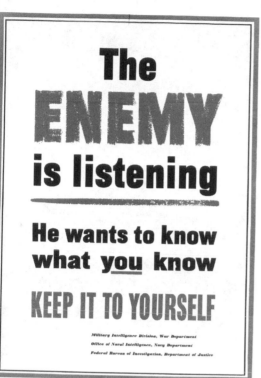

Office of Facts and Figures

Office of War Information

Office of War Information

Office of War Information

Office For Emergency Management

Office of Civilian Defense

This photograph appeared in *Time* with the caption: "National Legion of Mothers of America. Their idea: to pick off descending parachutists." UPI/ Bettmann.

THE FIFTH HORSEMAN

Editorial cartoon from *New York Herald Tribune*, June 9, 1940.

Editorial cartoon from *The New York Times*, June 26, 1938. Copyright © *Providence Journal.*

Henderson in The Providence Journal

Within our gates.

In a baffling misallocation of superhero manpower, Superman insists on protecting the home front against Fifth Column adversaries rather than meeting Axis enemies on the battlefield. Comic strip from *Washington Post*, March 10, 1942. Courtesy of DC Comics.

In 1940, Issue 1 of *Captain America* introduced a new champion of home front security. Courtesy of Marvel Comics.

Back cover of anonymous pamphlet, *Hitler Doomed to Madness* (Greenwich, Conn.: Country Press Inc., 1940).

FIVE

"Perfidious Albion"

Great Britain and the Fifth Column

Winston Churchill replaced Neville Chamberlain as the Prime Minister of Great Britain on May 10, 1940. The Churchill government initiated a new intimacy in Anglo-American relations. From the beginning of his tenure in office, Churchill pursued policies aimed at fully involving the United States in the war effort against Hitler. In 1940 and 1941 the United States and Great Britain jointly undertook a series of dramatic steps which served to draw the two English-speaking powers together: these steps included the destroyers for bases deal (August 1940), the Lend-Lease bill (March 1941), and the drafting of the Atlantic Charter (August 1941). When word reached the Prime Minister of the Japanese attack on the American naval base at Pearl Harbor he was ecstatic, for this attack now meant that "the United States was in the war, up to the neck and in to the death." A long worked-for end had now been achieved; when Churchill went to bed he "slept the sleep of the saved and the thankful."[1]

Churchill's effort to draw the United States into the war marked a departure from the policies of his predecessor. Throughout the period of the "phoney war," Neville Chamberlain intentionally avoided an overly close relationship with the United States. He viewed America as an undependable ally, doubted whether effective American help could be supplied quickly enough to influence the outcome of the war, and feared that if Washington did indeed offer aid to Britain, it would be at an exorbitant price. British caution toward the United States derived from the apparently stalemated continental military situation. Whitehall hoped this stalemate would force the Germans to accept a negotiated settlement. While the "phoney war" lingered on, and hopes of a compromise peace with the Germans were still alive, London saw no need to complicate European matters by involving the unreliable Americans in continental affairs.[2]

With the fall of France and the rise of Churchill, Britain's primary objective in dealing with the Roosevelt administration was to gain active American participation in the fight against Hitler. In order to help draw the United States into the war, London sought to make both the Roosevelt administration and the citizenry of the U.S. aware of the dangers which a seemingly distant Nazi regime posed to the American way of life. One way in which the British brought this threat home was to suggest that Nazi agents had already penetrated the Western Hemisphere in preparation for a future invasion. With authorization from Winston Churchill, the British established a large intelligence organization in the United States. This organization worked covertly to expose alleged espionage in North and South America.

The Churchill government also facilitated the transmission of the existing English spy fever across the Atlantic to the United States. Thus, uneasiness in the United States regarding the dangers posed by Axis subversion, specifically a German Fifth Column, derived in part from English influences. London did not simply attempt to dupe the Americans with bogus warnings of Axis intrigue. In fact, Churchill's government genuinely feared subversion in both Britain and the United States. This fear combined with the practical fact that it served the larger interests of British foreign policy to publicize subversive Nazi activities, not only in Europe, but also in North and South America. Thus, there was a willingness by London to give an overblown account of the menace which the German Fifth Column posed to the United States. The special cultural ties between the two nations also helped to amplify American fears of Nazi treachery. British books and motion pictures stressing the threat of German subversion found a receptive audience across the Atlantic. These tales supplemented the large number of Fifth Column suspense thrillers that originated in the United States.

This chapter considers the ways in which the British heightened American fears of a Nazi Trojan Horse. First, covert British intelligence activities in the United States exposed real and imaginary Fifth Column plots. Second, policymakers in London passed their fears of German treachery in Britain to their American counterparts. Finally, British spy thrillers—both novels and films—reinforced American thinking regarding the threat of a Nazi Trojan Horse in the United States. In effect, the British established their own Fifth Column in America, devoted to counter-Fifth Column activities.

British Intelligence in the United States

The British clearly won the clandestine struggle fought in America prior to 1917. When war erupted on the continent in 1939, decisionmakers in Whitehall no doubt remembered the experiences of the First World War, when German espionage and subversion in the United States had been thwarted and exposed. The hope of uncovering a second Zimmermann telegram or making some similar intelligence coup which would draw America into the conflict must have been strong. No other British statesman could have seen the potential for secret operations in America more fully than Winston Churchill. It was, after all, Churchill who as First Lord of the Admiralty supervised the espionage work of "Blinker" Hall and British naval intelligence.

However, in the interwar period the American public increasingly questioned the wisdom of United States participation in the Great War. It became a commonly held supposition in many circles that clever propaganda by the British had duped Washington into an unwise intervention in World War I. The British Embassy at Washington was sensitive to these charges. Therefore when World War II began, the British ambassador to the United States, Lord Lothian (Sir Philip Henry Kerr), sought to pursue a "no propaganda" campaign which would depend strictly on the distribution of "facts through the Embassy and the British Library of Information." Lothian argued against a large-scale public relations offensive in the United States:

> There is no need whatever for arguing the ideological case for the Allies. The United States is unanimous except for small interested groups, in its hatred of Hitlerism and Americans can be relied upon to conduct the ideological argument better and more effectively, so far as their own public opinion can do. The situation is quite different from the ignorance of 1914.[3]

As time passed a bureaucratic struggle erupted between the Foreign Office and the Ministry of Information over the control of propaganda in the United States. Duff Cooper, head of the Ministry of Information, thought that more had to be done in the public relations battle. Lothian was willing to bend a bit in the fight but continued to warn of the need to combat the "constant suggestion that we are working over-time to inveigle America into war by subtle and almost invisible coercion."[5]

In London the controversy over the nature of British policy in America was discussed at the highest levels of government. In the summer of 1940, Emery Reves proposed to Winston Churchill a scheme for an enlarged and more emphatic program of political action in the Western Hemisphere. Reves was born in Hungary and had only recently been naturalized as a British subject. Before the war he had headed a European press service which, among its many tasks, arranged for articles written by Winston Churchill to be syndicated to newspapers throughout the continent. In this capacity Reves had become a frequent correspondent with Churchill, informing him of developing events in Europe. The two men were thus on intimate terms both professionally and personally. (In fact, after the war Reves became Churchill's literary agent for his wartime memoirs.)[6] The propaganda campaign which Reves now put forth to the British Prime Minister had three goals: first, to persuade the American people that Hitler directly menaced the American nations "and will conquer them one by one, just as he conquered Europe"; second, to attack the principles of neutrality, isolation, and nonintervention as unworkable; and third, to launch an "offensive campaign" against German propaganda.[7]

Duff Cooper saw Reves's plan as an attempt to build "a Fifth Column . . . devoted to British interests." Cooper wrote to the Prime Minister that such an "offensive" propaganda policy "would be a revolution in our methods of propaganda." While Cooper remained noncommital on Reves's proposal, his subordinate Frank Pick expressed a positively hostile view of the scheme. Pick indignantly noted that "to use German methods of propaganda as recommended by Mr. Reves is contrary to our national character, is bound to recoil upon us dangerously, is in fact beyond our skill and capacity."[9] Reves's plan was eventually quashed but it was not without its supporters. Churchill observed that "Mr. Harcourt Johnstone, Dr. Dalton etc. were in principle in favor of something along on these lines."[10] Reves claimed that in addition to Dalton and Johnson "Mr. Attlee, Lord Lloyd, . . . Sir Robert Vansittard[sic], Mr. Rex Leeper, and many others are in full agreement with me." In December of 1940, Reves bitterly complained of those who had sabotaged his proposal, observing "that in the 16th month of the war we have still no organization for political warfare worthy of our armed forces."[11]

However, Reves lacked a full understanding of the situation. By late in the spring of 1940 Churchill had taken steps to develop an activist American policy. In May, Secret Intelligence Services appointed William Stephenson as liaison officer to American intelligence. Stephenson was a 44-year-old Canadian and a millionaire industrialist. During the First World War he had served with valor in the Royal Air Force. Just prior to his appointment in America, Stephenson had engaged in a variety of intelligence gathering operations for Britain. According to historian Anthony Cave Brown, he had volunteered to take part in a scheme with Colonel F. N. Mason-McFarlane to "shoot Hitler with high powered sporting rifles." Stephenson brought to his involvement in the "Great Game" the same sort of no-holds-barred toughness which had made him in his youth a successful amateur boxer.[12]

In his new position Stephenson's primary functions were to win U.S.

support for Britain, fight Nazi Fifth Column activity in the Western Hemisphere, and insure the safety of British material and property in America. Moreover, Churchill ordered Stephenson to pursue policies which would create a popular mood in America favorable to U.S. intervention in the war.[13] With the informal approval of President Franklin D. Roosevelt, Stephenson set up his organization, entitled British Security Coordination, in New York City. The agency operated out of the International Building of the Rockefeller Center under the cover of British Passport Control. BSC immediately became involved in a host of clandestine activities including wiretapping, political dirty tricks, and rumor-mongering.

BSC spent considerable time and energy in an effort to discredit isolationist groups and their representatives. One example of the campaign against supporters of United States neutrality involved the printing of false tickets to an America First meeting held at Madison Square Garden in New York City on October 30, 1941. Charles Lindbergh was scheduled to speak at the gathering, and British intelligence hoped to disrupt the "Lone Eagle's" lecture by planting interventionists in the audience. However, this plan backfired as the extra tickets only helped to fill a rather sparsely attended talk, thus creating an overblown impression of the level of interest in the isolationist program. British intelligence also worked to undermine American congressmen who adopted a strict position against intervention. For example, Stephenson directed an effort to bring to public attention the way in which isolationist congressmen were allowing the America First organization to send out pamphlets and correspondence under the congressional frank.[14]

BSC also engaged in a noteworthy disinformation campaign. By the summer of 1941 Earl "Sydney" Morrell, one of Stephenson's agents, claimed that "approximately 20 rumours daily are now dealt." Morrell worked in S.O.l—British subversive warfare operations—which was responsible for the dissemination of "black" propaganda in the United States. (Black propaganda was material whose true source was intentionally hidden.) BSC employed a variety of techniques in its distribution of black propaganda. Sometimes the British planted stories in the press of neutral countries, working under the assumption that such accounts would be picked up by American journals. S.O.l also maintained contact with the foreign-language press inside the United States. In particular Morrell cultivated a relationship with the Czech consul, to whom stories were forwarded, "rewritten by him and issued to the Czech press in the form of underground reports from Europe." British intelligence saw to it that these stories were cabled back to Europe and then transmitted again to the U.S. so as to give "a snowball effect to each rumor." BSC established contacts with many prominent American newspapers and journalists, usually through "cut-outs" (second-party intermediaries who were able to protect the identity of the source). Some of the more well-known figures included Dorothy Thompson, Walter Winchell, and Edgar Mowrer. The *New York Herald Tribune* was perhaps the most frequently used friendly newspaper, while magazines used by the British included *PM*, the *Nation*, and the *New Republic*.[15]

Morrell also made the boast that his organization had "controlled or acquired" a number of pro-Allied organizations in the U.S., including the Anti-Nazi League, the League for Human Rights, the Friends of Democracy, and the American Committee for Inter-American Cooperation. Morrell may very well have overstated the extent of his unit's influence on these American groups. Surely many of these organizations would have been attacking the isolationists regardless of British actions in the United States. Nonetheless, it is worth noting that historian Wayne Cole has identified the Friends of Democracy as one of the organizations most active in labeling the America First group as "the Axis Transmission Belt."[16] Indeed, it is quite plausible that BSC aided groups like the Friends of Democracy in portraying America First as a cat's-paw for the Nazis.[17]

British intelligence helped to generate heightened anxieties regarding the dangers of Axis penetration in Latin America.[18] In June of 1941 Stephenson aide H. Montgomery Hyde visited Bolivia to investigate rumours of a potential coup by Nazi sympathizers. J. P. Belmonte, the Bolivian military attaché in Berlin, was said to be at the center of the plot. However, Hyde could not come up with hard evidence to back his suspicions. Not to be deterred, the British agent arranged to forge a letter which suggested an impending coup by a fascist Fifth Column in Bolivia. The British assigned authorship of the letter to Belmonte. In Washington, William Stephenson told the FBI he had heard word of a courier carrying a German diplomatic bag holding "incriminating documents of the highest order." Next, BSC let the Bureau's field agent in Buenos Aires know that a German courier had been deprived of important papers while standing in a crowded elevator of the local German bank. According to Hyde's account, Hoover requested the filched document, and Stephenson, always willing to be the loyal ally, passed on the bogus coup plot to the Bureau. FDR then forwarded the information to the Bolivian government, which shut down the German embassy and rounded up 150 fascist sympathizers. The publicity surrounding the event further raised public awareness regarding the immediacy of the Fifth Column threat.[19]

As Hyde tells it, the BSC had launched a flawless operation, duping Roosevelt into accepting "cooked" material. In fact, Washington remained highly circumspect about the entire Belmonte conspiracy. A July 7 memo from Adolf Berle to Undersecretary of State Sumner Welles noted that "the F.B.I. tells us that they are not by any means convinced that the letter is genuine. In another similar case they suspected British intelligence of having 'planted' documents of dubious authenticity on them."[20] Washington had witnessed British deception campaigns frequently enough that any word of fascist plots was treated with suspicion. For example, in August of 1940, the British asked the American embassy in Bogotá to cooperate in a scheme to plant false documents which placed responsibility for an antigovernment riot on the German embassy (the very same British agent involved in this scheme later suggested to the American ambassador to Colombia, Spruille Braden, that perhaps some arrangement should be worked out "by which Dr. Lopez de Mesa, the Foreign Minister, might be killed"[21]). In a September 5, 1941, memorandum to Secretary of State Cordell Hull, Berle noted that in Latin America "British intelligence has been very active in making things appear dangerous. . . . I think we have to be a little on our guard against false scares."[22]

Later in 1941, British intelligence passed on to the White House a map which appeared to display the Axis master plan for remaking Latin America. In this map the fourteen states of Central and South America were condensed into five regions. FDR went to the public on October 27 and denounced the Nazi blueprint for aggression. He concluded that the map made clear Germany's "design not only against South America but against the United States as well."[23] The Germans quickly dismissed the map as a forgery. When questioned about the authenticity of the document FDR claimed it came from a source which was "undoubtedly reliable."[24] Surely this was an exaggeration, since intelligence from the British had in the past been found to be of questionable validity.[25]

The range of British espionage activity in the U.S. alarmed both Assistant Secretary of State Adolf Berle and FBI director J. Edgar Hoover. In April of 1941 Berle told Under-Secretary of State Sumner Welles of a "full size secret police and intelligence service" rapidly evolving in America.[26] Berle noted that BSC had district offices in Boston, New York City, Philadelphia, Baltimore, Charleston, Houston, and San Fransisco. He claimed Stephenson's organization had entered "the whole field of political, financial, industrial, and probably military intelligence," and he warned that with each passing day BSC established informal links with a variety of governmental organizations ranging from the New York City Police Department to certain agencies of the War Department.[27] Thus, it became clear that even though the British government had officially rejected Emery Reves's proposal for an offensive propaganda campaign, they had in fact implemented such a program in the United States.

Adolf Berle eventually became one of the most persistent critics of British intelligence operations in the United States. Berle was the son of a prominent Boston Congregationalist minister and a graduate of Harvard College and Harvard Law School. He was an original member of President Roosevelt's Brains Trust and he remained an important ally of FDR throughout his tenure in office. On questions of foreign policy Berle was a Wilsonian liberal. This made him not only an opponent of Soviet and Nazi totalitarianism, but also an adversary of British imperialism. The President appointed Berle to serve as Assistant Secretary of State in 1938. As part of his job he assumed responsibilities as the State Department Coordinator for Intelligence.[28] In this capacity, he became anxious over the activity of BSC. Throughout 1941 Berle strongly urged the President to limit Stephenson's organization strictly "to the actual and necessary operations of protecting British ships and British munitions."[29]

Berle soon became a figure thoroughly hated by London's officialdom. In September of 1940 the Washington-based manager of London's *Financial News* wrote the Foreign Office that Berle was "so anti-British that he takes visitors—including Dominion Ministers!—to the window, and shows the White House, and says 'the British burnt it in 1812,' with foam in his mouth."[30] This analysis was not entirely inaccurate, for Berle clearly harbored deep distrust of "perfidious Albion." At the outbreak of World War II, he called the history of past relations with London one of "half-truths, broken faith, intrigue behind the back of the State Department and even the President." Still, Berle viewed himself as a moderate and a realist on questions relating to Britain. Though convinced that England would be found to be "no more truthful with us now than they were in 1917," he nonetheless believed aid to Britain an essential component of American foreign policy. He based his reasoning on the hard fact that "we ourselves will be in difficulties if they go under."[31]

Berle presented quite sensible and compelling reasons for putting a halt to the extraordinary operations engaged in by Stephenson's group:

> I do not see that any of us can safely take the position that we should grant blanket immunity for any foreign spy system, no matter whose it is. Logically, why have it? If our interests diverge, it is adverse; if they are the same, our own people ought to be able to do the job with such assistance as they may want.[32]

Berle believed that the activities of BSC constituted a violation of the Espionage Act. He also complained that British espionage supplied London with vital strategic information which if England fell would end up in German hands. Even more important, Berle noted that Stephenson's organization was in a position to unduly influence American decisions by making "trouble for any individual in business or in public life to whom the British for some reason might take exception."[33] This concern weighed particularly heavily on the Assistant Secretary's mind as he believed that the British embassy was "gunning for [his] scalp."[34] Berle's fears were justified; as early as 1940 Victor Perowne of the Foreign Office suggested the creation of a file on Berle.[35] In January 1942, the FBI alerted the Assistant Secretary of a smear campaign being directed against him by Denis Paine of BSC. Washington ordered Paine to leave the United States within twenty-four hours. Stephenson denied involvement in the affair, claiming his agent had acted independently. However, the Justice Department used this incident to press for a curtailment of British operations in the U.S.

In a meeting on March 5, 1942, Attorney General Francis Biddle complained to British ambassador Halifax about the pattern of unauthorized activities engaged in by Stephenson's organization. Biddle claimed that in the wake of recent events the President and the cabinet had reached two conclusions. First, British intelligence's role in the U.S. should take the form of liaison rather than operations; second, a new man should probably be brought in to head BSC. Halifax expressed astonishment at Biddle's statement, claiming that Stephenson had assured him that the closest possible relations were maintained with the FBI. At this point in the discussion Berle telephoned J. Edgar Hoover in order to respond to Halifax's claim of intimate cooperation between BSC and the Bureau. Hoover bluntly commented that on those occasions when Stephenson did report what he was doing it was usually after the fact. The FBI chief noted that when his agents dealt with BSC "they were never sure of whether they were getting the whole story; and they knew in many cases they were not." The Americans then detailed to the Ambassador a number of specific examples of British intelligence excesses. After hearing all this, Halifax claimed that his thinking had been altered, though he made no firm commitment to institute reforms. On March 10, 1942, when Halifax met again with Berle and Biddle, he came prepared to stonewall. The ambassador flatly denied that British intelligence had done anything "except with the direct authority and cooperation of American officials." The Attorney General and Assistant Secretary of State reminded Halifax of Hoover's earlier comments, but this made no apparent impression on the ambassador. Finally, after much wrangling, Halifax "seemed to agree" on limiting BSC to liaison functions unless prior American approval had been granted for direct operations. With the United States already involved in the war, wildcat operations by BSC on American soil became less necessary and more difficult to justify.[36]

Why did President Roosevelt tolerate espionage by a foreign power on American soil? First, FDR was concerned about the potential dangers of Axis activities in the United States, and Stephenson's organization helped combat German spying in a number of legitimate ways. BSC both protected lend-lease supplies and opened access to new intelligence sources. After all, one more agency doing battle against the enemy made for better national security. Second, Roosevelt's toleration of the excesses of British intelligence suited his broader foreign policy goals. The President's willingness to work with Stephenson was a gesture of cooperation and support for England at a time when more dramatic public assistance may have been politically difficult. And of course BSC worked to discredit Roosevelt's domestic foreign policy critics.

Spy Fever in Britain

At times British intelligence intentionally exaggerated the threat of the Axis Fifth Column. Nonetheless, genuine fears of foreign intrigue lay behind much of the action taken by London. If anything, Britain saw the techniques of Nazi Fifth Column subversion as an even greater danger than the United States did. In May of 1940, the British Joint Intelligence Committee, a body including the heads of intelligence in the army, navy, and air force, as well as representatives from MI5 and MI6, claimed that the collapse of Norway and Denmark had been in large measure due to Fifth Column activity. Moreover, it warned that in England Nazi subversion "might well play a very active and highly dangerous part at the appropriate moment selected by the enemy." The JIC held that the lack "of sabotage up to date reinforces the view that such activities will only take place as part of a prearranged military plan." The Chiefs of Staff, noting the JIC findings, argued that subversion would be a dangerous component of any German plan against England.[37]

During the First World War the British government had placed 30,000 enemy aliens in detention camps. However, after the war this policy was viewed as an overreaction, and the government took measures to prevent such a mistake in any future national emergency. But with the rush of events in the spring and summer of 1940 the possibility of evenhanded treatment for enemy aliens vanished. Pressure from the War Office, Foreign Office, Joint Intelligence Committee, and Chiefs of Staff forced Sir John Anderson of the Home Office to implement a stern policy of internment. Ironically, 30 percent of the Germans confined in a typical camp in November of 1940 had been at one time in Nazi prisons or concentration camps; furthermore, 70 percent were classified by British tribunals in 1939 as "refugees from Nazi oppression." In fact, over 80 percent of those interned indicated a desire to perform some national service for England. However, the fear that Hitler had slipped agents in among the refugees discouraged a gentler policy toward enemy aliens. Eventually a total of 27,200 individuals were either placed in camps or deported, from an overall estimated enemy alien population of 73,000 (a figure not dissimilar from the number of World War I internees, in spite of the overall desire for a policy which fairly treated aliens). The willingness to waste limited resources in such an effort indicates the sincerity of Whitehall's concerns regarding potential problems caused by a Nazi Fifth Column.[38]

London's genuine concerns regarding the problem of subversion were transmitted to policymakers in Washington. For example, in July of 1940 Secretary of the Navy Frank Knox sent Colonel William Donovan on a mission to England. Knox gave Donovan two assignments: first, he was to evaluate Britain's morale and fighting capacity; second, he was to undertake a study of German subversive tactics in England. Washington sent journalist Edgar Ansel Mowrer along with Donovan to assist in the second assignment. Lord Lothian explained to the British Foreign Office that Knox sought information on techniques of Axis subversion in order to assist the FBI and to "warn the public about characteristic Fifth Column activities against which they should be on their guard."[39]

While in England, Mowrer and Donovan were supplied with background material on German subversive techniques. They relayed this back to the States, where it appeared as a four-part newspaper series and also as a national radio broadcast. The series reached chilling conclusions. Donovan noted: "In the United States an organization of Nazis is being trained in arms. As matters now stand, it is conceivable that the United States possesses the finest Nazi-schooled fifth column in the world, one which, in case of war with Germany could be our undoing."[40] Knox endorsed the finding of his agents, labeling their work "the most thoroughgoing survey of German 'fifth column' methods" yet done.[41] The whole affair unduly raised public fears of possible Axis subversion in the U.S.[42] While it is possible that the British intentionally supplied false information to the two Americans, such an interpretation is hardly necessary. With the shocking events of the spring of 1940 in mind, officials from both countries were ready to credit much of Hitler's success to his ability to weaken his adversaries' home-front morale. In August 1940, Ambassador Joseph Kennedy sent a report to Cordell Hull emphasizing the danger London believed America faced from home-front subversion: "Those with whom I have talked here are of the opinion that the United States has more to fear from Fifth Column activities than any other nation. They point to our tradition of violence, to the widespread ownership of firearms, and above all, to the polyglot character of our population."[43]

The British Spy Thriller in America

Espionage and spy thrillers imported into the United States from Britain influenced American attitudes toward the danger posed by a Nazi Fifth Column. These novels and films presented Germany as a nation particularly skillful in espionage. A stock character in British spy adventures was the German superagent. Usually this villain was portrayed as a man of extraordinary qualities: cultivated, fanatically brave, murderously cunning, and utterly ruthless. Such figures proved challenging foes, especially given the fact that England and America were open societies. The British had pioneered the development of the thriller/invasion story in the late nineteenth century. Hence by the time World War II began, the German spy had become a familiar figure in popular culture in both Britain and America. One could discuss any number of British authors and filmmakers who gained some degree of popularity in America through the spy thriller genre (for example, William LeQueux, E. Phillips Oppenheim, Sidney Horler, Geoffrey Household, Eric Ambler, and Alexander Korda). Two of the more prominent masters of this form were novelist John Buchan and filmmaker Alfred Hitchcock.

John Buchan was a man of unusual talents. He was a gifted and prolific writer as well as an important political activist. Buchan's career in public service included membership in Parliament (1927-35) and an appointmentment in 1935 as governor general of Canada. During the First World War, Buchan worked for the British government's propaganda bureau, where he oversaw the reorganization of the Department of Information. Later when that agency was again reorganized and made a cabinet-level position, he stayed on in the newly created Ministry of Information, working under Lord Beaverbrook. Here Buchan actively sought to improve Anglo-American relations. He encouraged the sending of lecturers to the United States and worked to bring American journalists to London and to the Western Front.[44]

In 1915, Buchan reaped fame and profits on both sides of the Atlantic with the release of *The Thirty-nine Steps*, the first of several Richard Hannay adventures. The plot line of this book follows the efforts of Hannay to crack a deadly spy ring which has penetrated England. At the start of the story, Buchan's hero is pursued by the police as a murder suspect; eventually, he clears himself and captures the real villains. In the process, Hannay unravels a German plot to steal British naval plans. The German spies in this work display extraordinary cunning and skill. Buchan's chief antagonist, the unnamed "man with the hooded eyes," shows a talent for disguise unmatched even by Sherlock Holmes. The Kaiser's agent successfully poses as a minister in Britain's war cabinet in order to gain intelligence on the royal navy. Earlier in the book he passes himself off as a scholarly archaeologist. Only through good luck and quick thinking is Hannay able to win the day.

With the 1916 publication of *Greenmantle*, the next Hannay adventure, Buchan again focused on the dangers of German espionage. Here Hilda von Eimen is the principal enemy agent. Buchan presents this character as a villainness of almost supernatural evil. Her plans envision the creation of a pro-German Persian empire, an empire which she intends to run. The efforts of Hannay, his American partner Bleinkiron, and his mysterious friend Sandy Arbuthnot prevent the onset of revolution in the Middle East. Nonetheless, von Eimen's razor-sharp mind, fanatical courage, and mesmerizing beauty nearly enable her to pull off the scheme.

Finally, in *Mr. Standfast* Buchan describes the misdeeds of Mr. Horace Ivery. Ivery is a German agent posing as a peace activist in Britain. Sir Walter Bullivant, Buchan's fictional head of British intelligence, warns of the dangers presented by men like Ivery to open democracies. "We're the leakiest society on earth, and we safeguard ourselves by keeping dangerous people out of it. We trust to our outer barrage. But any one who has really slipped inside has a million chances." With clubbish sexism Bullivant reinforces this point by asking Hannay and his friends to simply "think of women; how they talk."[45] Once again, however, justice triumphs and the Hun is defeated. German soldiers unwittingly kill Ivery, their own agent, while he is running for their trenches.

In his treatment of German spies film director Alfred Hitchcock stressed many of the same themes found in John Buchan's adventure stories. (In fact, in 1936 he offered a brilliant cinematic rendition of *The Thirty-nine Steps*, Buchan's most popular work.)[46] Like Buchan, Hitchcock made his German agents into human chameleons. Hitchcock's sophisticated villains hid their true identies as easily as the spies described in the Hannay stories. In *The Secret Agent* (1935), actor Robert Young plays a ruthless German assassin disguised as a wise-cracking American traveler. Paul Lukas is a cultivated but murderous Nazi operative masquerading as a physician in *The Lady Vanishes* (1938), and *Foreign Correspondent* (1940) features actor Herbert Marshall as a distinguished peace activist whose noble façade is merely a cover for pro-German schemes. The Nazi agents in Hitchcock's motion pictures were gifted and resourceful scoundrels. To the innocent and uninformed these villains appeared to be decent and trustworthy chaps, men of polish, breeding, and impeccable manners. In fact, one needed to scratch only slightly below the surface to discover a deadly and treacherous adversary.

In 1939 Alfred Hitchcock left Britain and came to America. At the time he had directed a number of successful motion pictures in Britain and was widely respected throughout the film industry. Anxious to work with the larger resources available in Hollywood, he signed with producer David O. Selznick to direct *Rebecca*. Some in England attacked Hitchcock for abandoning his native country at the time of its greatest need. In fact, the British government had requested that he continue making films in the U.S. so as to help win American popular support for the Allies.[47] Hitchcock immediately proceeded to produce anti-German thrillers, releasing *Foreign Correspondent* in 1940 and *Saboteur* in 1942.

Foreign Correspondent tells the story of an American journalist who, though initially unfamiliar with the situation in Europe, eventually comes to see the dangers posed by Nazi Germany. The film stresses the theme of Anglo-American cooperation as a United States reporter teams up with an English journalist to smash a Nazi spy ring in Britain.

In *Saboteur*, which went into production prior to the Pearl Harbor attack, Hitchcock took a more ardently interventionist stand. In this story, which he both wrote and directed, Hitchcock presented an America in which seemingly respectable members of society were fascist operatives. In later years he told François Truffaut that the film intentionally sought to show the links between isolationists and Nazis. "We were in 1941 and there were pro-German elements who called themselves America Firsters and who were, in fact, American Fascists. This was the group I had in mind while writing the scenario."[48] In *Saboteur*, Robert Cummings plays an average American on the run from the police and from Nazi agents. In the closing moments of the movie he confronts Tobin, a sinister Fifth Columnist. They exchange barbs, which reveals the way in which Hollywood tended to depict Americans and their German foes.

KANE: Why is it that you sneer every time you refer to this country? You've done pretty well here. I don't get it.

TOBIN: No, you wouldn't. You're one of the ardent believers—a good American. Oh, there are millions like you—people who plod along without asking questions. I hate to use the word stupid, but it seems to be the only one that applies. The great masses—the moron millions. Well, there are a few of us who are unwilling to just troop along—a few of us that are clever enough to see that there is much more to be done than live small complacent lives. A few of us in America who desire a more profitable type of government. When you think about it, Mr. Kane, the competence of the totalitarian nations is much higher than ours. They get things done.

KANE: Yes—they get things done. They bomb cities, sink ships, torture and murder—so you and your friends can eat off gold plates. It's a great philosophy.

TOBIN: I neither intend to be bombed nor sunk, Mr. Kane. That's why I'm leaving now. And if things don't go right for you—if we should win—then I'll be back. Perhaps I can get what I want then—power. Yes, I want that just as much as you want your comfort or your job—or that girl. We all have different tastes as you can see, only I'm willing to back my tastes with the necessary force.

KANE: You certainly make it sound smooth and easy. Well, that's a trick. I know the results of that power you believe in. It killed my friend and it's killed thousands like him. That's what you're aiming at, but it doesn't bother you. I can see that. Because you really hate all people. Let me tell you something. The last four or five days I've learned a lot. I've met guys like you and I've met others—people who are helpful and eager to do the right thing. People that get a kick out of helping each other fight the bad guys. Love and hate, the world is choosing up sides. I know who I'm with and there are a lot of people on my side—millions of us in every country. We're not soft. We're plenty strong. And we'll fight standing up on two feet and we'll win no matter what you guys do. We'll win if it takes from now until the cows come home![49]

It is hard to measure precisely the influence of works of popular culture on the thinking of either individual policymakers or a mass public. Nonetheless, artists like Buchan and Hitchcock helped create a widely prevalent image of Germany as a society which possessed a coolly competent secret service full of cultivated brutes. The works of both these men suggested that there was something inherent in the German character which made that nation's agents adept practitioners of the Great Game of espionage. The German spy who inhabited Buchan's novels and Hitchcock's films was part Prussian tactician, part university professor, and part barbarian. The works of these two tremendously popular artists thus played on and strengthened ancient ethnic and national stereotypes.[50]

The British attempt to influence American public and governmental opinion was broad-based, concerted, and quite effective. Stephenson's intelligence organization successfully publicized alleged penetration of the hemisphere by the Axis. The informational pipeline from Britain to both Washington insiders and the American media exploited the general fears of the Fifth Column, and British novels and films helped raise anxieties in the United States by portraying German espionage as a grave threat to open, democratic societies.

The Germans cooperated with Britain's effort to spark a Trojan Horse panic in America. Hitler's aggressive blitzkreig operations suggested the possibility that the Third Reich desired world conquest. Even more significant, the string of half-baked subversive activities Germany directed against the United States terrified ordinary Americans and confirmed the worst Fifth Column fears that London sought to inspire.

Of course, the British influence would have hardly mattered were it not for a complex cluster of domestic factors which made tales of the Fifth Column resonate throughout the country. The White House, the Congress, the emerging national security establishment (specifically the FBI), and the various popular media all cultivated the notion of widespread Axis espionage in America. Moreover, the self-image of the United States public encouraged citizens to regard their country as a vulnerable target for Axis espionage. In sum, the British influences did not instigate the notion of a Fifth Column, but exacerbated already existing American fears.

SIX

The Fifth Column
in Europe

In July 1941, the citizens of Anderson, South Carolina (population 20,000) staged a mock invasion of their own town. Over 1300 people played the parts of Fifth Columnists and supporting German troops. They set off fireworks as substitutes for exploding bombs and ignited blazing smoke pots to simulate burning buildings. An airplane dropped handbills urging Anderson residents to surrender. Meanwhile, Fifth Columnists disguised as tourists seized vital points in the city. They arrested employees at the local post office, newspaper, radio station, power plant, and railroad depot. Fifth Columnists also took into custody the town's mayor, police chief, and fire chief, forcing these local dignitaries to raise their hands above their heads while pistols were jabbed into their sides. Two columns of uniformed troops arrived shortly thereafter to cement the gains won by Trojan Horse treachery. With Anderson's capitulation, the invaders placed captured town officials in a concentration camp. After the mock attack's conclusion, the *New York Herald Tribune* reported that the town "entertained the Fifth Columnists and troops at a dance."[1]

The purpose of Anderson's mock invasion was to instruct cadets at Clemson University in the nefarious tactics which Hitler was thought to have used in Europe. In South Carolina and throughout America, commentators linked Nazi advances in Austria, Czechoslovakia, Poland, Norway, Holland, Belgium, and France to the employment of Trojan Horse techniques. Having observed the Reich's apparent ability to destroy its adversaries from within, most Americans believed that Germany directed similar tactics against the United States.

The Nazi Fifth Column was by no means a pure fiction.[2] The major propaganda, diplomatic, and intelligence organizations of the Reich frequently resorted to Trojan Horse activities. Joseph Goebbels's Propaganda Ministry tried both to win foreign sympathy for Hitler's policies and to generate internal dissension among Germany's enemies. Goebbels used a variety of channels to spread the Nazi message: news agencies, short-wave radio broadcasts, cultural exhibitions, travel bureaus, and so on.[3] The Foreign Ministry (Auswartiges Amt, or A.A.) also participated in Fifth Column operations. The A.A. provided subsidies for pro-German propaganda and pro-German organizations abroad. The Reich's diplomatic agents also collected intelligence on military, political, economic, social, and cultural matters in the countries where they were stationed.[4] Germany's intelligence organizations were even more fully involved in foreign intrigue. The Abwehr, the official intelligence agency of the German military, participated in wide ranging espionage, sabotage, and subversive operations across the Reich's borders. The Nazi party supported an additional intelligence agency which performed the same sort of covert activities as the Abwehr. Initially, Branch III of the Sicherheitsdienst (Security Service, or S.D.) handled foreign intelligence for the party. In the autumn of 1939, the S.D. was absorbed into the Reichssicherheitshauptamt (Reich Security Administration, or RSHA); Department VI of the RSHA took over responsiblities for foreign intelligence, and considerably expanded upon work performed by the S.D.[5]

Ultimately, Germans living outside the frontiers of the Reich proved the most effective agents of the Fifth Column. The Nazis maintained several agencies which wooed, monitored, and advised both *Reichsdeutsche* (German nationals living abroad) and *Volksdeutsche* (ethnic Germans who were not citizens of the Reich). Organizations such as the Volksbund für das Deutschum im Ausland (VDA) and the Deutsches Ausland-Institut (German Foreign Institute) endeavored to strengthen the racial and cultural ties between Germans living abroad and the Fatherland. The VDA and DAI were ostensibly private agencies, but in fact each group supported official government policy. General supervision of *Volksdeutschen* communities was exerted by the Volksdeutsche Mittelstelle (Liaison Office for Minority Germans), a secret Nazi party agency staffed by members of Heinrich Himmler's Schutzstaffeen (S.S.). In 1938, Hitler authorized the Volksdeutsche Mittelstelle to handle all nationalities questions. However, other government ministries frustrated its attempts to implement policy (especially the Foreign Ministry). Another Nazi party agency, the Auslandsorganisation, had primary responsibility for all party members living outside of the Reich. The agency served as a pool for the recruitment of spies and also generated intelligence reports on conditions abroad.[6]

In spite of all of Germany's various efforts to spy, propagandize, sabotage, and subvert its enemies, Fifth Column methods proved consequential only in Austria, Czechoslovakia, and Poland. In these three states Hitler played on Pan-German sentiments frustrated by the Versailles treaty. Norway, Belgium, Holland, and France were not victims of the Nazi Trojan Horse. Rather, they were undone by the ingenuity, audacity, and skill of Germany's armed forces. Yet, it was not until the Wehrmacht's blitzkrieg triumphs in the spring and early summer of 1940 that the German Trojan Horse became an object of international dread and terror. The fear of the Fifth Column drastically escalated just as Trojan Horse tactics ceased to play any real part in Germany's victories.

Germany's apparently successful use of subversive tactics in Europe had a powerful impact in the United States. The events which transpired between March 1938 and July 1940 catalyzed America's Fifth Column fears and transformed a nagging worry into a national hysteria. In the wake of the fall of France, United States government officials, foreign refugees, and the mass media all issued grave warnings regarding the threat which the Fifth Column posed to America. The public's worries peaked in the aftermath of the French surrender to Hitler. This chapter discusses Germany's victories in Austria, Czechoslovakia, Poland, Norway, France and the Low Countries, and describes the lessons for domestic security which Americans read into these developments.

Austria, Czechoslovakia, and Poland

The unification of Austria with Germany was one of Hitler's principal foreign policy objectives. Early in 1938, the Germans pursued a series of steps which brought about the realization of this goal. On February 12, Austrian Chancellor Kurt Schuschnigg met with Adolf Hitler at Berchtesgaden. Hitler bullied Schuschnigg into accepting an agreement which greatly limited Vienna's independence from Berlin. The Austrian Chancellor promised to accept several Nazis into his government, to offer a general amnesty for imprisoned Nazis, and to consult with Germany prior to finalizing all foreign policy decisions. After the Berchtesgaden conference, Schuschnigg desperately attempted to stave off his country's de facto absorption into Germany. Early in March, he decided to call for a plebiscite on the Anschluss issue. The government framed the plebiscite question in such a way as to ensure that a majority of Austrians would vote for continuing independence. Schuschnigg planned to call for the vote on March 13, so as to leave opposition elements little time to organize. These actions enraged Hitler, who feared that his plans for Austria might be thwarted. The Fuehrer demanded a cancelation of the plebiscite, the resignation of Schuschnigg, and the appointment of Austrian Nazi Arthur Seyss-Inquart as Chancellor. Cowed by the threat of invasion, Vienna complied with Hitler's demands. On March 12 German troops crossed the Austrian border. Berlin claimed that the Wehrmacht was simply responding to a request from Chancellor Seyss-

Inquart to restore order in Austria. (In fact, Seyss-Inquart attempted to rescind this request, but the Germans claimed to have received the message too late to hold back the Wehrmacht.) One day later the unification of Austria and Germany was officially announced.[7]

The Anschluss was achieved with minimal resistance. Vienna lacked a credible military deterrent to Berlin's aggression and received no support from the international community. More important, the Austrian state never developed a strong sense of national identity. Pan-German sentiment ran deeply throughout the nation's most important political parties. Hitler was able to capitalize on such feelings, presenting Anschluss as part of a natural process of unifying all Germans within one Fatherland. When the Wehrmacht finally did enter Austria it was greeted with enthusiastic cheers from the native population.[8]

The Fifth Column tactics of the Austrian Nazi party helped bring about Anschluss. These extremists employed a host of techniques, both legal and illegal, to bring down the legitimate government. In 1934, the Nazis launched an abortive coup which left Chancellor Engelbert Dollfuss mortally wounded. After a brief period of government repression, the Austrian Nazi party was able to reassert an influential position in the country's political life. In the final moments before the Anschluss, Arthur Seyss-Inquart and his fellow Austrian Nazis proved indispensable allies to Adolf Hitler. The Nazis leaked information to Berlin regarding Schuschnigg's schemes, and when finally in power they supplied the Wehrmacht with a pretext to enter the country. Bruce Pauley, a historian of the Austrian Nazi movement, has concluded that the party's behavior during the thirties demonstrates "how a small, fanatical band, supplied in part by smuggled weapons and fueled by propaganda, can infiltrate institutions, undermine governments, and destabilize society itself."[9] Thus, Austria proved the first and perhaps the most total victim of the Nazi Fifth Column.

After annexing Austria, Hitler determined to move against Czechoslovakia. Here again, he was able to take advantage of simmering German nationalism. When peacemakers at Versailles created the state of Czechoslovakia, they incorporated within its borders a hodgepodge of ethnic minorities. In order to make the new nation militarily defensible, a region along the frontiers of Bohemia and Moravia was ceded to the Czechs. This area, known as the Sudetenland, was home to approximately three and a half million Germans. The Nazis used this population to mount a Fifth Column attack against the Prague government.

The most prominent leader of Czechoslovakia's minority Germans was Konrad Henlein. In 1935, the German Foreign Ministry began funneling large amounts of money to Henlein's organization, the Sudeten German Party (SdP). Over the next few years the Reich exerted an ever-increasing influence over the SdP. On March 28, 1938, Hitler met with Henlein to map out strategy. The SdP was told to pursue negotiations with the Czechs, but to make demands that Prague would never be able to accept. In April, Henlein outlined a plan, the Karlsbad program, calling for the complete autonomy of the Sudetenland, and stopping just short of a demand for union with Germany. The SdP believed that President Eduard Benes's government would never accept these proposals. However, on September 7 the Czechs acceded to the Karlsbad agenda. (The Prague government took this step largely because of pressure from Great Britain.) Henlein avoided a negotiated resolution to the crisis, using the arrest of several SdP members as a pretext to cut off talks with the Czechs.

On September 12, at the Nazi party rally at Nuremberg, Hitler spoke out against the alleged persecution of the Sudeten Germans. The day after this speech, rioting broke out along the Czech borderlands. Henlein fled to Germany, where he issued a statement which demanded the incorporation of the Sudetenland into the Reich. Along Germany's frontier, refugees from Czechoslovakia were organized into Freikorps units and launched raids into the Asch-Eger district.[10]

The crisis threatened to turn into a general European war. Czechoslovakia had defensive alliances with both the Soviet Union and France. Because of its obligations to France, Great Britain feared that it might be drawn into a conflict resulting from the Czech crisis. On September 14 British Prime Minister Neville Chamberlain requested a meeting with Hitler to discuss the Sudeten situation. The next day the two heads of state met at Berchtesgaden. Chamberlain tentatively suggested a willingness to accept German control over the Sudetenland. The British Prime Minister consulted with the French and persuaded President Edouard Daladier to accept the Reich's annexation of Czech areas in which over half the population was German. Hitler rejected this offer and demanded more territory. War seemed likely. However, on September 29, a conference was held at Munich. Representatives attended from France, England, Italy, and Germany. Determined to avoid hurling the continent into a disastrous conflagration, Neville Chamberlain and Eduord Daldier acceded to Hitler's demands. As a result, Czechoslovakia's defenses were irreparably compromised.

The booty that he won at Munich did not appease Hitler; he remained committed to the complete destruction of Czechoslovakia. As a result of the Munich conference, Czechoslovakia's government was divided into three federated provinces: Bohemia-Moravia, Slovakia, and Ruthenia. In an effort to bring about the disintegration of the Czech state, the Nazis began to encourage Slovak and Ruthenian separatism. These efforts were not particularly successful, and it was the deployment of the Wehrmacht, not Hitler's "divide and conquer" tactics, which effected the final dismemberment of Czechoslovakia.[11] Nonetheless, Hitler's attempt to play one ethnic group off another did not go unremarked. Such techniques were recognized as characteristic of the Nazi Trojan Horse.

Hitler next directed his acquisitive energies toward Poland. Here again he justified his aggression by denouncing the Versailles treaty and by championing the cause of Germans living outside the Reich. Berlin insisted upon the restoration of the ethnically German city of Danzig to the Reich, as well as free German access across the Polish corridor to Danzig. Warsaw refused to give in to Hitler on these issues.

On September 1, 1939, Germany launched several coordinated thrusts along Poland's long exposed frontiers. Armored and motorized units of the Wehrmacht rolled forward, crushing the largely unmechanized forces opposing them. Britain and France declared war on Germany on September 3, but neither nation was able to relieve the pressure on the doomed Poles. When the Soviets crossed Poland's eastern frontier on September 17, the government in Warsaw fled the country. The Germans and Russians snuffed out large-scale Polish resistance by October 5.

The Wehrmacht received noteworthy assistance from Poland's large German minority. After World War I, the Versailles treaty transferred portions of Germany to the newly revived state of Poland. As a result, approximately 13,000 *Reichsdeutschen* and 1,000,000 *Volksdeutschen* were brought under Warsaw's governance. These Germans felt little affection for the Polish state, and many of them proved willing traitors. Before the Nazi invasion, *Volksdeutschen* disseminated propaganda and assisted in German espionage. During the Wehrmacht's blitzkrieg, several thousand Fifth Columnists supplied intelligence, served as guides, and even participated in scattered guerilla operations. The home-grown Polish Fifth Column was supplemented by agents of the Abwehr and Sicherheitsdienst, who mounted covert behind-the-lines actions.[12]

Interestingly, the Third Reich's moves against Poland, Czechoslovakia, and Austria did not generate a Fifth Column panic in America. Prior to the spring and summer of 1940 most of United States worries about a Nazi Trojan Horse were based on German operations in the Western Hemisphere, not on a perceived pattern of conquest displayed in Europe. Of course, Hitler's use of German minorities to stir up dissension within prospective foes did not go wholly unremarked. For example, a *Reader's Digest* piece published in January of 1939 observed that the Nazi technique "successful in Germany, Austria, and Czechoslovakia is to stir up dissatisfaction and internal dissension, then to step in and, through the German minority they control, to dominate the chaos they have created."[13] However, in the United States, a Fifth Column hysteria emerged only with the collapse of Norway in April of 1940, Holland and Belgium in May, and France in June. After these cataclysmic events, Americans began to discern Fifth Column lessons to be drawn from Germany's European victories. With the disasters of 1940, Hitler's Trojan Horse tactics were viewed as part of the preferred modus operandi of Berlin's rapacious leader.

Norway

On April 9, 1940, Germany launched a two-pronged offensive against Denmark and Norway. The Reich quickly overwhelmed both Scandinavian nations. Denmark's fall caused little international surprise. However, Hitler's seemingly effortless triumph over Norway dismayed observers worldwide. A far tougher fight had been expected from the Norwegians, who appeared to have capitulated without offering any resistance. The press soon came to explain Germany's victory as a triumph for the Fifth Column. This interpretation of events quickly gained acceptance throughout Europe, North America, and South America.

Chicago Daily News reporter Leland Stowe was in Norway at the time of the German invasion. Stowe became convinced that the Nazis" attack had succeeded because of Trojan Horse tactics. On April 14, he wrote a dispatch which unequivocally credited Norway's fall to treachery:

> Norway's capital and great seaports were not captured by armed force. They were seized with unparalleled speed by means of a gigantic conspiracy which must undoubtedly rank among the most audacious and most perfectly oiled political plots of the past century. By bribery and extraordinary infiltration on the part of Nazi agents, and by treason on the part of a few highly placed Norwegian civilians, and defense officials, the German dictatorship built its Trojan Horse.[14]

Stowe's analysis eventually became the conventional explanation for Germany's Scandinavian victory. News reports disseminated stories of German agents who had penetrated Norway disguised as students, vacationers, and seamen. The press credited Fifth Columnists with spiking guns, disconnecting mines, spreading false rumors, and serving as guides for the invading Germans.[15]

Throughout America, press accounts downplayed the military skill of the Germans, focusing instead on the Fifth Column. *Time* magazine wrote that Oslo and other points of entry "were betrayed from within by their sworn defenders before the people knew what was happening."[16] The *Indianapolis Times* called the Nazi victory "a story for which a place must be reserved alongside those of Judas and Benedict Arnold."[17] The *St. Louis Post-Dispatch* saw Hitler's Norwegian invasion as part of a pattern of Fifth Column treachery: "Just as in Austria, in Czechoslovakia, and in Danzig, the Nazi tempters preceded the army, sowing the seeds of treason. As they found a Seyss-Inquart in Vienna, a Henlein in the Sudetenland, and a Forster in Danzig, so they find a

Quisling in Oslo."[18] *U.S. News and World Report* observed that the fall of Norway had raised questions about America's ability to resist Fifth Column techniques:

> In Washington, as everywhere in the United States, Americans are asking: Can it happen here? Could any Foreign Power move a "Trojan Horse" into the country, enlist traitors, purchase the support of political and military leaders and land an army of occupation as the Nazis appear to have done in Norway?[19]

In fact, Trojan Horse tactics played an inconsequential role in the fall of Norway. Of course, the Scandinavian country was not entirely free of disloyalty. Vidkun Quisling, the head of Norway's Fascist party, the Nasjonal Samling (N.S.), had established treasonous communications with Berlin prior to the German invasion. Quisling repeatedly urged the Reich to invade his homeland, arguing that it was the only way to preempt a similar action by the British. Before the Nazi invasion, members of the N.S. gathered intelligence on Norway's coastal defenses and passed this information on to the Germans. Furthermore, the Nazis supplied Quisling with money to initiate subversive operations. However, none of these treasonous activities counted for much when Germany finally mounted its Scandinavian offensive.[20]

Hitler had originally hoped to keep Norway out of the war, but over time he became persuaded that such an invasion was necessary. The German navy lobbied hard for a move north. Admiral Erich Raeder argued that the establishment of submarine bases and airfields in Norway would improve Germany's ability to harass British shipping and would help to string out the British blockade. More important, Hitler feared a possible occupation of Norway by Great Britain. Such a step would have allowed the British to cut off the shipments of Swedish iron ore which were transported to the Reich along the Norwegian coast. In February, the British violated Norwegian territorial waters, boarding the German supply ship *Altmark* and removing 300 captured British seamen. This step helped finalize Hitler's determination to attack Norway.[21]

Speed, daring, and skill were the key ingredients of Germany's military success. German naval transports ran the British blockade, debarking troops at critical points along Norway's 1000 mile-plus coastline. In a single day Hitler's soldiers captured Oslo, Christiansand, Bergen, Trondheim, and Narvik. The Reich also employed parachute units to take airfields near Oslo and Stavangar. Though the Fifth Column was widely perceived as having singlehandedly undone Norway, Nazi agents and Norwegian turncoats received unjust credit for a victory belonging to Germany's military forces.

Holland, Belgium, and France

On May 10, 1940, Germany began a series of coordinated offensives which brought about the surrender of Holland, Belgium, and France. It was an astonishingly successful military campaign. In a few weeks the Wehrmacht accomplished what it had failed to achieve in four years of trench warfare during the First World War. Germany destroyed the French army and set Britain's expeditionary force on an ignominious retreat. Newly won air bases and submarine pens left Berlin in a position to increase its attacks on Great Britain. Germany accomplished all of this with remarkably few casualties. Many observers came to see the Wehrmacht's victories as a partial product of Trojan Horse operations.

The Germans opened their campaign in Holland with several coordinated strikes. In the eastern part of the country special Abwehr units were asked to seize control of bridges along the Maas and Waal rivers. These troops included Dutch-speaking Germans and thirty Dutch Nazis; their special mission was code-named "Trojan Horse." The Abwehr commando units largely failed to accomplish their assignments as Dutch soldiers successfully destroyed several important bridges in eastern Holland. However, the Nazis secured a bridgehead at Gennep and they immediately took advantage of this achievement, pouring infantrymen and tanks through the Dutch defensive lines. The deployment of German airborne forces in the Dutch rear proved even more disastrous. The Reich's elite paratrooper units seized several key bridges behind the Dutch lines of defense, clearing the way for advancing Panzer divisions. These airborne forces also prevented Holland from sending its reserve units to the Eastern Front, and without additional manpower support the Dutch lines of defense collapsed. Five days after the German invasion Holland surrendered.[22]

Within Holland the German attack produced a deluge of rumors. German paratroopers were said to have disguised themselves as farmers, railroad workers, police officers, priests, and Dutch soldiers. There were whispers that traitors had poisoned meat, water, chocolates, and cigarettes. Such tales seeped across the frontiers of Holland where they were accepted with credulity. In fact, documented examples of Fifth Column activity in Holland are hard to find, despite the use of Dutch Nazis and disguised Abwehr units in operation "Trojan Horse." The precision work of German paratroopers accounts for the rapid debacle of Dutch resistance.[23]

In Belgium, airborne units again played a crucial role in the Wehrmacht's success. At dawn on May 10, 1940, glider aircraft carried specially trained German soldiers across the Belgian frontier. These forces captured vital bridgeheads along the Albert Canal and also compelled the surrender of the Belgian fortress Eben Emael. The Reich's opening success allowed the Germans to overwhelm their adversaries' first line of defense. In less than two days the Wehrmacht took positions which the Belgians had hoped would hold out for at least one week. On May 11, the Belgian army withdrew to the Dyle river, where it formed a defensive front with French and British forces—the German assault on the Low Countries had prompted the allies to rush troops into Belgium. Unfortunately, the collapse of the French lines along the Meuse required the abandonment of the Dyle line and the Allied armies soon found themselves pushed closer to Atlantic.

On May 12, 1940, German tanks broke through the Ardennes and began racing toward the coast. Eight days later the Reich's armored spearhead had divided the French forces in two, leaving the Belgian army, the British Expeditionary Force, and the French 1st Army surrounded. On May 27, faced with an untenable military situation, King Leopold III of Belgium surrendered. On that same day the British began evacuating their own troops from the beaches of Dunkirk. The German forces then turned their attention southward, launching an offensive against the French army. The demoralized French quickly gave ground; on the 14th the Wehrmacht controlled Paris and on the 22nd an armistice was reached.

Belgium and France fell prey to the same sort of hysteria which pervaded Holland. Fifth Columnists were said to have spread false orders, obstructed transportation networks, poisoned food, and transmitted intelligence to the invading foes. German paratroopers were rumored to be wandering about Belgium and France in a multitude of disguises. In Belgium, prisons overflowed with individuals whom the government suspected of disloyalty. The French also interned thousands of suspected Fifth Columnists, shipping them to concentration camps near the Pyrennes.[24]

Throughout America much of the press asserted that the Fifth Column had been crucial to Germany's triumphs in Holland, Belgium, and France. A Buffalo paper concluded that the Dutch had been prevented from opening the dikes in time by "parachute troops, Fifth Columnists and plain every day traitors for hire. . . ."[25] CBS reporter Edwin Hartwich filed a dispatch which claimed that Fifth Columnists were responsible for distracting large elements of the Dutch army.[26] A newspaper in Flint, Michigan, observed that activities of the Fifth Column in Belgium and France had been attested to by "reporters whose professional reputation has been too lofty all these years to be impeached."[27] *Newsweek* commented that at the time of the French surrender, "Fifth Columnists, the dreaded secret enemy of this war, were appearing in many places in French uniforms giving false orders which added to the confusion."[28] On June 15, 1940, shortly before France's capitulation, the *Atlanta Constitution* observed: "It is but the course of common sense that the country should take every precaution needed to prevent, immediately, any 'fifth column' work in the United States. The evidence is too recent and too clear to forget what traitors, saboteurs and spies did in Norway, in Denmark, in Holland and in Belgium."[29]

Most reporters saw the Fifth Column as only one cause for Germany's success against Holland, Belgium, and France. In an October 1940 article in *Foreign Affairs*, journalist M. W. Fodor offered a multifactorial explanation for the Wehrmacht's most recent blitzkrieg victories. "The causes of German successes in the Netherlands, as in Belgium and Northern France were partly superiority in numbers of planes and tanks, partly better armament, such as double breasted armorplate on tanks and rapid fire large-caliber anti-tank guns. But all of this, I believe would not have availed them had they not enlisted other allies—incompetence, treason and fifth column sympathies."[30] *New York Times* reporter Otto Tolischus wrote that Fifth Column activities were "an important but only one of many important new weapons employed by Germany in her total war." Tolischus suggested that the Fifth Column had played a decisive role in Holland's collapse but had been much less significant in the attacks on Belgium and France.[31]

Hitler's overall success in Europe was repeatedly presented to the American public as a cautionary tale. Informed observers of all stripes—refugees from Europe, newspaper reporters, and government officials—warned against the Fifth Column.

Refugees from Europe seemed to supply authoritative confirmation of Germany's involvement in Trojan Horse techniques. In the late thirties Herman von Rauschning, an ex-Nazi party member and the former president of the senate of Danzig, began writing on Hitler's devotion to Fifth Column tactics.[32] In his widely read books and articles Rauschning quoted top Nazi leaders boasting about their ability to destroy their enemies through the Fifth Column. In *The Voice of Destruction* (1939) Rauschning claimed that Hitler had once stated: "I shall never start a war without the certainty that a demoralized enemy will succumb to the first stroke of a gigantic attack." Readers were told that Hitler had publicly avowed his desire to "conquer the enemy from within, to conquer him through himself." Rauschning observed that America was a prime target for Nazi subversion. He offered quotations from both Hitler and Goebbels which suggested Germany's intention to activate a Fifth Column in the United States. Hitler was said to have remarked: "America is permanently on the brink of revolution. It will be a simple matter for me to produce unrest and revolts in the United States, so that these gentry will have their hands full with their own affairs." Rauschning accused Goebbels of singling out the United States as a country where "divide and conquer" techniques might prove unusually productive: "No other country has so many social and religious tensions. We shall be able to play on many strings there."[33] Rauschning gradually gained a reputation as a prescient and knowledgable commentator on the Third

Reich and the Fifth Column. With each advance by Germany and each apparent triumph of the Trojan Horse, Rauschning's observations appeared ever more convincing. Newspapers, magazines, and government publications frequently quoted his comments regarding the Fifth Column.[34]

A number of American journalists and writers issued the same type of alarmist reports as Rauschning. In 1941, Leland Stowe, the man who had first exposed the Fifth Column in Norway, produced a best-selling book entitled *No Other Road to Freedom*. In this work, Stowe claimed that Hitler had conquered twelve countries, "first and foremost, from the inside." Stowe noted that the Reich now planned on using these very same techniques against the United States:

> Hitler would concentrate on seizing us from inside. In fact, he has already been concentrating upon that for many years. Nazi Germany will never fight to dominate North America unless her Trojan-horse methods fail, or as a last paralysing stroke to unlease a civil war already fully prepared within our borders and to deliver a perfectly synchronized coup de grace to embattled, divided America. This is the undeviating and classical Nazi strategy of revolutionary conquest—never to allow armed force for more than blackmail purposes if the same goal can be achieved internally, subtly and secretively.[35]

Other writers issued similar warnings. In his book *Strategy of Terror*, Edmond Taylor remarked on the Nazis' ability to create confusion and disunity within their European victims prior to attack. Taylor argued that rumours of treason destroyed a nation more effectively than actual treason. He claimed that a whispering campaign which spread panic and defeatism led to France's collapse. Taylor concluded that a Fifth Column already existed in America and that it could be thwarted only through "the vigilance of the whole loyal population and by a clear insight into what it is and how it works."[36]

The fall of France and the Low Countries also evoked a nervous response from leading government officials. During the Nazi blitzkrieg, William Bullitt served as America's ambassador in Paris. On May 17, 1940, Bullitt reported to Secretary of State Hull that a combined Nazi-Soviet Fifth Column attack was being directed against France. The ambassador claimed that Communist railway workers had disrupted train service, an act which clogged roads in Belgium and France and limited the mobility of Allied armies. He asserted that hundreds of Nazi and Communist agents were stationed behind the French lines, and were using short wave radio transmitters to report on Allied troop movements. Upon his return to America the former ambassador continued to insist that France had been defeated from within. In early August, Bullitt met with Secretary of War Stimson. After the session, Stimson noted that Bullitt had "laid great stress on the diabolically efficient organization of Germany as to its Fifth Column."[38] A few weeks later the ambassador delivered an address to the American Philosophical Association. He urged the nation to avoid the fate of France and to remain alive to the threat posed by hidden enemies. Bullitt cautioned that while Hitler and Stalin were not yet ready to attack the United States, ". . . their campaign of befuddlement, their preparatory assault is following the same lines in America that it followed in France."[39]

Several intelligence officials concluded that the Fifth Column eased the way for German advances through the Low Countries and France. America's naval attaché in London, A. G. Kirk, observed that in the Netherlands "Fifth Column activities were very hard to combat."[40] After the Wehrmacht had smashed France, Kirk wrote to Walter Anderson, the chief of naval intelligence, suggesting that America needed to be wary of hidden enemies:

To you I don't need to say much about the Fifth Column, but I can assure you it has proved very helpful to Mr. Hitler. How strong the 5th Column is in the United States you know better than I, but we must be awfully careful to make sure we are not caught trying to steal second when the power play is put on by the Nazis.[41]

In February 1941, Sherman Miles, the head of United States military intelligence, wrote a memo to Chief of Staff George Marshall expressing concern over the menace of an American Trojan Horse:

Working on the internal question for the past eight months, I have become almost a fanatic on morale and the possibilities of disintegration in the rear. For I am convinced that the fall of France was not due primarily to the defeat of her armies by superior German force or material, but to disintegration, to collapse of morale. Unquestionably the Germans had a fertile field on which to work— French pacifism, socialism and communism—but it is obvious they worked on it industriously and intelligently.[42]

Other important government officials publicly denounced the Fifth Column after Germany's success in France. In late May 1940, the President repeatedly warned Americans that the Nazis' Trojan Horse techniques had proved deadly in Europe and were now being applied in America. Various members of the cabinet also voiced both public and private concerns over the Fifth Column's success in Europe. Certain members of Congress were particularly vocal about the problem and helped to fuel public panic. In a speech carried nationally over CBS radio, Senator James Byrnes informed Americans that "Fifth Columns are already active in America, and those who consciously or unconsciously retard the efforts of this government to provide for the defense of the American people are the fifth column's most effective fellow travellers."[44] Representative Martin Dies announced that his House Un-American Activities Committee had uncovered evidence of a Nazi, fascist, and Communist plot against America's defense plants. Senator Robert Reynolds of North Carolina introduced a bill to ban any Nazi or Communist from employment on WPA projects. Congress passed additional legislation aimed at better keeping track of resident aliens and foreign-controlled organizations.

The fall of France, the Low Countries, and Norway confirmed the public's Fifth Column fears. A Roper poll taken in June of 1940 showed that only 2.7 percent of Americans felt that the government was doing enough to handle the Trojan Horse problem. Some 46 percent of those surveyed backed the deportation of all Nazi sympathizers, while 28 percent suggested that Nazi sympathizers should be prevented from agitating and organizing in America.[45] Bizarre stories began appearing in the press, which indicated the nervous state of the popular mind. San Antonio mayor Maury Maverick warned of a Fifth Column invasion from Mexico.[46] A group of American Legionnares in New York State promised to guard the Canadian frontier against similar incursions.[47] Georgia governor E. D. Rivers called for the deportation of all alien enemies as a security measure to protect Forts Benning and McPherson.[48] Leaders of the Navajo tribe in New Mexico outlawed all subversive and un-American activities.[49] The president of the University of Michigan vowed to counter on-campus Fifth Column agitation.[50] A parachute enthusiast in Nebraska wrote a letter to an Omaha paper requesting that citizens refrain from randomly shooting at skydivers during county fair season.[51] Outside of St. Louis a German-American sports club was burned to the ground.[52] Countless civic groups publicly pledged to battle Fifth Column activities. Among the more unusual of such vows was that of Jeff Davis, "King of the Hoboes," who announced a program "to stamp out fifth-column stuff" among the nation's tramps. This vow was made at the annual meeting of the Hoboes of America, Inc., held in Milwaukee.[53] Organizations as diverse as the National Grange, the Sleeping Car Porters Union, the National Council of Women, and the Lions International all urged vigilance against America's hidden enemies. Sensing the public's heightened concern with the Trojan Horse, the Mutual Broadcasting System announced in July 1940 the creation of a radio program entitled "Wings of America." The new show followed the adventures of fictional newswoman Lorna Carroll as she sought to combat Fifth Columnists working for an organization which called itself the Advance Front.[55] Countless other bits of evidence revealed the hysteria which the fall of France, Belgium, and Holland had precipitated in America.

In mid-June 1940, Hearst newsman Karl von Wiegand held an interview with Adolf Hitler. During the course of the meeting Wiegand brought up the tremendous fear which the Nazi Fifth Column had aroused in the United States. Hitler pooh-poohed the whole notion of Trojan Horse warfare:

> This so-called "Fifth Column" conveys nothing to me because it doesn't exist except in the imagination of fantastic minds or as a phantom created by unscrupulous propaganda for obvious purposes. Incompetent governments drive their peoples into war, and when they pitiably collapse, it is understandable that they prefer to shift the responsiblity elsewhere.[56]

Hitler's denials doubtlessly failed to persuade many Americans of Germany's innocence. After all, the President, cabinet members, State Department officials, congressmen, journalists, and European refugees all had testified to the horrible reality of the Nazi Fifth Column in Europe and America.

SEVEN

Keeping the Panic Alive

German Propaganda, Espionage, and Sabotage in the United States

Hitler dismissed the significance of the Fifth Column in America. Nonetheless, between 1940 and 1942, the Third Reich participated in propaganda, espionage, and sabotage activities on United States soil. The Nazis won few gains from these badly managed, low-priority operations. Instead, German intrigue simply helped convince the American government and public that an undeclared guerilla war had been initiated. The nation's news media gave extensive coverage to reports of German wrongdoing and other popular cultural forms (film, comic books, fiction) drew on press and radio reports of Nazi intrigue to create the legend of an omnipresent pro-Hitler Fifth Column. An examination of the Reich's efforts at propaganda, espionage, and sabotage makes America's Trojan Horse hysteria a bit more understandable.

Propaganda

Germany engaged in a spectacularly unsuccessful propaganda campaign in the United States. Berlin principally sought to encourage American neutrality. In order to achieve this end the Reich's propagandists tried to foster American distrust of the Allied nations and to soften American hostility toward Adolf Hitler and his Nazi regime. Germany carried out this campaign of manipulation with little tact or skill. Consequently, the Reich's efforts at persuasion became a source of national indignation.[1]

Much of the Nazis' propagandizing in the United States was overt. The German Library of Information and the German Railroads Information Office, both based in New York City, did little to disguise their dissemination of pro-German materials. However, the Nazis also attempted to influence public opinion through covert means. The resort to "black" propaganda infuriated Americans. Germany subsidized and guided front organizations such as the Transocean News Service and the American Fellowship Forum. Both of these groups falsely claimed independence from Berlin. The Reich also tried to influence American public policy secretly. In fact, the Germans' most successful propaganda agent was able to exert influence over several isolationist congressmen.

The German Library of Information served as one of the Reich's major propaganda outlets in America. The library distributed pro-German books, periodicals, and pamphlets. A sampling of titles published by the agency includes: *German White Book: Documents Concerning the Last Phase of the German-Polish Campaign, Polish Acts of Atrocity Against the German Minority, German White Book: Documents Preceding the Outbreak of the War, German White Book: Britain's Designs on Norway, Allied Intrigue in the Low Countries,* and *The Second Hunger Blockade.* The organization printed a number of less political publications, such as *German Forests, Treasures of a Nation* and *German Christmas Carols and Christmas Toys.* The library also produced *Facts in Review,* a weekly bulletin that defended the actions of Hitler's government.[2] In 1939 this newsletter averaged four pages in length with a circulation of 20,000. Two years later the publication averaged sixteen pages and circulation figures stood at 100,000.[3] In addition to its literary efforts, the Library of Information also supported pro-German lectures and distributed pro-German films.

The German Railroads Information Office presented itself as an agency designed to increase tourism to Germany. The government-backed organization produced travel booklets which presented a candy-coated picture of Hitler and his Nazi Government. Congressional investigators noted with suspicion that the Railroads Information Office vastly expanded its budget just when the war had brought to a virtual halt all United States travel to the Reich.[4]

In the fall of 1940, congressional investigators revealed the Transocean News Service and the American Fellowship Forum as front organizations for the Nazis.[5] Transocean was founded in Germany during the First World War era and originally functioned as a German version of the Associated Press and the United Press. However, when the Nazis came to power they brought the agency under their authority. Despite this change, the news service posed as an independent organization. In the wake of Dies committee revelations, Transocean was asked to leave the United States, and its two principal representatives in America were prosecuted for violations of the Foreign Agents Registration Act. HUAC also played a role in publicizing Berlin's control of the American Fellowship Forum. Frederic Auhagen, an émigré from Germany and a former German-language instructor at Columbia University, headed this group.

The forum attempted to unify German-Americans behind a peace platform. Auhagen established a magazine, *Today's Challenge*, which argued for an isolationist foreign policy. The leader of the American Fellowship Forum was eventually imprisoned for failing to inform the United States government of his involvement in propaganda activities.[6]

In the months preceding Japan's attack on Pearl Harbor, Germany was embarrassed by the exposure of its most important propaganda agent, George Sylvester Viereck. Viereck masterminded efforts to manipulate American legislators and to abuse the congressional franking privilege.[7]

Viereck had a long history of pro-German propagandizing in America. In August 1914, he began work as an editor on *The Fatherland*, a publication which urged "fair play" for the Central Powers. Viereck became one of the most notorious defenders of the Kaiser. In 1929, he wrote a series of articles for the *Saturday Evening Post* on World War I propaganda. He eventually turned these pieces into a book entitled *Spreading Germs of Hate*. Viereck's past connection with German propaganda was thus common knowledge. The Nazis' willingness to employ such a suspected figure typifies the overall carelessness of German intrigue in America.

In 1932, the American publicity firm Carl Byoir and Associates hired Viereck. A year later he traveled to Germany and worked out a deal whereby Byoir was hired to consult with the German Railroads Information Bureau. In 1934, the McCormack-Dickstein committee investigated Byoir's links to the Reich as well as those of Ivy Lee, another American public relations outfit. As a result of this congressional inquiry the German embassy ended its contracts with both Byoir and Ivy Lee.

In 1939, Berlin once again employed Viereck as a propaganda agent. He worked for the German Library of Information, serving as the editor of *Facts in Review*. Viereck also supplied intelligence on American affairs to the German Foreign Office. He did this under journalistic cover. *Muenchner Nueuste Nachrichten,* a small Munich newspaper, hired him to analyze conditions in the United States. He sent his reports to the German government as well as to his putative employer in Munich.

In 1940, Viereck achieved controlling interest in a small publishing house, Flanders Hall. This company sponsored the release of a handful of anti-Allied pamphlets. Typical publications included *Seven Periods of Irish History* by Shaemas O'Sheel, *One Hundred Families That Rule the Empire* by Giselher Wirsing (this piece attacked English financiers), and *Lord Lothian Against Lord Lothian*, attributed to Senator Ernest Lundeen, but actually written by Viereck. In September 1941, newspaper columnist Drew Pearson broke a story showing that most of Flanders Hall's publications were translations of material which the German Foreign Office had sent to the German Library of Information. Pearson also revealed Viereck's part in the propaganda scheme.

The most shocking aspect of Viereck's work was the scandalous intimacy which he established with several isolationist congressmen and members of their staff. Viereck was especially friendly with Senator Ernest Lundeen, for whom he wrote several speeches. He persuaded Lundeen to form the Make Europe Pay War Debts Committee. This anti-Allied group urged the confiscation of British and French holdings in the Western Hemisphere as compensation for unpaid bills from World War I. The organization attracted a number of prominent legislators: Senator Rush Holt, Senator Robert Reynolds, Senator Smith Brookhart, Representative Hamilton Fish, Representative Stephen Day, Representative Martin Sweeney, and Representative Jennings Randolph. Viereck shunned an official post in the new organization, opting to exert his influence from behind the scenes. He urged the committee's treasurer, Prescott Dennett, to have isolationist propaganda—newspaper editorials, magazine articles, book excerpts, congressional speeches, and so on—inserted in the *Congressional Record*. Viereck then suggested that these pieces be reprinted and sent out to the public under congressional frank. He was assisted in this effort by George Hill, secretary to isolationist legislator Hamilton Fish. Hill placed Congressman Fish's frank at Viereck's disposal in exchange for monetary renumeration. The Justice Department estimated that Viereck played a part in placing at least 38 pieces in the *Congressional Record*; between 5000 and 125,000 copies of each article were distributed through the federal mails free of postal charges.[8]

In the fall of 1941 a federal grand jury convened to examine Viereck's propaganda activities. Front-page news stories revealed how the paid German propagandist had managed to manipulate American congressmen and flood the American mails with anti-interventionist literature.[9] Viereck's actions smeared the entire isolationist movement by suggesting that puppetmasters in Berlin controlled Roosevelt's foreign policy critics.

Espionage

German espionage activities in the United States were badly flawed.[10] First, Germany took unnecessary risks by engaging in espionage for data which might have been obtained openly. Second, most of the Nazi operatives in America were poor spies. Few had received professional training and many were already compromised by past associations with pro-German movements. Third, Germany failed to compartmentalize properly its operations. Hence, the apprehension of one agent often led to many additional arrests. Fourth, the information which the Nazis collected in America did not prove of much value. (For example, historian Thomas Etzold notes that Germany's greatest intelligence coup in America, the theft of the Norden bomb sight, produced few results. The sight was not installed in time for the Battle of Britain and after that point the Luftwaffe's bombing activities were not as important a part of the Reich's air war.)[11]

Superior counterespionage work by the Federal Bureau of Investigation resulted in the frequent exposure of German spying in America. During the summer and autumn of 1941 the G-men rounded up three different German spy rings. The capture of these organizations was greeted with much media fanfare and offered all Americans proof of Hitler's hostile attitude toward the United States.

In February 1939, William Sebold, a former mechanic at Consolidated Aircraft in San Diego, California, went to Germany in order to visit relatives. Sebold was a naturalized American citizen who had emigrated to the United States following the First World War. Shortly after returning to Germany, he was approached by the Gestapo and asked to perform undercover work in the United States. Sebold initially put off such requests. However, he feared that refusal to cooperate would lead to his imprisonment in a concentration camp or retaliation against members of his family. He finally agreed to become a spy. The Germans sent their reluctant recruit to an espionage training school in Hamburg where he received cursory instruction in setting up short-wave radio transmitters, microphotography, and other aspects of spycraft.[12]

After having acceded to the Abwehr's demand that he spy on the United States, Sebold requested permission to visit the American consulate in Cologne in order to replace his passport. (German intelligence appears to have stolen this document.) Sebold told Vice Consul Dale Maher his predicament. Maher counseled the anxious visitor to play along with the Abwehr's scheme.[13]

The Germans finally sent Sebold back to America in January 1940. The Nazis gave him funds to support his espionage and the names of several contacts in New York City (Frederick Duquesne, Hermann Lang, Lilly Stein, and Everett Roeder).[14] FBI agents met with Sebold upon his return home. They helped their double-agent establish a radio transmitter in Centerport, Long Island. The G-men were able to monitor all meetings held in the spy nest.

Sebold was the contact man for Germany's principal agent in New York City, Frederick Joubert Duquesne. During the First World War, the New York police had arrested Duquesne for planting a time bomb aboard the British vessel S.S. *Tennyson*. Germany's willingness to rely on such a notorious figure underscored once again its careless approach to intelligence-gathering in the United States. Duquesne sent Sebold production figures for various defense plants, photographs of American military hardware, and information on the sailing dates of Allied cargo vessels. The FBI allowed intelligence of little value to go through to Berlin, but they withheld or changed information deemed important to national security. Hoover's men held off on making arrests until they were certain that they had identified all Nazi agents working through Sebold.

German carelessness allowed the FBI to uncover other Nazi spy rings. Carl Reuper worked as a mechanic for Air Associates in Bendix, New Jersey. He also doubled as a German spymaster, running agents in defense plants in New Jersey and Pennsylvania. A short-wave radio transmitter in the Bronx sent intelligence collected by the secret ring back to Germany. In January 1941, Reuper asked Walter Nipkin, a fellow employee at Air Associates, to spy for Germany. Nipkin pretended to accept the offer. In fact, he went to the FBI and reported the German intelligence-gathering effort. The Bureau used their new recruit to pass on disinformation to Berlin and to determine the full scope of Reuper's spy operation.[15]

Hoover decided to roll up both the Duquesne and Reuper rings at the same time. In mid-summer of 1941, authorities placed 33 German agents under arrest. The roundup made headlines. When the German operatives were put on trial in the fall, the public learned with amazement of the FBI's ability to plant double-agents inside the Nazi spy apparatus. The Sebold and Nipken affairs displayed the Bureau at its best, and became a central part of G-man folklore.

Shortly after moving in on the Duquesne and Reuper groups, the Bureau broke the back of yet another Nazi spy ring operating out of New York. Early in 1941, the British Censorship Bureau in Hamilton, Bermuda, detected a number of unusual letters bearing a New York postmark and signed "Joe K." This correspondence was destined for addresses in Spain and Portugal. The prose style of "Joe K's" letters aroused British suspicions. Consequently, various chemical tests were performed in order to determine whether or not the correspondence contained secret messages. The tests revealed data on Allied shipments across the Atlantic, the positioning of Allied troops, and aircraft construction in the United States.[16] The British then informed the FBI that an enemy spy, codenamed "Joe K," was at large in the New York area.

On March 18, 1941, a traffic accident in Times Square helped the FBI advance their investigation of this case. A taxi cab hit a man bearing papers identifying him as Julio Lopez Lido. Lido was rushed to St. Vincent's Hospital, but died a day later. Witnesses to the accident noted that the injured man's briefcase had been taken away by his companion, a short, bespectacled man with a pronounced German accent. A manager at the Hotel Taft, where Lido had been staying, called the police to inform them of strange calls which he had received regarding Lido's luggage. The police examined the dead man's hotel room and discovered materials suggesting espionage.[17] The FBI was brought into the case. An examination of Lido's possessions uncovered material that revealed the deceased's true identity to be Ulrich von der Osten, a captain in German military intelligence. Further, leads were developed that allowed the Bureau to positively identify one Frederick Ludwig as "Joe K."

Ludwig was born in the United States, but had spent most of his adult life in Germany. In March 1940, he began espionage activities for the Reich. He was asked to gather intelligence on the "size, equipment, location and morale of American army units; on the routing of convoys between the United States and England; and on aircraft production figures."[18] Ludwig visited defense plants, harbors, and military installations along the eastern seaboard. He mailed detailed reports to Germany on ship sinkings, troop placements, and American supplies to Britain. He controlled eight sub-agents who gathered additional military intelligence.[19]

The FBI placed Ludwig under surveillance after discovering his identity. In late July, after the arrest of Duquesne, he began to suspect that his operations had been compromised. Ludwig left New York for the West Coast, with the intention of returning to Germany via the Pacific Ocean. FBI agents pursued him and made an arrest in Washington State. At the same time the Bureau apprehended Ludwig's associates.

Sabotage

In 1945, the Federal Bureau of Investigation proudly boasted that no verified acts of sabotage had been committed in the United States during the Second World War. Nonetheless, throughout the Fifth Column scare the public worried that Nazi agents were busily planting bombs and setting fires throughout the country. These fears peaked in the middle of 1942, when the government repelled a German sabotage mission to the United States.

Before America's formal entry into the Second World War, the Germans refrained from involvement in any sabotage in the United States. However, a number of unexplained industrial accidents provided reasonable grounds for the public to suspect Germany of attacking America. In September 1940, an explosion occurred at the Hercules Powder plant in Kenvil, New Jersey. This blast was widely believed to have been the work of saboteurs. News reports noted that the German-American Bund maintained a camp only fourteen miles from the munitions factory. The *New York Times* speculated that the disaster may have been another Black Tom.[20] However, multiple investigations into the affair discounted the likelihood of Axis sabotage.

On November 12, 1940, three powder plants, two in New Jersey and one in Pennsylvania, experienced mysterious explosions. HUAC chairman Martin Dies warned that "the acts of sabotage the past twenty-four hours are only a beginning."[21] Fellow Dies committee member J. Parnell Thomas added that the disasters "can hardly be placed in the category of coincidence."[22] Secretary of War Henry Stimson noted that

the explosions had occurred with "teutonic precision." Despite such con-
jecture an FBI inquiry into the diasasters found no evidence of Axis
intrigue.

The false tales of German sabotage which were spreading throughout
the country deeply troubled Attorney General Robert Jackson. He
spelled out his concerns in an interdepartmental meeting attended by
Harold Ickes, Henry Stimson, Frank Knox, Frank Walker, Louis Brownlow, and Clarence Dykstra on November 28, 1940:

> Now let me tell you the sort of thing that is making us trouble, and
> if it makes us trouble it is going to make trouble for everyone else
> sooner or later. Last Sunday Night, Walter Winchell, who probably
> has the largest audience of any man in America on the air, related
> a gruesome case of sabotage which consisted of a workman driving
> a nail through a cable which it was said would set fire to the cable
> in one of your War Department buildings. I suppose we got hun-
> dreds of inquiries "why don't you get this rat"?
>
> Now the "rat" was an ordinary carpenter who drove a nail
> through, which happens in every building. It did strike a cable and
> the worst that would happen would be to blow a fuse. It happens
> in every building. There is no sabotage in it. It might have been
> deliberate, but the chances are there is no more sabotage involved
> than what I related.
>
> I could give you a dozen instances of things that have been pub-
> licized, and we get terrific reactions from them as sabotage in which
> there is just no credible evidence of sabotage. You are getting, in
> this country today, a state of mind that you cannot deal with the
> labor problem on its merits. I think it is becoming a very dangerous
> thing.[23]

Winchell was not the only broadcaster who irritated government officials by exaggerating the Fifth Column threat. In December 1940, an
FBI report commented angrily on a series of radio programs which
Wythe Williams had aired on the Mutual Broadcasting System. The Bureau noted that Williams had described a number of alleged acts of
sabotage which were "totally unfounded, as well as deliberate distor-
tions of the facts obtained from his sources of information." The MBS
announcer's most shocking revelation detailed an attempt by Nazi agents
to blow up two arsenals in New Jersey. (The plot called for the installations to be bombarded with trench mortars.) Williams followed up his
radio shows with an article in *Liberty* magazine on Hitler's attempts to
manipulate U.S. elections.[24]

Despite its concerns over false alarms, the government took the threat
of Axis sabotage quite seriously. The Justice Department instructed the
FBI to conduct surveys of plants involved in defense-related work. These

surveys were intended to help factories improve security and frustrate would-be saboteurs. As part of its counter-sabotage effort, the Bureau also planted undercover agents within many of America's defense plants and recruited informants from the work force. The FBI saw this type of spying as an essential defense against Fifth Columnists and wondered little about the ramifications for civil liberties.

Unexplained mishaps in defense-related areas continued to be attributed to enemy agents. On February 9, 1942, the *Normandie* (recently renamed the USS *Lafayette*) caught fire and capsized while it was docked in New York harbor. Rumors quickly spread that Axis arson had caused the conflagration. It was said that fire hoses had been mysteriously cut and that gasoline had been secretly poured into the ship's sprinkler system.[25] John Franklin Carter reported to President Roosevelt that most New Yorkers, "from expert shipping men to subway gossipers," believed that the fire was of incendiary origin.[26] Multiple investigations into the affair ensued. The FBI found "no indication that sabotage was the cause of the burning or subsequent capsizing of the vessel."[27] Separate House and Senate committees concluded that the *Normandie*'s sinking was an accident. Investigators found that while the vessel was being converted into an Army troop ship careless workmen had employed an acetylene torch in close proximity to a bale of highly flammable kapok life preservers. Sparks from the torch set the life preservers ablaze and led to the *Normandie*'s destruction.[28]

In January 1942, the Third Reich initiated a U-boat offensive in America's coastal waters. Over the next six months, enemy subs sank 171 merchant vessels in the Eastern Sea Frontier. (The ESF stretched from Maine to northern Florida.) The extension of Germany's submarine warfare to America's shores raised fears of increased sabotage. It was thought that the U-boats might serve as a ferry service for Axis agents.[29]

Such concerns were not without foundation. In April 1942, the Abwehr brought eight men to a Nazi sabotage school forty miles from Berlin and trained them for a mission in the United States.[30] The agents learned how to use explosives, detonators, and timing devices. The Germans gave each man a legend—a false life history—complete with counterfeit birth certificate, Social Security card, draft deferment card, and driver's license. All of the men had spent several years living in the United States. In fact, two of the saboteurs were American citizens.[31]

The Abwehr's sabotage mission, code-named Operation Pastorius, aimed at destroying a diverse range of targets, including bridges, railroad stations, power plants, water facilities, and Jewish-owned businesses. However, the saboteurs' main objective was America's light metal industry. The Germans targeted for destruction three plants belonging to the Aluminum Company of America (one in Alcoa, Tennessee, another in Massena, New York, and a third in East St. Louis, Missouri), as well as a cryolite plant in Philadelphia. The Nazis hoped to slow down American aircraft production.

The Abwehr agents were divided into two teams of four men. George John Dasch headed the first group. His subordinates included Ernest Burger, Heinrich Heinck, and Richard Quirin. A U-boat transported Dasch's team to Long Island, New York. Edward Quirlin led the second group of saboteurs. He and his men—Herman Neubauer, Werner Thiel, and Herbert Haupt—were dropped off along the Florida coast. The Abwehr instructed both teams to scatter throughout the United States and provided the eight saboteurs with $175,000.

The German sabotage mission met with bad luck from the outset. Dasch's team was dropped off near Amagansett, Long Island, at approximately midnight, June 13, 1942. The saboteurs began unloading their supplies immediately after landing. An unidentified figure bearing a flashlight approached them while they were in the midst of this project. Dasch rushed forward to intercept the man, who turned out to be a young American Coast Guard officer named John Cullen. Hoping to get rid of Cullen, Dasch claimed to be a fisherman who had run aground in the evening fog. After hearing this explanation Cullen asked the German spy to accompany him to a nearby Coast Guard station. Dasch refused. He threatened Cullen and at the same time offered him a bribe of $260 to keep quiet. Unaware of what he was up against, the Coast Guardsman accepted the cash and returned to his station. Cullen immediately informed his superiors of the strange happenings. The next morning a search of the beach uncovered the saboteurs' supplies. However, the four enemy agents had disappeared.

As a result of his early run-in with the Coast Guard, Dasch developed cold feet. He and his compatriot Ernest Burger resolved to turn themselves in. On June 15, Dasch called the FBI's office in New York City and claimed to possess important information. Four days later he surrendered to the Bureau's headquarters in Washington. Dasch completely compromised the Abwehr's sabotage scheme, revealing his compatriot's identities, contacts, and objectives. The G-men used this information to round up the enemy intruders, all of whom were in government custody by June 27.

Germany's attempt at sabotage deeply troubled the FBI. On June 22 Hoover sent a worried note to the White House: "The lack of protection of our beaches and coasts is making it possible for these groups to enter freely and with minimum possibility of detection and presents a very pressing problem warranting immediate consideration."[32] After announcing the capture of the saboteurs, Hoover told the public that enemy infiltration remained a serious problem:

> The recent landing of saboteurs from Nazi submarines sounds a
> new alert for all Americans. These saboteurs were apprehended before
> they could carry out their plans of destruction.

But other saboteurs may try to come to our shores. They must be stopped.

Every citizen should immediately report any information regarding espionage, sabotage or un-American activities to the Federal Bureau of Investigation.[33]

The G-men's victory over Operation Pastorius won considerable plaudits for the Bureau and J. Edgar Hoover. Without much encouraging war news to report, the media triumphantly announced the capture of all eight saboteurs. No one doubted that the possibility of future sabotage missions remained. However, most Americans found comfort in the FBI's proven record of competence.

FDR was keenly interested in the sabotage case. He wrote to the Attorney General urging that the two American citizens captured were "just as guilty as it is possible to be" and that "the death penalty is almost obligatory." With regard to the six remaining saboteurs of German citizenship, Roosevelt urged that they be tried by court-martial, "as were Andre and Hale."[34] The would-be saboteurs met a sad fate. On July 2, Roosevelt authorized the captured Germans to be prosecuted in a military court. After a speedy trial the defendants were found guilty and sentenced to death. (FDR converted Dasch's sentence to thirty years and Burger's to life imprisonment based upon the two men's willingness to cooperate with the Bureau.) Given the state of public opinion anything less than the death penalty would have left the Roosevelt administration subject to charges of coddling Nazis and encouraging future sabotage. Moreover, the sentence was entirely just under the rules of war.

The failure of Operation Pastorius led Hitler to rebuke Abwehr chief Admiral Canaris. The fiasco also discouraged the Nazis from attempting similar sabotage missions. During the remaining years of the war, the Germans only once more dispatched agents to America by submarine. Late in 1944, U-boats dropped two RSHA spies off the coast of Maine. The FBI captured both men shortly thereafter.[35] These agents benefited from the calmer state of public nerves in the later years of the war and received prison sentences rather than the death penalty.

German Intrigue and Popular Culture

Real accounts of Nazi intrigue helped inspire an avalanche of comic books, dime novels, and motion pictures on the Trojan Horse problem. The public thrilled to wild tales of dangerous propagandists, cunning spies, and murderous saboteurs. Stories of pro-Nazi Fifth Column activities struck a responsive chord in the nation, lasting long after the end of World War II.

In 1941, Joe Simon and Jack Kirby created the character of Captain America. Issue no.1 of the comic book dealt with the superhero's origins.

The story begins with U.S. government officials in a state of panic over the Fifth Column. Working under special authority from President Roosevelt, a brilliant scientist named Reinstein develops a secret formula to create an army of supermen. Steve Rogers, a 4-F recruit, volunteers for an experiment involving the new serum. The test exponentially increases Rogers's physical and mental strength. His creator, Reinstein, gives the young man a new mission and a new identity:

> Behold! The crowning achievement of all my years of hard work! The first of a corps of super-agents whose mental and physical ability will make them a terror to spies and saboteurs. We shall call you Captain America, Son! Because, like you—America shall gain the strength and the will to safeguard our shores.[36]

Immediately after the successful experiment, a Fifth Columnist shoots and kills Reinstein. Captain America pursues the Axis operative, who is electrocuted in laboratory equipment. Amidst the chaos, Reinstein's secret formula is destroyed, so that no more super-agents can be turned out. Steve Rogers goes on to battle hidden foes of American democracy.

Countless other superheroes locked horns with the Fifth Column, including Batman, the Green Hornet, Spy Smasher, and Wonder Woman. On March 10, 1942, a comic strip appeared in the *Washington Post* in which Superman dedicated himself solely to fighting spies and saboteurs. In a speech before a joint session of Congress, the Man of Steel observed:

> I believe I can best serve the nation on the home front, battling our most insidious foes . . . the hidden maggots—the traitors, the Fifth Columnists, the potential Quislings who will do all in their power to halt our production of war materials. I will be on the alert for the old totalitarian trick of creating disunity by spreading race hatreds.[37]

Immediately after delivering this message, Superman frustrates a German effort to blow up Congress. Comic strip Fifth Columnists proved capable of almost any outrage, going so far as to kidnap Little Orphan Annie.[38]

Dime novels also mined themes of subversion and sabotage. With the onset of the European war, pulp editor Jerry Westerfeld wrote a letter to *Writer's Digest* soliciting stories on Nazi intrigue in the United States for his publications *Fantastic Adventures* and *Amazing Stories*.[39] Other editors also welcomed similar suspense yarns. *Ace G-Man Stories* and *G-Men Detective* published stories almost exclusively focused on the Fifth Column menace. Recurring heroes such as the Voice, Dan Fowlair, and the Suicide Squad (a trio of FBI agents named Klaw, Kerrigan, and Murdoch) regularly did battle against diverse Axis plots to undermine the home front. Trojan horse schemes included campaigns to elect a Nazi "sleeper" agent President of the United States (quite a popular theme), to penetrate the armed forces with Bundsmen, to kidnap British diplomats, to destroy American defense production, and to blow up the Panama canal. Nazi Fifth Columnists proved eager to blow up teenage boys or menace young women with razor blades in order to achieve their goals. FBI pulps regularly featured the head of Germany's Secret Service at work in the States. Usually these spymasters offered patronizing homilies to their American adversaries on the efficacy of Nazi intelligence work. In "The Suicide Squad's Private War," Wolfgang von Reichenstein gloated:

Incredible? Not at all, my dear friend. In the Secret Service of the Greater Reich, nothing is incredible—and nothing is impossible. The poorest spy in our service is adept at disguise, even in his natural self. You will note that there is nothing wrong with my eye, yet for years as Wolfang Von Reichenstein, I wore this eyepatch, so that it became associated with me. Those who sought me always looked for a man with only one eye. Therefore, they never found me! As for the character of old Pappy Ricks, I had a double build up that character for me, years before your country thought that the Reich would ever be a menace to America. And now, Pappy Ricks is above suspicion."

In an effort to link fact and fiction, *Ace G-Man Stories* regularly featured J. Edgar Hoover's speeches on the Fifth Column menace at the front of their novels.[40]

Black Mask offered fans of pulp detective fiction the most hard-boiled and stylish stories of Fifth Column intrigue. Peter Paige's ". . . And God Won't Tell" is written in the form of a confession to a priest by a murderous Irish-American, Dan Ryan. Ryan awaits the electric chair for killing a Jewish tailor at the behest of German agents. The story featured Nazis playing on the blue-collar protagonist's ethnic and class resentments. Ryan's recruitment to the Reich is solidified by a seductress, "built like an old time burlesque queen. Everything big—where it counted." In another *Black Mask* entry, "Conspiracy in Sunlight," a London sunbather turns out to be a German agent who uses himself as a human compass in order to direct the Luftwaffe to vulnerable targets. The agent is undone when he falls victim to sunstroke, becomes delirious, and blurts out a few German phrases while undergoing treatment in an English hospital.[41]

Trojan Horse tales appeared most frequently in detective pulps, but adventure, science-fiction, and fantasy magazines were eager to deal with the problem as well. In recounting Cortes's conquest of Mexico, *Thrilling Adventures* argued that the Spanish used a Fifth Column, propaganda, and terror to defeat the Aztecs. The same pulp ran a multi-part series on Germany's alleged effort to undermine the timber industry in the American Northwest. A sage woodsman named Pegleg detects signs of forest sabotage and opines in a dialect of indeterminate origins: "looks like some o' that Fifth Colyum stuff we were readin' about." A few science-fiction dime novels of the period feature Nazi spies seeking to steal secret weapons, usually some form of disintegration ray, from the Americans. One fantasy story emphasized the Fifth Column's alliances with the forces of darkness. In "Speak of the Devil," an American actor learns that Hitler's success has been due to an agreement with the devil. In this story the Nazi Fifth Columnist proves so loathsome that even Satan disdains his company.[42]

As has already been discussed, Hollywood increasingly addressed the Fifth Column problem after the release of *Confessions of a Nazi Spy* in 1939. The studios produced dramas featuring serious actors such as Humphrey Bogart, Alan Ladd, and Robert Young, as well as comic features starring performers such as Bob Hope, Abbott and Costello, the Dead End Kids, the Three Stooges and Joe E. Brown. A host of B movies brought Charlie Chan, Sherlock Holmes, Ellery Queen, the Invisible Man, Roy Rogers, and Tarzan into conflict with Axis agents. *The Encyclopedia of American Spy Films* notes that in 1942 alone Hollywood produced over 70 films dealing with the Fifth Column.[43]

The Rumrich spy case set off the first media frenzy over Hitler's Fifth Column. Succeeding examples of bungled Nazi intrigue encouraged more elaborate and fanciful tales of hidden enemies. Extensive press coverage of actual German outrages led the way for the multitude of popular fictions on the Fifth Column that bombarded ordinary American citizens in the early forties. Yet not comic strips, pulps, films, nor even newspaper reports could have generated a full-blown national hysteria, had trusted government officials not contributed to the burgeoning fear. At the center of Washington's handling of the Trojan Horse problem, we find the President himself, cagy yet credulous, when it came to this attack on American integrity.

EIGHT

—⟨✺⟩—

Franklin Roosevelt
and the Fifth Column

During a two-year period (from 1940 through 1942), President Franklin Roosevelt repeatedly spoke out on the gravity of the Trojan Horse menace; he warned that enemy agents had already slipped into the U.S. and were threatening to destroy the nation from within. Roosevelt also took pains to assure the public that his administration was working hard to block such nefarious activity. Through his policymaking and rhetoric, FDR played a more influential role in shaping popular attitudes toward the Fifth Column than did any other single individual.

As the thirties wound down, FDR increasingly commented on the problem of German intrigue in America. In response to the revelations coming out of the Rumrich trial, the President promised to improve the government's counterintelligence operations.[1] With the outbreak of the European war, Roosevelt took dramatic steps to strengthen America's home defenses. On September 6, 1939, he announced that the Federal Bureau of Investigation had been placed in charge of investigating espionage, sabotage, subversion, and the violation of neutrality laws.[2] He ordered local law enforcement officers to hand over information on the spy problem to Hoover's G-men. On September 8, 1939, Roosevelt informed a press gathering that personnel were being added to various government investigative agencies in order to guard against "some of the things that happened over here in 1914 and 1915 and 1916 and the beginning of 1917 before we got into the war." The President reminded journalists that the period preceding American involvement in World War I had witnessed sabotage, propaganda, and "a good many definite plans which would tend to be subversive."[3]

FDR did not turn his full attention to the Trojan Horse menace until the Nazi invasion of France. In a May 16, 1940, message to Congress, Roosevelt urged Americans to "recast their thinking about national protection." He cautioned that Germany's blitzkrieg victories were directly linked to a new kind of "Fifth Column" warfare which entailed efforts to soften up an adversary before attack.[4] At a May 24 press conference FDR was asked to specify what form Trojan Horse activities had taken in America. He responded evasively to the query, advising reporters only that they should examine the Dies committee findings, where they would encounter some "good information" and some "not so good" on the spy problem.[5] In a fireside chat delivered two days later, the President finally clarified the nature of the Fifth Column danger which he felt America faced:

> Today's threat to our national security is not a matter of military weapons alone. We know of new methods of attack.
> The Trojan Horse. The Fifth Column that betrays a nation unprepared for treachery.
> Spies, saboteurs and traitors are the actors in this new strategy. With all of these we must and will deal vigorously.

Roosevelt added that the principal Fifth Column threat lay in the Nazis' application of "divide and conquer" techniques.

> As a result of these techniques, armament programs may be dangerously delayed. Singleness of national purpose may be undermined. Men can lose confidence in each other and therefore in the efficacy of their own united action. Faith and courage can yield to doubt and fear. The unity of the state can be so sapped that its strength can be destroyed.[6]

On May 30, FDR reinforced these observations by telling a gathering of reporters that "this Fifth Column thing . . . is altogether too widespread through the country."[7]

Several members of the media believed that Roosevelt's rhetoric was fanning the flame of public hysteria. On June 5, 1940, a skeptical reporter asked the President whether the Fifth Column activities actually existed. FDR replied, "They do, very definitely." The President added that there had been 40 to 50 attempts to sabotage American defense plants.[8]

Long after the fall of France, FDR continued to stress the threat which spies, saboteurs, and propagandists posed to national security. He tirelessly reminded Americans that "secret emissaries are active in our own and neighboring countries" seeking to exacerbate class, racial, and religious divisions.[9] Roosevelt spoke of Hitler's effort to destroy America through " 'an inside job'—a job accomplished not by overpowering invasion from without but by confusion and division and moral disintegration from within."[10] Almost every message which Roosevelt delivered on national security matters made at least a passing reference to the need to better insulate the home front against Axis intrigue.[11]

Roosevelt effectively used the Fifth Column issue to discredit and disgrace his isolationist opponents. He argued that the presence of totalitarian agents in America highlighted the immediacy of the German threat and the folly of isolationism. However, the President did not merely attack the cogency of his opponent's foreign policy views; he also challenged their loyalty. FDR lumped together actual spies in the employ of Hitler with his isolationist critics. The President held that the isolationists were lulling the public into a false sense of security and weakening the nation's moral and mental defenses.[12] He branded opponents of his style of internationalism as "appeaser fifth columnists."[13] Roosevelt contended that the isolationists—knowingly or not—acted as agents for Hitler's propaganda office.[14]

FDR's unwillingness to recognize a distinction between legitimate opposition and treason is best seen in his treatment of Charles Lindbergh. Lindbergh was one of America's most forceful and outspoken advocates of isolation. He repeatedly accused the White House of recklessly leading America toward war. Lindbergh's status as a national folk hero ensured that his criticisms of Roosevelt's foreign policy received widespread media coverage. The President retaliated by publicly vilifying the celebrated airman. FDR equated Lindbergh with Civil War Copperhead Clement L. Vallandigham.[15] Roosevelt's attacks were not cynically motivated, but reflected his genuine feelings. In May of 1940, FDR wrote Henry Stimson a private letter expressing sorrow that Lindbergh "has completely abandoned his belief in our form of government and has accepted Nazi methods for America because apparently they are efficient."[16] Roosevelt also confided to his Secretary of the Treasury, Henry Morgenthau, that he was "absolutely convinced that Lindbergh was a Nazi."[17] Roosevelt's frustration with the "Lone Eagle" is not mysterious. Lindbergh advocated policies which delighted Berlin. His isolationism was exasperatingly naive and, in the view of many contemporaries, tinged with anti-semitism. Lindbergh, of course, was no turncoat. After the Pearl Harbor attack he desperately sought to serve his country in a military capacity. However, a bitter White House refused to restore Lindbergh's commission in the Army Air Force. Ultimately the airman was able to play a role in the fighting as a private citizen. United Aircraft Corporation hired Lindbergh as a technical adviser. In this capacity, he ended up flying over 50 combat missions in the Pacific and even shot down a Japanese aircraft.[18]

As Geoffrey Smith has written, the Roosevelt administration was not the only source of accusations of disloyalty. Far-right extremists such as

Fritz Kuhn, Charles Coughlin, and William Dudley Pelley claimed the White House was in cahoots with a "Judeo-Bolshevik" conspiracy. America Firsters, while usually more restrained, also linked the New Deal to un-American behavior.[19] The *Chicago Tribune*, the primary isolationist organ of the mainstream press, accused Harry Hopkins, Harold Ickes, and Frances Perkins of giving "aid and comfort to the Fifth Column." For the *Tribune* the main Trojan Horse menace emanated from the Soviet Union, not Nazi Germany (although the editorial page insinuated that New Deal bureaus were tending to create a Nazified state). The paper bitterly complained of Roosevelt's efforts to employ the bogey of a German Fifth Column in the United States as a means of advancing interventionist programs. While the *Tribune*'s editorial pages denounced such tactics, news stories and features admitted the centrality of the Trojan Horse to Hitler's success in Europe. Throughout June 1940, the Sunday paper ran a multi-part series which concluded: "Germany does not have the only great spy system. But Germany has the best, judged by known accomplishments to date." A *Tribune* analysis of the "phony war" contended that Hitler had delayed his blitzkrieg in accord with the desires of Fifth Columnists who asked for more time to soften up the Western democracies. Thanks to the Trojan Horse, the paper noted, Hitler "knew exactly what they were doing and what they would not take up until he struck."[20] If the most ardent isolationist newspaper ran stories admitting the danger of Hitler's Fifth Column, it is hardly surprising that Roosevelt reached similar if more exaggerated conclusions.

By and large, FDR's savage attacks on the loyalty of the isolationists were unfair. Still, the White House possessed considerable evidence suggesting an alliance between Hitler and the isolationists. German propaganda consistently praised the America First Committee. For example, in seeking to prove Britain's responsibility for the war, Hitler cited a speech delivered by the chairman of the America First Committee, Leonard Wood. In fact, there were scattered attempts by pro-Nazi operatives to infiltrate the America First movement. The Third Reich gave financial support to aviator Laura Ingles, a popular isolationist speaker.[21] Additionally, the German embassy in Washington subsidized a variety of publications espousing the isolationist viewpoint.[22] Nazi efforts to aid his domestic opponents genuinely concerned the President. In November 1941, he asked the Attorney General to "please speak to me about the possibility of a Grand Jury investigation of the money sources behind the America First Committee. . . ."[23] It is not hard to forgive Roosevelt for his tendency to doubt the patriotism of his isolationist critics.

FDR took a lively personal interest in domestic security matters. He maintained excellent relations with his intelligence chiefs, meeting regularly with them. Walter S. Anderson, FDR's Chief of Naval Intelligence from 1940 to 1941, noted: "President Roosevelt was quite intelligence-minded. He directed that an officer from Naval Intelligence and one from Military Intelligence should visit him about three times a week, to brief him on the current situation."[24] Roosevelt worked particularly closely with his FBI director, J. Edgar Hoover. Hoover sent thousands of reports to the White House between 1940 and 1945. FDR did not respond passively to these intelligence reports. Instead, he played an activist role in battling Axis intrigue. In meetings with the Attorney General, Roosevelt frequently suggested the investigation of individuals whom he suspected of having Nazi sympathies.[25] FDR also felt few compunctions about having the FBI look into very specific Fifth Column problems which he thought were being ignored. For example, on April 3, 1942, the President sent the following query to Hoover: "Have you pretty well cleaned out the alien waiters in the principal Washington hotels. Altogether too much conversation in the dining rooms! FDR."[26] Roosevelt occasionally asked the Justice Department to consider the suppression of extremist publications which he believed encouraged internal division.[27] FDR's interest in the Axis Fifth Column threat was also revealed by the fact that he found time to read the *Hour* and *PM* magazines—both private publications largely concerned with exposing fascist activities in America.[28]

Like the vast majority of Americans, Roosevelt believed that the Axis Fifth Column endangered national security. FDR's concerns were entirely understandable; as commander-in-chief he was ultimately responsible for home-front defense. The FBI, military intelligence, and the Office of Naval Intelligence all presented the Nazi Trojan Horse as a serious threat. As has already been shown, the Germans did indeed engage in a host of clandestine activities directed against the United States. Though such activities were small in scale, poorly conducted, and successfully controlled, they raised dire possibilities. Policymakers could never be entirely sure whether or not the enemy was conducting undetected Fifth Column operations. Moreover, there were lingering fears in many informed quarters that the Reich planned to unleash one overwhelming Trojan Horse offensive sometime in the future.[29]

While Roosevelt received much reliable data on the state of domestic security, he was also fed a stream of alarmist rumors. Even the usually trustworthy FBI passed on reports to the White House inaccurately predicting a spurt of secret German operations. In February 1940, the Bureau warned of a sabotage scheme aimed at paralyzing Los Angeles. In May 1941, Hoover forwarded data from the British which predicted that the Nazis would launch a campaign of destruction against America's factories during the Decoration Day weekend. In June 1942, while the FBI was pursuing two groups of German saboteurs, Hoover warned that similar units were likely to "be sent from Germany to the United States every six weeks to initiate a wave of terror. . . ."[30]

Roosevelt received a particularly frightening analysis of the Fifth Column problem from journalist John Franklin Carter. On December 31,

1941, Carter wrote FDR a memo which predicted an all-out Axis sabotage campaign in the spring of 1942.[31] On January 9, 1942, Carter forwarded a report to the White House which held that "there is a definite wealthy and well entrenched fifth column in this country." The study claimed that this subversive group was simply waiting for the "green light" from its superiors in Berlin. American citizens, not resident aliens, were presented as the most fearsome Fifth Columnists:

> In the Nazi plan of campaign they have undoubtedly instructed their better agents as far back as 1932 and probably even earlier to come to the United States and immediately take out citizenship papers in order to get the protection of this status. This is borne out by the files of our Intelligence Services which show the worst elements are American.

The report offered two ways to "get at these people": first, suspend habeas corpus "as Lincoln did during the Civil War"; second, send suspected Fifth Columnists to work "plowing and rolling flat a field in South Dakota."[32] After reading this document Roosevelt asked Carter to talk the matter over with Attorney General Francis Biddle and FBI boss J. Edgar Hoover. Biddle refused to act on the report, leaving a miffed Carter to inform FDR that "the problem of U.S. citizens who are Axis agents remains as is. . . ."[33]

By the autumn of 1942 a range of factors combined to assuage FDR's Fifth Column jitters. In October, Roosevelt suggested that the threat of German intrigue was on the wane. He concluded that the Nazi's "War of Nerves" was "now turning into a boomerang." The President observed that Hitler would soon be faced with a Fifth Column problem of his own as the repulse of German forces at Stalingrad and the rising casualties of the Wehrmacht fostered defeatism and disillusionment throughout the Reich.[34] Just as the Allies' shift to the offensive boosted Roosevelt's confidence about the state of home-front security, so too did the FBI's increasingly apparent mastery over all forms of Nazi Trojan Horse activity. In July 1942, an FBI survey of domestic security downplayed the hazards posed by German intrigue. The Bureau noted that "extreme difficulty apparently exists in the establishment of accounts for the use of axis agents. . . ." The report added that fascist-inspired propaganda was on the wane and reassuringly concluded that "German organizations which in the past exhibited pro-Nazi sympathies are practically defunct at the present time. . . ."[35] The capture of a group of German saboteurs in July 1942 and the destruction of several spy rings offered the President fairly conclusive evidence that Hitler's secret war in America was failing. Finally, the political value of the Fifth Column threat diminished sharply after Hitler's declaration of war against the

United States. FDR no longer needed to prod the country toward internationalism nor was he forced to parry attacks from isolationist critics.

With the benefit of hindsight, Roosevelt's concern about the Fifth Column may appear excessive. However, compared with many of his contemporaries, the President met the Trojan Horse menace with considerable equanimity. Even so level-headed a New Dealer as Attorney General Robert Jackson informed listeners of Drew Pearson's radio program that there were three forms of Fifth Column activity: "First, there is the propaganda activity—the attempt to turn Americans from our traditional political and economic system to Fascism, Nazism or Communism. The second is the process of 'softening' a nation in preparation for invasion—to divide the people in order to conquer them, to stir up race-hatreds, to create confusion in order to sabotage their morale, *to discredit the nation's leaders* [my italics] and to make it ineffective as a competitor or weak as an enemy. The third force is just plain appeasement."[36] In fact, Roosevelt's failure to back more stringent anti-Fifth Column measures exasperated most administration figures. The pressure which various advisers placed upon FDR to counteract enemy intrigue can be seen clearly in the battle over the creation of a centralized morale agency. Secretary of the Interior Harold Ickes spearheaded an effort to create a government apparatus responsible for combating enemy propaganda. President Roosevelt saw to it that no powerful morale organization came into being. The administration's debate over government propaganda highlights FDR's canny response to the Fifth Column problem. The President used his own personal power to play up the Trojan Horse threat and encouraged his political allies to do the same. However, he avoided the establishment of an influential propaganda agency which might have alienated the public or recreated the virulent anti-German sentiment of the First World War.[37]

Protecting National Morale

Germany's successes in the spring of 1940 generated tremendous momentum within the Roosevelt administration for the creation of a powerful counterpropaganda agency. FDR's advisers feared that Hitler would find America as vulnerable to Trojan Horse tactics as Europe appeared to have been. United States policymakers were not so much worried that Germany planned an imminent invasion—though they conceded that such an invasion might come. Rather, they saw Hitler working to aid the isolationists, disaffect the public from Roosevelt, and sap the nation's will to resist aggression. Interventionists worried that German propaganda might keep the U.S. neutral until England was defeated. After that, the Reich would be free to direct its full energy toward the Western Hemisphere.

Many in the Roosevelt administration saw a centralized program of government propaganda as the only effective response to the German Fifth Column. Supporters of an energetic morale-building effort included Secretary of the Interior Harold Ickes, Secretary of War Henry Stimson, Secretary of the Navy Frank Knox, Secretary of Labor Frances Perkins, Vice President Henry Wallace, Director of the Budget Harold Smith, Army Chief of Staff George C. Marshall, and Assistant Secretary of War John C. McCloy. For administration supporters of propaganda, the line between German Fifth Columnists and critics of Roosevelt's foreign policy was virtually nonexistent. For example, Harold Ickes claimed that the isolationists were running a "carefully planned campaign" of defeatism in order to assist Germany.[38] He publicly rebuked Charles Lindbergh, describing "the Lone Eagle" as America's "No. 1 Nazi fellow traveller."[39] Ickes pushed for a coordinated government counterattack which would support the Allied cause and explicitly address the arguments of prominent isolationists such as Lindbergh, Senator Burton Wheeler, and Senator Gerald Nye.

President Roosevelt remained circumspect regarding Ickes's proposals. Nonetheless, pressure from within the administration led him to experiment with three different morale agencies: the Office of Civilian Defense (OCD), the Office of Facts and Figures (OFF), and the Office of War Information (OWI). Roosevelt's support for these organizations proved tepid and erratic. FDR was determined to use his power and influence to fight the Fifth Column, but he did not wish to behave in a way which would recall America's unpleasant experience with government propaganda during World War I. Ultimately, OCD, OFF, and OWI played only a small role in the Fifth Column story. However, the discussions that preceded the establishment of a government morale program revealed the intense anxiety which the Nazi Trojan Horse menace aroused among Roosevelt's most trusted advisers.

During the interwar period, Americans came to cast a jaundiced eye upon the work of the Creel committee, blaming the Committee on Public Information for fostering a national climate of intolerance and hysteria. Wartime excesses directed against German-Americans, pacifists, aliens, and various other dissenters were linked to the government's patriotic oversell. Additionally, President Wilson's establishment of a centralized propaganda agency seemed to be a dangerous concentration of power in the hands of government. The Creel committee's popular reputation suffered further damage from the general revulsion against the idea of "propaganda" which developed in the thirties.[40] President Franklin Roosevelt fully understood the public's hostility toward government propaganda and deplored the anti-German excesses of the First World War. Hence, he proceeded with great circumspection when his advisers began to argue in the fall of 1940 for a morale agency to counteract the Nazi

Fifth Column and to woo support for a more vigorous American foreign policy.

Throughout the summer of 1940, the President wrestled with various proposals aimed at bolstering domestic morale and creating greater civilian participation in the government's preparedness campaign. On June 7, Lauchlin Currie urged FDR to create local defense committees to help with the administration's defense program. Working along similar lines, Archibald MacLeish, the Librarian of Congress, called for an organization to coordinate civilian volunteer activities for defense. MacLeish hoped to persuade the public of the need for a more active U.S. role in the struggle against Hitler. From May until September President Roosevelt held discussions with adviser Louis Brownlow on the possibility of creating a single government information agency. Brownlow drafted plans for an organization divided into three separate parts: one unit was to defend the country from German propaganda; a second unit was to provide the public with news pertaining to the progress of national defense; and a third unit was left to handle "the ordinary informational services of the Government as it goes along."[41]

Roosevelt's cabinet soon joined in the push for more systematic efforts to improve domestic morale. At a cabinet meeting held on November 8, 1940, Harold Ickes proposed the establishment of "some machinery for propaganda."[42] Frank Knox and Henry Stimson promptly seconded this suggestion. After the proposal won general cabinet approval, President Roosevelt created a committee to consider the formation of a federal morale agency. Ickes assumed leadership of the committee.[43] Others serving with him included Robert Jackson, Henry Stimson, Frank Knox, Frances Perkins, Louis Brownlow, Clarence Dykstra (Selective Service Director), and Frank Walker (Postmaster General).

Assistant Secretary of War John McCloy became an important figure in the discussions held by Ickes's cabinet committee. McCloy attended several meetings as a representative for Henry Stimson. The committee listened to the Assistant Secretary of War's counsel with great respect, as his role in prosecuting the Black Tom and Kingsland sabotage cases made him an expert on the Fifth Column problem. McCloy told the committee that a federal propaganda agency should be a cabinet-level appointment. He noted that Germany as a matter of pre-invasion strategy assaulted its adversaries with "a super barrage to precede the artillery barrage—the barrage of ideas." Ickes was confirmed in his own support for a counter-Fifth Column program by McCloy's conclusion that propaganda was "a really essential military weapon in this day and age."[44]

Ickes's committee based its discussion upon Louis Brownlow's plan to create a super information agency to coordinate counterpropaganda, defense news, and miscellaneous government information. The cabinet committee considered only Brownlow's proposals relating to counter-propaganda. Ickes believed the task of protecting morale so important as to require an independent government bureau. He feared that a propaganda unit buried within a larger information organization would lack the influence and independence needed to be effective. In a letter to the President, Ickes spelled out the primary functions of a morale organization: "To analyze and combat propaganda menacing the national security and defense, to fortify the national morale, to let the people of other countries know the nature and direction of the American way of life and to acquaint the people of this country with the nature and sources of the present threat to their liberties, civil, economic, and political."[45] Ickes called for the new organization to be set up in the executive office of the President. He proposed the department be run by a single chief, assisted by an advisory council. Ickes forwarded his committee's recommendation for the establishment of a morale agency to FDR on November 28, 1940. The President did not formally reply to this proposal until March 3, 1941. FDR's foot-dragging revealed his deep reservations over instituting a second Creel committee.[46]

Lowell Mellett reinforced Roosevelt's doubts about government propaganda. Mellett was the chief of the Office of Government Reports, an agency created in September 1939 as part of the administration's emergency reorganization. The OGR cleared news stories from various government departments; answered informational inquiries from the public; produced press releases, news stories, and posters on the administration's defense programs; and monitored news and editorial coverage of current events, keeping government officials up to date on shifts in journalistic opinion. Mellett attempted to work with the media in a voluntary, cooperative fashion. As a former editor of the *Washington Times*, he knew that the press was wary of government propaganda and would react with hostility to any attempts by the President to dictate news coverage. (Mellett's own organization was viewed with suspicion by journalists who derisively described the OGR as OGRe.) Mellett thought that Ickes's effort to create a morale unit would prove disastrously unpopular with the press and the public. Moreover, he did not believe such an organization necessary, especially given the mounting support tendered by the media to Roosevelt's foreign policy after the fall of France.[47]

FDR used Mellett to block progress toward a morale agency. When Ickes pressed for action on the propaganda problem, the President would ask him to consult with Lowell Mellett. In a February 24 meeting with Ickes, McCloy, and Undersecretary of the Navy James Forrestal, Mellett spelled out his distaste for propaganda. The OGR chief claimed: "No one could tell Americans what to do or how to think!" He protested that Hitler's methods in Germany were unsuitable for the United States. McCloy countered that a propaganda apparatus was needed "as badly as we need airplanes." He argued that the weakness of navy intelligence, army intelligence, and the Federal Bureau of Investigation all made a government morale agency an essential element of national defense. Ickes expressed astonishment at Mellett's failure to appreciate "the fact that Hitler's method of breaking down the morale of other people had proved to be pretty effective in Austria and Czechoslovakia and Belgium and France etc."[48]

Ickes's involvement with the Council for Democracy solidified his support for propaganda. This organization was made up of academics, public opinion experts, journalists, labor leaders, and businessmen. Arthur Upham Pope, an expert on Persian art, headed the group. The Council for Democracy was an interventionist organization, concerned primarily with the state of public morale. In February, Ickes requested a report from the group outlining how a national propaganda agency might be structured. Pope's organization forwarded a "Plan for National Morale" to the Secretary of the Interior. Ickes expressed enthusiasm for the proposal.[49] However, Mellett saw the scheme as unworkable and he viewed Pope as an impractical academic. Solicitor General Francis Biddle joined Mellett in opposing the "Plan." Biddle noted that much of the work suggested for a morale service was already in the hands of other agencies; that the press and the public were likely to disapprove of a federal morale agency; and that "the vast private 'propaganda' now going on [was] preferable to a more unified and central control."[50] Over time, Ickes was to become completely frustrated with those who opposed a federal counterpropaganda agency; Mellett particularly irked him. In mid-March the Secretary of the Interior dashed off an angry note to the OGR chief warning that the administraton's dismissive treatment of the morale problem would result in America paying "the same cost as France and other countries have paid for their stupidity."[51] For his part, Mellett saw Ickes as a meddlesome amateur who failed to understand the role of the media in American democracy.

On March 3, 1941, FDR told Ickes that he approved of his November 28 recommendations "in principle." However, the President expressed a desire for a list of candidates who might serve as head of the morale agency and also possible staff members for the Bureau's advisory committee. Ickes quickly replied, proposing either John McCloy of the War Department or Ralph Ingersoll of *PM* magazine as possible directors. He also submitted a lengthy roll call of prominent citizens to serve on the propaganda board, including many members of the Council for Democracy (such as Arthur Upham Pope, Alfred E. Cohn, George Gallup, and Edgar Ansel Mowrer).[52] Again President Roosevelt delayed. Ickes found the President's behavior deplorable. His frustrations about the failure to set up a morale unit eventually led him to express doubts in his diary about FDR's leadership: "If I could have looked this far ahead and seen an inactive and uninspiring President, I would not have supported him for a third term. My desire for him was due entirely to the fact that I believed he would prove to be a great leader in the time of grave crisis that I saw approaching."[53]

The President hoped to shape public opinion in a less heavyhanded way than that proposed by Ickes. In March of 1941, FDR created the Division of Information in the Office of Emergency Management. This new organization did not handle morale issues, but merely generated information on the progress of the defense program. (In 1942, the Office of War Information absorbed this body.)[54] It was believed that such an agency would help to keep the public interested in the progress of the nation's defense buildup.

Roosevelt was strongly attracted to the idea of voluntary participation in the defense effort—especially civilian defense. He hoped to elevate morale by directly involving citizens in preparedness programs. Early in 1941, newspaperman George Fort Milton outlined a blueprint for an Office of Peace Security and forwarded it to the President. Milton held a deep interest in America's historical vulnerability to internal enemies. (In 1942 he released a lengthy monograph entitled *Abraham Lincoln and the Fifth Column*.)[55] FDR formed a subcommittee to use Milton's memorandum as the basis for an Office of Home Defense. The members of this committee—former ambassador to France William C. Bullitt, Director of the Budget Harold Smith, and presidential assistant Wayne Coy—worked out plans for a civilian defense agency. The triumvirate's proposal did not focus on the explicit manipulation of American public opinion.

At a cabinet meeting in mid-April, Secretary of War Stimson asked Ickes about the status of the proposed propaganda organization.[56] Once the subject was broached, FDR tried to stall discussion by asking the Secretary of the Interior to meet with Lowell Mellett. Ickes flatly refused to do so, leading the President to burst out in good-natured laughter. Roosevelt then asked his cabinet for possible candidates to run the propaganda organization. A desultory discussion followed. Ickes finally interrupted the proceedings and suggested that Henry Wallace be made temporary acting director of the morale unit in order to get the organization off the ground. FDR agreed. However, Ickes uneasily noted that Roosevelt "had this morale idea all mixed up with home guards, voluntary firemen, etc."[57]

It was apparent that Roosevelt intended to submerge morale building within a larger civilian defense agency. Ickes vainly fought against such a move. He told Henry Morgenthau that this approach would kill a serious morale program, and he asked the Secretary of the Treasury to "put in a few words" with the President on the matter.[58] On April 30, Ickes wrote FDR that Harold Smith and "some of the rest of us" believe "that the morale and counter-propaganda effort should be separate from home defense and that such an organization should be provided as soon as possible."[59] Roosevelt was unmoved. He simply suggested that Ickes, along with Lowell Mellett and Ulric Bell, meet with the new director of civilian defense in order to discuss "the whole subject of effective publicity to offset the propaganda of the Wheelers, Nyes, Lindburghs [*sic*] etc."[60]

On May 20, 1941, FDR issued an executive order establishing the Office of Civilian Defense. OCD was given the following mandate:

> to assure effective coordination of the Federal relations with State and local governments engaged in defense activities, to provide for necessary cooperation with State and local governments in respect to measures for adequate protection of the civilian population in emergency periods, to facilitate constructive civilian participation in the defense program, and *to sustain national morale* [my emphasis].[61]

FDR appointed Fiorello La Guardia to head OCD. This selection indicated that Roosevelt did not really take the new agency all that seriously. La Guardia already served as mayor of New York City and as the acting chairman on the Permanent Joint Board of Defense between Canada and the United States. Harold Ickes bitterly complained to FDR that "Fiorello is not God and he has to eat and sleep like other human beings."[62] What effort La Guardia did expend as OCD chief was directed almost entirely toward civilian defense projects—air raid precautions, first aid training, and the like. LaGuardia did establish a Bureau of Facts and Figures to handle morale questions. However, this unit proved to be an inconsequential component of OCD.

Significant protest arose within the Roosevelt administration over La Guardia's failure to adequately deal with the morale problem. Ickes, McCloy, and Smith all expressed concern.[63] In September of 1941, the President received a warning from General George Marshall that morale among recent draftees was extremely low. Marshall called for a more energetic government propaganda initiative.[64] Such complaints led the President to remove propaganda from La Guardia's control and create a new organization.

In October of 1941, Franklin Roosevelt appointed Librarian of Congress Archibald MacLeish to head up an Office of Facts and Figures. The executive order establishing OFF outlined two functions for the new agency. First, it was to "formulate programs designed to facilitate a widespread and accurate understanding of the national defense effort and of the defense policies and activities of the government. . . ." Second, it was asked to coordinate the dissemination of information emerging from the various departments involved in defense. OFF director MacLeish saw his primary job as one of education. He believed OFF should supply "the country with the factual information to demonstrate the necessity of decisions taken or proposed or the advisability of policies now adopted or proposed for adoption in the near future."[65] In short, the Librarian of Congress wanted to justify administration policy to the public.

MacLeish's agency proved a dismal failure. Only six months after its creation the Office of War Information absorbed OFF. From the outset MacLeish noted that his organization could succeed only if it were given access to relevant government intelligence, real authority to coordinate different government departments, and an open door to the President's office.[66] None of these conditions was met. Moreover, MacLeish's agency never enjoyed good relations with the press. Journalists viewed OFF with suspicion. Arthur Krock observed that if MacLeish's unit lived up to its promise to deliver only straight facts "it will be the first government bureau to do that."[67] Some papers scornfully derided OFF as the Office of Fun and Frolic.

During its brief existence OFF attempted to control rumors and counter enemy propaganda. In February 1942, *Divide and Conquer*, OFF's first publication, appeared. This booklet alerted citizens to the Reich's ingenious ability "to sow seeds of hate and disunity, turning people against their own governments, governments against their own allies, class against class." It warned against complacency:

> The United States is still intact but Hitler hopes to destroy that unity, physically and mentally. All his tricks are now being directed against us. Our job is one of individual awareness, in order to avoid falling into Hitler's trap. Hitler's propaganda wears a thousand false faces. It never announces itself as "Nazi." It appears where least expected, often turning up as the latest joke issued by the government.

Divide and Conquer was lent a scholarly air by its reliance on footnotes from earlier works denouncing the Fifth Column (pieces by Leland Stowe, Hermann von Rauschning, Edmond Taylor, and William Donovan were cited). The piece gained widespread circulation when it was reprinted in the *Saturday Evening Post*. Even after its incorporation into OWI, OFF continued to produce counter-Fifth Column pieces.[68]

By the winter of 1942, OFF's inadequacy became apparent. Frustrated by his organization's impotence, Archibald MacLeish called for FDR to establish a more powerful centralized agency. FDR concurred and assigned Milton Eisenhower the task of drafting a blueprint for a reorganized government information bureau. On June 13, 1942, Executive Order #9182 created the Office of War Information. The new agency was divided into a foreign branch and a domestic branch. The Office of Government Reports, the Division of Information in the Office of Emergency Management, and the Office of Facts and Figures formed the domestic unit. The Foreign Information Service of William Donovan's Coordinator of Information Office was also transferred to OWI, and became the basis of the agency's foreign unit. The President called on OWI to coordinate government information, establish cooperative ties with the media, and improve public understanding of the war. Roosevelt selected widely respected newsman Elmer Davis to head the agency.

In the area of foreign propaganda, OWI backed away from policies that might have allowed the United States to develop fully its own Trojan Horse weapon. Franklin Roosevelt endorsed such an approach as he stripped Robert Sherwood's Foreign Information Service from the control of William Donovan and placed it under the umbrella of OWI. Donovan and Sherwood bitterly disagreed over the proper way to use propaganda. The latter favored a "strategy of truth", which emphasized the virtues of democracy and the horrors of fascism; the former supported a "strategy of terror" aimed at disrupting, dividing, and confusing the enemy. Donovan wanted to beat Germany at its own Fifth Column game, softening up the Nazi state through the employment of deception and rumor. Sherwood disliked the notion of the United States modeling its policies on those of Adolf Hitler. He believed that once the United States disseminated outright lies the FIS's credibility would be badly undermined.

Donovan had hoped to keep FIS within his newly created Office of Strategic Services. Even after the President decided to place Sherwood's operation under civilian control, Donovan maintained an interest in propaganda, especially as it related to subversion. In December 1942 the Joint Chiefs of Staff issued a directive placing psychological warfare in the hands of OSS. This action prompted a number of senior members of OWI to threaten resignation. Davis complained directly to the White House. Roosevelt responded by asserting OWI's authority over all overseas propaganda; at the same time he issued an order that would have disassembled OSS, farming out its constituent branches to other agencies. Only last minute aid from the Joint Chiefs of Staff prevented implementation of the order. In the resulting compromise, OSS gained the right to handle black propaganda directly tied to military operations, but the broader category of psychological warfare was left in the hands of Davis's organization.

Allan Winkler has demonstrated that as the war progressed OWI increasingly worked in direct support of military operations. The effort of evangelizing the world to the benefits of the Four Freedoms and the Atlantic Charter gave way to more immediate military needs. By 1944, campaigns sought to persuade both the Germans and the Japanese to recognize the overpowering strength of the Allies and surrender. In seeking to defeat the Axis, OWI agents under control of the military sometimes dispensed information that diverged from the "strategy of truth." To the extent that OWI sought to sap the will of the enemy to resist, it was indeed imitating some of the tactics that Hitler had allegedly used in France. However, the harder edge of Fifth Column propaganda (for example, the forgery of documents and the dissemination of cooked-up stories) remained primarily in the hands of the OSS.[69]

Throughout its existence, divisive problems plagued OWI's domestic branch. First, each individual government agency still retained final control over the information which it produced. Consequently, defense organizations had to be cajoled and nagged into releasing material. Second, OWI's varied tasks led to considerable confusion over the agencies' primary function. Some claimed OWI was simply to supply the public with news; others saw its job as one of selling the war to America; and still others believed it was primarily a public relations unit for the Roosevelt administration. These competing visions helped to generate sharp internal divisions within OWI. Third, the failure to win the trust of Congress undermined Davis's organization. Capitol Hill suspected that the executive branch controlled OWI. In 1943, Congress put the financial squeeze on the agency's domestic branch. Elmer Davis noted that Congress had supplied the OWI with "just enough money to relieve them of the odium of having put us out of business . . . and not enough to let us accomplish anything."[70] In fact, the appropriation for fiscal year 1944 allotted 90 percent of OWI's budget to the overseas branch.[71]

Only a few months after the creation of OWI, America's spy hysteria began to die down. As a result, Elmer Davis's organization devoted only slight attention to the Trojan Horse menace. In the modest attention it did give to the Fifth Column problem, OWI followed somewhat contradictory approaches. Some units, such as the Bureau of Graphics and Printing, produced material likely to reinforce spy fears. Other branches of OWI, such as the Bureau of Motion Pictures, treated the Nazi Trojan Horse as a fanciful hobgoblin and followed policies aimed at quelling popular anxieties.

Many of the posters which OWI produced focused on the Axis spy menace. These works of art carried slogans such as: "Loose Talk Causes Loss of Life," "Don't Talk Too Much—I Mean You," "A Careless Word—A Needless Loss," "Keep It Under Your Hat," and "Foreign Agents Have Big Ears." The posters reached a large audience. Billboards, trains, buses, subways, federal buildings, and defense plants all prominently displayed the images. The artwork produced by OWI's Graphics Bureau suggested the omnipresence of Axis eavesdroppers and the inadequacy of America's attempts to fully root out enemy agents.[72]

While the Graphics Bureau warned of the Axis spy onslaught, OWI's Bureau of Motion Pictures (BMP) tried to reduce spy hysteria. Lowell Mellett headed BMP. He had begun liaison work with Hollywood in 1940 while fulfilling his duties at OGR. Mellett used his post in OWI to encourage the introduction of patriotic themes into Hollywood films. BMP established an office in Hollywood which reviewed movie scripts.

This office often suggested additions or deletions to film story lines, although Mellett lacked coercive authority over the studio moguls. Nonetheless, he received a certain degree of voluntary cooperation from moviemakers.[73]

One area in which BMP expressed dissatisfaction was Hollywood's obsessive interest in the Axis Fifth Column threat. The year 1942 proved to be the heyday of the spy film; 60 percent of the nation's 122 war features released in that year focused on the theme of espionage. In September of 1942, BMP issued a report which criticized the superabundance of spy pictures and publicly blamed the studios for giving Americans "an exaggerated idea of this menace."[74] Hollywood rapidly cut down on its output of espionage features. In 1943, only 25 of 105 films centered around enemy spies. In 1944 a more precipitous decline occurred as only 12 of 76 war pictures principally treated matters of enemy intrigue.[75] Mellett may have been partially responsible for dampening the studios' enthusiasm with Axis spies. However, it is more likely that Hollywood decided to shift its focus to other wartime problems because public interest in espionage was petering out.

Throughout the fall of 1940 and the spring of 1941, Secretary of the Interior Harold Ickes pressured FDR to create a morale agency aimed at battling the German Fifth Column. However, FDR shrewdly noted that the media, Congress, and various executive departments were all independently alerting the public to the problem of German intrigue. Roosevelt himself joined in with the chorus of voices denouncing the Fifth Column. Given this situation, the President saw a powerful government propaganda organization as superfluous and possibly harmful. He decided that it was best to fight the Nazi Trojan Horse in a decentralized way.[76]

None of the morale agencies built by the Roosevelt administration played a determining role in generating, sustaining, or terminating the Fifth Column scare. At most such organizations had a marginal impact, sometimes heightening fears of a German Trojan Horse, and in a few cases calming them. OCD remained almost completely disinterested in the spy menace and never fulfilled the morale-building function which was expected of it. OFF did attempt to counter enemy propaganda and to bolster domestic unity. MacLeish's organization released a few publications which addressed the Fifth Column problem. Still, these releases probably had only a slight impact on popular attitudes, and at best simply reinforced already existing concerns about the Nazi Trojan Horse. OWI's treatment of the spy problem at home was mixed. Some of its departments trumpeted the espionage threat, while others downplayed it. OWI's poster campaigns almost certainly were the agency's primary contribution to the fight against enemy espionage. However, by and large, OWI's domestic branch spent very little time dealing with the Fifth Column issue. The Foreign Information Service sought to weaken enemy morale, but left the "black" propaganda techniques associated with the Nazis primarily in the control of OSS.

OCD, OFF, and OWI all were assigned a wide range of responsibilities having little to do with directly answering the Fifth Column challenge. OCD focused upon civilian defense work. OFF and OWI were asked to serve as news bureaus; each agency cleared and coordinated information produced by different government departments. Moreover, OFF and OWI's responsibilities for morale-building went far beyond countering the Axis Trojan Horse. They often entailed developing campaigns to sell bonds, encourage conservation, improve worker productivity, and cultivate a greater public understanding of the war.

Franklin Roosevelt soothed the nerves of his fretful advisers by partially following through on their suggestion that he create a government morale program. However, he purposely curbed OCD, OFF, and OWI, limiting their mandates and offering them little support when they were criticized. America never developed a propaganda agency similar in scope to that run by Joseph Goebbels in Germany; it did not even come close to recreating another Committee on Public Information. Franklin Roosevelt understood far better than his advisers the tremendous political costs which would be incurred by too blatant an attempt to shape public opinion. In the end Roosevelt achieved the goals which Ickes had desired without resorting to a formal counter-Fifth Column organization. FDR used the Trojan Horse issue to attack the isolationists, to rally support for the Allies, and to rouse the public from its apparent indifference to European affairs. He also tried to reassure Americans that the government worked to protect home-front security.

Roosevelt's handling of the Fifth Column issue has been harshly criticized in important scholarly studies by historians Richard Steele and Leo Ribuffo. Steele sees FDR's assault on anti-interventionist critics as intolerant, reckless, and conspiratorial. Ribuffo finds that Roosevelt's fomenting of a Brown Scare along with his internment of Japanese-Americans demonstrate him to have been "a president little concerned about civil liberties." Arthur Schlesinger, Jr., vigorously protests that such conclusions fail to give "due recognition of the context in which a historical figure has acted and of the standards by which action was judged in his epoch."[77] Viewing Roosevelt against the tumultuous environment in which he operated, I find Schlesinger's assessment especially persuasive. After all, a significant body of scholarship holds that Hitler ultimately desired world conquest.[78] As this book has shown, newspaper reporters, diplomats, and intelligence officers all warned Roosevelt of the danger the country faced from internal enemies. Much of the contemporary discussion of FDR's Fifth Column policies attacked the President for not doing *enough* to protect the nation. While major anti-interventionists denounced administration efforts to paint them as Nazi dupes, many of these same individuals leveled charges of un-

American behavior against Roosevelt and suggested that the White House was preparing the way for fascism or else providing cover for a Red Fifth Column.[79]

It does not take too much imagination to envision policies that could have been far worse than those instituted by Roosevelt. Steele's own excellent study of the origins of government propaganda before Pearl Harbor shows how FDR repeatedly thwarted plans for a potentially repressive morale agency. In foreign propaganda as well, Roosevelt curbed the tendency toward a mirror-imaging of alleged Nazi Fifth Column tactics. Even the expansion of FBI power, which Ribuffo decries, was at least in part designed to limit ad hoc vigilantes from administering rough justice to suspected subversives. The one major sedition case brought against a group of Bundists, Nazi sympathizers, propagandists, and extremists resulted in a mistrial with no jailings.

None of this is to deny Steele and Ribuffo's significant findings that FDR manipulated the Fifth Column issue to weaken the anti-interventionist movement, nor that public fear of Axis enemies strengthened instruments of state power such as the Federal Bureau of Investigation. However, Leo Ribuffo's pairing of Roosevelt's internment of the Japanese with his policies regarding the Brown Scare goes too far. In retrospect, we all might wish Roosevelt had risen above the conventional use of the term Fifth Column, which made little distinction between unwitting accomplices of a foreign power and actual enemy agents. FDR certainly gave as good as he got in the bare-knuckled street fight over the direction of American foreign policy. Roosevelt's handling of the Axis Fifth Column does not entitle him to lavish praise. However, given the difficult conditions in which he operated, the censure of historians is unfair.

NINE

J. Edgar Hoover versus the Nazis

No government agency was more intimately involved in the fight against the Axis Fifth Column than the Federal Bureau of Investigation. After battling with several other bureaucracies, the Bureau garnered primary responsibility for protecting the home front. This new assignment was accompanied by the authority to maintain ongoing surveillance over suspicious extremist organizations even when there was no government intent to prosecute a crime. (In the past FBI surveillance was sanctioned only in instances where the government was preparing a case involving the violation of a specific federal law.) As a result of its expansion into the field of counterintelligence, the Bureau was transformed. Budgets skyrocketed and the number of agents grew fivefold (898 agents in 1940; 4,886 in 1945[1]). The successful fight against the Fifth Column also further solidified the position which J. Edgar Hoover and his G-men had won in the pantheon of American heroes.

The FBI won considerable fame and glory for its anti-spy work. Nonetheless, in the period before Pearl Harbor, the Bureau's counterintelligence activities were not entirely spared from public scrutiny and criticism. Many Americans feared the establishment of a home-grown Gestapo and only reluctantly ceded more power to Franklin Roosevelt and the federal government. Civil libertarians expressed misgivings about Hoover, doubting that he could be trusted to protect individual rights. Examples of past excesses by the Bureau were cited as warnings of what might lie ahead if the G-men were not kept tightly in check. Hoover also had to face charges that his organization failed to pursue internal enemies with enough vigor. Such attacks came principally from members of Martin Dies's House Un-American Activities Committee. HUAC contended that enemy spies, both Communist and fascist, ran wild throughout America, inspiring labor unrest, sabotaging industrial plants, and flooding the country with propaganda.

Though such criticism irked the director, he outlasted it. Even at those moments when the Bureau was under heavy attack, most Americans remained satisfied with the way in which Hoover protected the home front. By and large, the public believed that the Bureau effectively combated the Fifth Column without resorting to either Nazi or Stalinist tactics.

In the late thirties and early forties Hoover was a figure of widespread popular adulation. Consequently, his response to the Fifth Column problem was crucial. As the nation's most respected law enforcement officer, Hoover had the power to reassure or to terrify the nation. He gave numerous speeches and wrote countless articles addressing the Fifth Column menace. His approach to the problem was complex. While he confirmed public hysteria, he also helped to contain and control it.

Between 1940 and 1942 Hoover repeatedly characterized America's Trojan Horse as a severe threat to national security. He warned that Fifth Columnists had penetrated into every layer of American society. He claimed that public indifference had allowed enemies of democracy to burrow deeply within the United States, and he called for the nation's citizens to pay greater care to the spy menace. Hoover tempered this alarmism by praising the efficiency of the bureau's counterintelligence work, publicizing Bureau triumphs, and predicting the ultimate defeat of the Fifth Column. Nonetheless, the overall effect of the director's speeches and writings was to augment popular dread of internal enemies.

Though Hoover sought to keep the citizenry on edge, he strenuously endeavored to prevent public fear from manifesting itself in the form of mob violence. He cautioned Americans against vigilante actions, noting that this sort of activity played into the hands of the Fifth Column. Hoover was convinced that many of the violations of civil liberties that had occurred during the First World War were due to the government's past willingness to use a decentralized approach to counterintelligence. Thus, he worked hard to eliminate volunteer groups from active involvement in the fight against the Trojan Horse. Citizens were to act only as "listening posts" for FBI professionals. The director also sought to prevent other intelligence agencies from poaching in domestic anti-spy work. Hoover argued that the overlapping of responsibilities among competing intelligence bureaucracies on the home front undermined counterespionage, heightened public confusion, and opened the door to mass hysteria. (Such an argument was clearly in the interests of the FBI, but it did not lack persuasive force.)

The Bureau's defeat of the Fifth Column was one of its greatest triumphs. By the end of the Second World War J. Edgar Hoover's successes against the Nazi Trojan Horse left the FBI firmly in control of domestic counterintelligence. With the rapid emergence of a Cold War with the Soviet Union, Hoover appeared to many Americans as the man best suited to thwart Communist espionage, sabotage, and subversion.

The Bureau of Investigation 1908-1933: In and Out of Domestic Surveillance

On July 26, 1908, President Theodore Roosevelt ordered Attorney General Charles J. Bonaparte to create a special investigative force within the Justice Department. Bonaparte complied with the presidential order and organized the Bureau of Investigation.

The early history of the B.I. was rather disreputable. The slacker raids of the First World War, the "Red Scare" of 1919–20, and the scandals of the Harding era implicated the B.I. in divisive and sometimes illegal activities. These events resulted in a downsizing of the Bureau and a curtailment of the agency's power. In particular, the B.I. lost its authority to engage in ongoing domestic political surveillance. It would not be until the New Deal that this power was restored.

During the First World War, the Bureau monitored enemy aliens and enforced the Selective Service Act. At the start of the war the government had only 300 agents to perform these tasks. In order to compensate for this personnel shortage, Bureau director A. Bruce Bielaski looked for civilian assistance. Bielaski and Attorney General Thomas Gregory both agreed to work with a volunteer organization known as the American Protective League. The APL was started in March of 1917 by a Chicago advertising executive. Within three months the group had 100,000 members, and at its height reached a total membership of 260,000. The use of such amateur detectives proved to be ill-advised, as APL members frequently engaged in unconstitutional activities. They conducted illegal searches, harassed "suspicious" fellow citizens, and posed as Secret Service agents.[2]

The most controversial actions of the wartime Bureau were its efforts to uncover violators of the Selective Service Act. In order to track down draft dodgers, Bielaski endorsed a policy of "slacker" raids. These raids occurred from April to September, 1918, in cities throughout the nation. The most important round-ups took place in Manhattan, Brooklyn, Jersey City, and Newark, from September 3 to 5, 1918. Individuals who were unable to prove compliance with the draft law (those who were not carrying draft cards) were brought to holding areas by law enforcement officials. In executing the operation Bielaski used 35 Bureau agents and over 2000 members of the APL. (He also engaged police officers, National Guardsmen, and members of the United States Armed Forces.) Some 50,000 men between the ages of 21 and 31 were rounded up from baseball stadiums, movie houses, restaurants, and city streets. Eventually the raid unearthed 15,000 individuals who had not met the requirements of the Selective Service Act.[3]

The draft enforcement program produced a furor. Attorney General Thomas Gregory backed the government's action and he received tacit support from President Wilson. However, many elements in Congress and the press voiced outrage. Republicans in the Senate and House decried the raids. Senator Hiram Johnson of California challenged the holding of so many citizens "merely because they are suspects." He called the episode "a spectacle never before presented in the Republic." The *New York World* labeled the raids "a shameful abuse of power."[4] Rather than unify popular support behind the Bureau, the slacker raids became a source of embarrassment.

In the immediate aftermath of the First World War, the Bureau once again became involved in activities threatening civil liberties. As American doughboys began to return from Europe the United States was caught up in an anti-Communist panic known as the Red Scare. A number of unsettling international and domestic developments inspired national fear. In 1919, Lenin created the Communist International. The Comintern's objective was to assist the spread of bolshevism worldwide, a goal which marked America as a possible target for Soviet-inspired revolution. Within the United States a wave of strikes swept the country. An unnerving outbreak of terrorist bombings accompanied this labor unrest. Postal officials discovered several letter bombs addressed to the homes of Supreme Court Justices, congressmen, cabinet members, and prominent industrialists. Though only a few radicals were involved in terrorist acts, many Americans thought that an attempt to overthrow the government was imminent.

One of the intended victims of the bombing campaign was the Attorney General of the United States, A. Mitchell Palmer. Late in the evening on June 2, 1919, an explosive device destroyed the front of Palmer's Washington home. (The man responsible for this act seems to have been blown up by his own device.) This action helped to shock the Attorney General into taking a harder line against Communism. Palmer decided that the most effective way to combat domestic bolshevism was to prosecute radical aliens (at this time the vast majority of Communist party members were aliens). Few legal barriers existed to protect noncitizens from deportation. The Immigration Statute of 1918 allowed for the expulsion of any aliens espousing the violent overthrow of the United States government or belonging to groups which advocated the same. Palmer selected the B.I. to spearhead his anti-Communist campaign. In particular, he relied upon the General Intelligence Division of the Bureau.[5]

Palmer's decision put a young Justice Department attorney named J. Edgar Hoover at the forefront of the government's campaign against radicalism. During the First World War Hoover had served in the Alien Enemy Registration section of the Justice Department. In this capacity he had reviewed cases of aliens placed in detention camps, recommending the internees' release, further detention, or their deportation. Hoover made himself indispensable by acquiring expertise in matters involving aliens and by establishing a close working relationship with the Labor Department's Immigration Bureau. In June 1919, Hoover was selected to head the Radical Division, renamed in 1920 the General Intelligence Division, the largest section of the Bureau of Investigation.

As overseer of the Radical Division, Hoover directed the compilation of files on over 200,000 groups and individuals. The files principally contained information on Communist targets, but also included reports on prominent liberals (for example, Jane Addams and Robert La Follette) and liberal organizations (such as the American Civil Liberties Union).[6] In the fall of 1919 Hoover successfully worked on the deportation cases of radicals Emma Goldman and Alexander Berkman. Goldman and Berkman were eventually sent to the Soviet Union along with 247 other deportees aboard the *Buford*. The Bureau received widespread popular acclaim for its role in the deportations. Hoover soon began preparations for a new assault on the left.

On January 2, 1920, the Bureau conducted raids in 33 different cities across America. The government held over 4000 individuals for deportation.[7] Hoover hoped to gather evidence to justify the deportation of aliens belonging to the Communist party. The Bureau conducted raids in restaurants, bars, bowling alleys, the homes of suspected aliens, and Communist meeting halls. Those arrested were frequently denied the benefit of counsel and were sometimes held in squalid, overcrowded facilities.

Initially, Hoover was applauded for his actions. However, a reaction soon set in against the Bureau. Due to the illness of Secretary of Labor William Wilson, Assistant Secretary of Labor Louis Post became acting chief of the department in March 1920. Post, a staunch civil libertarian, objected to Hoover's raids and began to throw out many of the deportation cases. Hoover believed that the listing of an individual's name on a Communist party register was enough evidence for prosecution. Post disagreed, demanding a higher standard of proof. The Acting Secretary of Labor also rejected any evidence which had been extracted from aliens who had not been represented by counsel. Due to Post's actions, only 556 of those held in the Palmer raids were eventually deported.[8]

A bitter fight ensued between the Justice Department and the Labor Department. Palmer, with coaching from Hoover, depicted Post as a Communist sympathizer and tried to have him impeached. A number of prominent lawyers rushed to Post's defense and prepared a report on the various instances of Justice Department lawbreaking which had taken place during the Red Scare. The lawyer's report charged the Bureau of Investigation with detaining individuals without warrants, making illegal searches and seizures, and abridging the constitutional rights of those arrested. In June 1920, the Attorney General appeared before a congressional committee and attempted to respond to attacks on the Justice Department. However, he failed to explain away the excesses of his raids.[9]

By the middle of 1920 the Red Scare came to an end. Internationally, Communism had failed to expand beyond the USSR. In the United States, radical activities had declined sharply, in part due to the Bureau's raids. Attorney General Palmer's bid for the Democratic presidential nomination failed, and the party's eventual nominee, James Cox, formally repudiated the government's response to the Red Scare. Hoover attempted to distance himself from the Palmer raids. The Bureau's roundups of aliens became a source of embarrassment. They also caused many civil libertarians to regard Hoover with lingering suspicion.

The Harding era brought the Bureau's public reputation to a new low. William J. Burns, a thoroughgoing scoundrel, was appointed to head the agency.[10] Burns's superior in the Justice Department was the equally unsavory figure Harry M. Daugherty. Together Burns and Daugherty turned the Bureau into an instrument of political intimidation. Break-ins and wiretaps became accepted practice. When Senator Burton Wheeler began pursuing corruption in the Harding administration, the Bureau unsuccessfully attempted to frame him on trumped-up charges of land fraud. This plot also included a failed attempt to involve Wheeler in a compromising relationship with a young woman.[11]

When Calvin Coolidge succeeded to the presidency he removed Daugherty from the Justice Department. Coolidge appointed Harlan Fiske Stone, a man of unquestioned probity, to become the new Attorney General. Stone entered the Justice Department determined to clean up the mess that he had inherited. One of his first steps was to fire Burns. Stone conducted a search for a new B.I. chief, and finally decided to appoint the 29-year-old assistant director of the Bureau, J. Edgar Hoover.

Hoover won the appointment because he was able to convince the Attorney General of his lack of involvement in B.I. scandals. Harlan Stone remained suspicious of the Bureau and he ordered Hoover to curtail the agency's activities: The Bureau was to limit its work to the investigation of violations of federal laws; to abolish its General Intelligence Division; to prohibit wiretaps; to reduce personnel and discharge problem employees; and to sever links with private investigative agencies and volunteer detectives.[12] Stone wanted the Bureau to worry about the conduct, not the opinions of citizens, and even then "only such conduct as is forbidden by the laws of the United States."[13] Hoover's biographer, Richard Gid Powers, has noted that the experiences of the slacker raids and Red Scare shaped the way in which the Bureau responded to threats of subversion during World War II.[14]

The New Deal, the FBI, and Domestic Counterintelligence

The New Deal brought the Bureau back out of obscurity. In 1933, Franklin Roosevelt appointed Homer S. Cummings as Attorney General of the United States. Keeping in line with the New Deal's spirit of activism, Cummings determined to place the federal government at the forefront of law enforcement. The Attorney General helped win more legal authority for the Bureau, pushing through a host of federal laws expanding the Bureau's jurisdiction. During his tenure in office Cummings increased the agency's budgets and manpower. He also fostered the development of an intense public relations campaign in support of the G-men. (Cummings renamed the Bureau of Investigation the Federal Bureau of Investigation.)

In the thirties a host of colorful hoodlums escaped local authorities by crossing state and county lines. Cummings decided to use the FBI to crack down on these lawbreakers. Hoover and his agents became national heroes as they systematically gunned down or apprehended gangsters such as George "Machine Gun" Kelly, Frank "Jelly" Nash, Alvin "Creepy" Karpis, Charles "Pretty Boy" Floyd, "Baby Face" Nelson, John Dillinger, Louis Lepke, and "Ma" Barker. The FBI captured the public's imagination and became one of the New Deal's most respected alphabet agencies.[15]

The Bureau's first forays into counterintelligence work began in the early thirties. In March 1933, the German embassy requested that the United States examine a death threat against Adolf Hitler. Secretary of State Hull called upon Hoover to run an investigation. One year later FDR asked the Bureau to gather material on Nazi groups in America. Right-wing extremists Joseph McWilliams, Lawrence Dennis, Gerald Winrod, and William Dudley Pelley were the focus of this FBI study. Both of these investigations were limited in scope, yet they helped to establish a pattern of White House reliance on the FBI for counterintelligence matters.

In August of 1936, Hoover sent Franklin Roosevelt a memorandum which detailed an apparent Communist conspiracy to win control over a number of important American industries. The director noted that the Communists would "be able to paralyze the country in that they stop all shipping in and out through Bridges' organization [West Coast Longshoreman's Union]; stop the operating of industry through the Mining Union of Lewis; and stop publication of any newspapers of the country through the Newspaper Guild." He added that radicals were penetrating the government, particularly the National Labor Relations Board.[16] The President responded to Hoover's warning with a call for coordinated intelligence regarding "subversive activities in the United States, particularly Fascism and Communism." Roosevelt asked the Bureau for "a broad picture of the general movement and its activities as may affect the economic and political life of the country as a whole."[17]

At a meeting with the President on August 25, Hoover noted that there was no government organization gathering general intelligence information on subversive groups. FDR then asked the Bureau to take up this work. The President unilaterally expanded the scope of FBI activity by taking advantage of a provision in the Bureau's appropriation bill which allowed Hoover's agency to conduct investigations at the request of the State Department. Roosevelt informed Cordell Hull that he wanted a survey of Communist and fascist activities in the U.S. When Hull told Hoover to "go ahead and investigate the ———," the Secretary of State's profane request elicited uproarious laughter from the President.[18]

FDR did not formally place the FBI in charge of counterintelligence until 1939. Between 1936 and 1939 Hoover monitored the activities of extremist groups in the United States on the verbal requests of Hull and Roosevelt. (The President assured the FBI director that he held a letter in his White House safe authorizing the Bureau's counterintelligence duties.) Hoover was not bothered by this situation. He noted that the word "espionage" was repugnant to the American people and therefore it was unwise "to draw attention to the fact that it was proposed to develop a counter-espionage drive of any magnitude." Hoover urged secrecy "in order to avoid criticism or objections which might be raised by either ill-informed persons or individuals with some ulterior motive."[19]

Hoover and the State Department

As the Second World War approached, the State Department attempted to assert a supervisory position over home-front security matters. The FBI strenuously resisted this effort. A bureaucratic power struggle took place in 1939, resulting in total victory for the Bureau. Cordell Hull offered little support to his subordinate, Assistant Secretary of State George Messersmith, the man assigned as the Coordinator of Intelligence. Conversely, Attorney General Frank Murphy consistently backed the FBI's efforts to gain unfettered control of domestic counterintelligence work.

On October 11, 1938, President Roosevelt informed the press of a government determination to reorganize and improve the nation's counterspy program. In 1938, four departments handled such work: Justice, War, Navy, and State. The Treasury Department and Post Office also had investigative arms and were occasionally drawn into counterespionage activity. However, there were no regular interdepartmental meetings. Hence, coordination of investigations and exchange of intelligence information occurred informally, haphazardly, and sporadically.[20]

The State Department proposed the creation of an Interdepartmental Intelligence Committee in order to ensure efficiency and cooperation in the struggle against foreign intrigue. The committee was to be composed of representatives from the Post Office and War, Navy, Justice, and Treasury departments. A State Department official would chair the group and serve as "a central receiving, distributing and coordinating officer." The chair was empowered to decide which government agency was to investigate any particular case. No agency was to take action without previously informing the State Department. In the wake of the concern generated by the Rumrich trial, FDR approved State's plan.[21]

This system remained faithful to the spirit of policies established by President Woodrow Wilson. During the First World War, the State Department oversaw the Bureau of Investigation, the Secret Service, the Office of Naval Intelligence, and the Military Intelligence Division (G-2). In 1927, the State Department Intelligence Liaison Agency (U-1) was dissolved, a step which decentralized domestic counterespionage. In spite of this change, State's directive role in domestic security matters was still the law.[22] In the early thirties FBI investigations into subversion, sabotage, and espionage could be legally conducted only at the request of the State Department. Cordell Hull willingly gave the Bureau a good deal of independence in its activities, and Hoover reported many of his findings directly to the President. The proposal of 1938 aimed at reinstituting a more certain State Department supervision over intelligence affairs.

Assistant Secretary of State George Messersmith was appointed to head the Interdepartmental Coordinating Committee. Messersmith's duties as Assistant Secretary of State distracted him from intelligence matters. As the State Department budget officer he devoted considerable energy to wrestling funds away from a parsimonious Congress. He was also responsible for the recruitment of foreign service personnel. Such work entailed the time-consuming supervision of State Department oral examinations. Finally, Messersmith expended much of his energy working to absorb commercial and agricultural attachés into the foreign service.[23]

Despite his many duties, the Assistant Secretary was determined to assert and exercise his authority as America's intelligence coordinator. He thought that the State Department was the logical control center for the battle against espionage: "We were neutral as we had no investigating agency and we did have a great deal of information coming from the field and we were able to give certain interpretations and background which were helpful to the investigating units."[24]

Hoover simply ignored State's authority. In February 1939, the Justice Department instructed all intelligence arms of the government to forward "information with regard to espionage and related activities to the local offices of the F.B.I." This step infuriated Messersmith, who held that such action ran "directly contrary to the wishes of the President that coordination should be established through this Department." The Assistant Secretary believed that the Justice Department letter was evidence of a Bureau plan to "take over all this [intelligence] work." Messersmith protested to Sumner Welles, who carried the complaint to FDR. The President reassured State that he intended no changes in the nation's intelligence command structure at present. Despite such consoling words Roosevelt failed to take steps to curtail FBI independence.[25]

By the spring of 1939, the State Department was becoming peripheral to America's counterespionage effort. On March 24, Messersmith's assistant, Fletcher Warren, reported that "every member of the other departments," with the possible exception of MID, opposed State Department coordination. Warren further noted that each department had indicated that its relationship with the FBI was "most friendly and satisfactory." He warned that Hoover had captured de facto control of domestic security matters: "Post Office and Treasury are currently referring to FBI any cases which do not normally fall within their scope. MID and ONI appear to be doing the same."[26]

Throughout the Second World War, Hoover was able to depend upon support from the Attorney General and a sympathetic hearing from the President. Hoover's links with Frank Murphy and FDR accounted for his ultimate victory over Messersmith. In May 1939, Murphy tried to pressure Messersmith into giving up the State Department's function as coordinator. The Attorney General described the existing situation as unworkable and harmful to Bureau counterespionage efforts. Messersmith held that all was well and pointedly rejected the Attorney General's proposals for change. Consequently, Murphy went to FDR complaining of State Department inefficiency and demanding "a concentration of investigation of all espionage, counterespionage, and sabotage matters in the Federal Bureau of Investigation of the Department of Justice, the G-2 section of the War Department, and the Office of Naval Intelligence."[27]

On June 26 Roosevelt issued the following memorandum to all government agencies involved in intelligence work: "After a careful checkup on this matter of espionage, counter-espionage and sabotage, I agree that the principal work in this country should be done under the leadership of the F.B.I., G-2 section of the War Department, and O.N.I. of the Navy Department."[28] Roosevelt asked the State Department to continue with intelligence work and to maintain close contact with the heads of MID, ONI, and the FBI. However, the President's June 26 directive ended Messersmith's supervision over counterintelligence work. Messersmith admitted in September 1939 that his duties as coordinator had "practically ceased."[29] President Roosevelt clarified the situation with another memo calling on the three principal intelligence agencies—FBI, G-2, ONI—to form a committee to coordinate their activities. All other investigative agencies were to "refer immediately to the nearest office of the Federal Bureau of Investigation any data, information, or material that may come to their notice bearing directly on espionage, counterespionage, or sabotage."[30]

When war broke out in Europe, President Roosevelt publicly announced the centralization of domestic counterespionage under the aegis of the FBI. On September 6, 1939, FDR called for Hoover's agency to handle "investigative work in matters relating to espionage, sabotage, and violations of the neutrality regulations." The President requested that all American law enforcement officers turn over to a representative of the Bureau any information which they had regarding domestic security matters.[31] Attorney General Murphy promised the nation that the FBI would see to it that the United States no longer remained "a happy hunting ground" for enemy agents.[32]

Hoover versus MID

The President's directive of June 26 placed three agencies in charge of the nation's intelligence affairs: the Federal Bureau of Investigation, the Office of Naval Intelligence, and the Military Intelligence Division. Hoover's primary responsibility was to protect home-front security. On June 5, 1940, MID, ONI, and the FBI formally agreed that the "FBI will assume responsibility for all investigations of cases involving citizens in the United States and its territories with the exception of the Panama Canal Zone, Guam, Samoa, and the Philippine Islands."[33] Outside the United States Roosevelt authorized the Bureau to counteract the Nazi Fifth Column in South America. However, the FBI's domestic counterintelligence work was by far its highest priority. (The maximum number of agents in Latin America at once was 360.)[34] In spite of presidential backing, Hoover soon found himself faced with challenges to Bureau authority at home and abroad.

The most serious jurisdictional conflict involved Hoover and General Sherman Miles, the chief of G-2. (The Bureau's relationship with ONI was far less troubled, though not entirely free of difficulty.)[35] The dispute was founded in Miles's desire to transfer responsibility for counter-Fifth Column operations from the Justice Department to MID in the event America became actively involved in hostilities. G-2 urged this policy for two reasons: "1. Operations against the fifth column are war operations, and hence military responsibilities in war. 2. Plans for these operations are military responsibilities in peace and war."[36] In preparation for taking over home-front security MID began to engage in preliminary investigations of domestic Fifth Column activities. Miles further alienated Hoover by questioning the wisdom of expanding FBI intelligence activities into Latin America.

Hoover tenaciously defended his bureaucratic turf. The FBI chief complained to Secretary Morgenthau that military intelligence was "expanding into the field of civil intelligence" and creating "undercover offices" around the country. He noted that these actions violated the President's "very wise directive" of June 26, 1939.[37] Hoover warned the Attorney General's office that MID involvement in counter-Fifth Column work would be confusing to the public. Even worse, the "injection of military authorities into civilian matters [was] very dangerous," likely to provoke "unfavorable public reaction" and best "kept at a minimum." Hoover noted that the British managed quite well by keeping counterespionage work in civilian hands. He added that even during the First World War, America's home-front security had been kept out of military hands. Hoover observed that the military's counter-Fifth Column plan was dangerously decentralized. He cautioned that MID's reliance on "loyal citizens or civil organizations—to minimize the use of line troops"—only increased the chances of vigilante activity.[38]

In October 1940, Hoover complained directly to the White House about the way in which MID officials were tending "to overstep their proper jurisdiction."[39] Aware of the possibility that President Roosevelt might step in and appoint an overall head of American intelligence, the director offered a slightly toned down version of his differences with Miles. He assured FDR that intelligence coordination was maintained on a constructive basis and characterized his imbroglio with MID as a "small situation." Hoover claimed that he only mentioned the dispute with Miles to keep events from getting out of control.[40]

The donnybrook between Hoover and Miles became a source of general administration concern. In October 1940, the chief of MID informed Secretary Stimson that the head of the FBI was a "prima donna."[41] Four months later Stimson was angered when he discovered that Hoover had attempted to discredit Miles with the President. In his diary Stimson noted that the FBI director had written "a very childish, petulant statement" to Roosevelt which called attention "to all sorts of little things which ought to have been the subject of mutual collaboration and a phone call rather than a formal letter."[42] In an effort to establish better "collaboration and cooperation" among G-2, ONI, and the FBI, Stimson arranged a conference with Attorney General Jackson and Secretary of the Navy Knox. At this gathering Jackson conceded to Stimson that Hoover was "a most difficult person to deal with."[43]

On February 12, 1941, Assistant Secretary of State Adolf Berle called a meeting of the heads of ONI, MID, and the FBI. Berle hoped to settle the row between Hoover and Miles. Only one week earlier the Assistant

Secretary had disavowed any willingness to get involved in the dispute: "I don't know anything about it and I don't want to know."[44] Nonetheless, Berle's post as State Department Coordinator of Intelligence and his ability to work with both Miles and Hoover made him a logical peacemaker. Berle found his mediation work "harder diplomacy than negotiating an inter-American agreement." However, he noted that after "two mortal hours" they reached an agreement "which will at least serve as an armistice if not a final peace."[45] The Assistant Secretary of State realized that an agreement suited the interests of both men since "the President may step in and appoint a coordinator."[46]

The Berle pact did not settle all the jurisdictional battles between the FBI, MID, and ONI. New York City remained an area where conflicts among America's three intelligence agencies were particularly severe. During World War I Berlin had centered much of its clandestine warfare in the New York area. In the late thirties and early forties this pattern of behavior seemed to repeat itself (for example, in the Rumrich case, the Ludwig case, and the Sebold case). Some 65 percent of United States Lend-Lease aid to Britain departed from New York harbor.[47] Consequently, all three of the nation's major intelligence agencies performed work in New York City.

Miles opened up a special branch of G-2 in New York under the command of Major Frederick Sharp. Among its many activities, Sharp's office sought information from companies doing business in Latin America. Hoover claimed that the FBI already collected such data. The director complained to the Attorney General that Miles's agents upset and confused American businessmen, who resented giving the same information to several different intelligence outfits.[48]

The bickering among his intelligence chiefs led FDR to act. In March 1941, he asked William Vincent Astor, a Hudson Valley neighbor and longtime friend, to serve as coordinator for intelligence in the New York area. As a private citizen Astor showed a special fondness for intelligence work. He used his position as managing director of Western Union and his close British connections to gather information for the White House.[49] Astor was eager to play an official role in espionage and counterespionage matters and he gladly accepted FDR's job offer. Roosevelt called on Astor to act as a "clearing house" for problems in the New York area and to "assign priorities and responsibilities" among ONI, MID, and the FBI.[50]

In and of itself, the appointment did not trouble the FBI. The new area controller was friendly to the G-men, describing the Bureau as "the best equipped and trained, and the most alert and competent of our various intelligence services."[51] Moreover, Astor lacked a bureaucratic and political base from which to exert power. Thus, he never turned his position into one of real authority. Astor continued on in his job until 1944 when he resigned.

Hoover versus the Office of Strategic Services

The appointment of Astor suggested a more threatening possibility for the FBI, ONI, and G-2. In April, rumors began circulating that President Roosevelt planned to appoint William Donovan as the overall coordinator for all American intelligence. In mid-May the chiefs of ONI, G-2 and the FBI quickly huddled and drafted a statement firmly rejecting the need for either an overall coordinator of intelligence or a referee to resolve conflicts in the area of countersubversion. The intelligence chiefs noted that they were currently taking all the steps required to control enemy agents.[52] On June 2, 1941, Hoover forwarded a report to the White House which voiced the belief that there was no need for the designation of a supervisor to coordinate the activities of the FBI, G-2, and ONI because "complete coordination and cooperation" presently existed.[53]

On April 26, 1941, William Donovan had sent a memorandum to Secretary of Navy Knox suggesting the creation of an American intelligence agency closely modeled on that of the British government. Donovan argued that the new service should perform three functions:

(1) to have sole charge of intelligence work abroad, (2) to coordinate the activities of military and naval attachés and others in the collection of information abroad, (3) to classify and interpret all information from whatever source obtained to be available for the President and for such of the services he would designate.[54]

Donovan noted that the new agency was not to "take over the home duties now performed by the F.B.I., nor the intelligence organizations of the Army and the Navy."[55]. He envisioned an organization which also would intercept mail, cable, and radio traffic; mount propaganda offensives against the enemy; and run covert operations behind enemy lines.

In July 1941, the President announced the establishment of the Office of Coordinator of Information (OCI) and the appointment of William Donovan as Coordinator of Information (COI). An executive order instructed Donovan to "collect and assemble information and data bearing on national security from the various departments . . . to analyze and collate such materials for the use of the President and such other officials as the President may designate."[56] One year later, in June 1942, the OCI was reconstituted as the Office of Strategic Services (OSS).

Hoover and Donovan had several run-ins. Repeated attempts by the OCI to become involved in Latin American affairs met opposition from both the Office of Inter-American Affairs and the FBI. FDR eventually stepped in and settled the dispute by issuing a directive barring the COI's office from involvement in the South American and Canadian fields.[57]

In October 1942, the FBI interrupted an OSS-sponsored burglary of the Spanish embassy in Washington. The OSS desired to gather intelligence on the codes and ciphers used in Spanish diplomatic traffic. While Donovan's men were inside the embassy, two cars from the Bureau pulled up with sirens blaring and lights flashing. The FBI agents arrested all of the OSS agents. Donovan later sent these men out of the United States in order to prevent Hoover from initiating a federal case against them.[58] Near the end of the Second World War, Hoover helped to undermine a plan which Donovan had proposed for the establishment of a postwar agency.[59] All of these conflicts were linked to the director's fear that Donovan would trespass in the Bureau's fiefdom. Despite Hoover's anxieties, the OSS did little to interfere with domestic counterintelligence.

While the FBI sought to blunt Axis efforts to undermine the American home front, the OSS endeavored to turn the Fifth Column weapon against Germany. An early student of Nazi subversion, William Donovan determined to enlist espionage, sabotage, guerilla warfare, and black propaganda in the cause of democracy. Bradley Smith has shown that the creation of OSS and its support by the Joint Chiefs of Staff grew out of a widely shared belief in the efficacy of Trojan Horse tactics. Smith further holds that Donovan's fascination with (and overestimation of) irregular warfare shaped CIA operations in the fifties and sixties.[60] Thus, the apparent Nazi Fifth Column successes persuaded officials in Washington of the need for the United States to develop its own capacity for subversive warfare.

Hoover's Critics

As the man responsible for America's counterintelligence effort, Hoover found himself subject to public criticism. Some argued that the FBI pursued an overly aggressive, liberty-threatening security campaign. Others held that the Bureau did not do enough to control the Fifth Column.

Between February and March 1940, Hoover came under fierce attack from radicals, liberals, and a few conservatives, all of whom voiced skepticism about the director's commitment to civil liberties and his personal suitability to handle domestic counterespionage. An ill-advised FBI raid on the Milwaukee and Detroit headquarters of the U.S. Veterans of the Spanish Civil War prompted the groundswell of anti-Hoover sentiment.

On February 3, 1940, Bureau agents arrested twelve veterans of the Abraham Lincoln Brigade, eleven in Detroit and one in Milwaukee. The FBI charged these individuals with illegally recruiting volunteers to fight against General Franco's Nationalists in Spain. The arrests proved a public relations disaster for the Bureau. In Detroit the ex-Lincoln Brigade vets were rounded up in the middle of the night, handcuffed together, and photographed for the press. Such methods conjured up shocking parallels with Nazi techniques. The *Milwaukee Journal* blasted the Bu-

reau for behaving like "a Gestapo that can haul citizens off to prison
and court in ignominy, imposing any kind of conditions without ac-
countability."[61] The lapse of time between the alleged commission of
illegal recruiting (1937) and the Bureau arrests (1940) alarmed civil libertarians. The fact that the Spanish Civil War had long since been
decided made the FBI raids appear to many to be petty political harassment.

At the same time that Hoover was drawing fire for the Detroit and
Milwaukee raids, civil libertarians expressed concern about the FBI's
General Intelligence Division. GID had been shut down in 1924, but
Hoover revived it in 1938. This Bureau unit collected information on
individuals and organizations "engaged in activities of Communism, Nazism, and various types of foreign espionage." The FBI established contacts with individuals in labor, business, and the professions. The
division also maintained a file of publications which included magazines,
pamphlets, and foreign-language newspapers. All of this aimed at limiting domestic subversion.

Hoover publicly informed a House appropriations committee of
GID's existence late in 1939. The director noted that the division was
"made necessary by the President's proclamation directing that all complaints of violations of national defense statutes be reported to the Federal Bureau of Investigation." Hoover told Congress that the FBI was
gathering information on individuals and groups "who might be a
source of grave danger to the security of this country."[62]

GID's reemergence raised questions about Hoover's part in the bad
old days of the Red Scare. The *New Republic* noted that it "is gravely
to be questioned whether J. Edgar Hoover in view of his background
and experience during its blackest period, after the Great War, is the
proper person to head this organization [FBI]."[63] The same publication
later observed that in 1919 Hoover had overseen the Bureau's GID and
had allowed "wholesale raids on thousands of defenseless and innocent
citizens and aliens, the breaking up of strikes and the violation of the
most sacred civil rights."[64] *The Philadelphia Inquirer* offered equally
acerbic criticisms of GID:

> If the Stage is being set for government surveillance and supervision
> of our daily activities and avocations, with no one knowing where
> the net will be spread next in an attempt to "get something" on
> persons who are not approved of by the powers that be; if things
> like these are forecast by the new and indefensible acts charged,
> then we may as well realize that what we are heading into is the
> wanton rule of a bludgeoning spy system, arrogant and menacing,
> such as has been developed by the totalitarian governments of Eu-
> rope . . . there must be no compromise with espionage. The place
> for OGPUs and Gestapos is the other side of the Atlantic.[65]

At the same time he was being attacked for threatening civil liberties, Hoover also found himself subject to ridicule and charges of incompetence. Late in February 1940, the director traveled to Florida where he directed raids on gambling and prostitution rings. A number of newspapers expressed puzzlement and concern at the Bureau's involvement in such matters. Hoover had only recently informed Congress that a large number of national defense investigations had been delayed due to an FBI manpower shortage. The *St. Louis Post-Dispatch* and the *New York Daily News* noted that prostitution and gambling were matters for local authorities, whereas domestic security was the FBI's most important task. The *Washington Times-Herald* echoed a similar concern about Hoover's misallocation of resources, running a story on the Miami round-ups with the headline: "G-men Bask in Florida as [Defense] Cases Pile Up."[66] Matters got worse when rumors began circulating that Hoover had been staying at a fancy hotel (apparently true) at government expense (partly false: government agents were given a limited expense account and Hoover paid all hotel costs above his allotted money).

In Congress, Senator George Norris, a liberal Republican from Nebraska, challenged Hoover's management of the FBI. The Bureau's behavior in the Detroit and Milwaukee arrests outraged Norris. He called for a Justice Department investigation of the episode. Norris expressed a general unhappiness with the expansion of FBI power which was taking place, worrying that excessive praise for the Bureau would produce "an organization [which] will itself in the end direct the government by tyrannical force."[67] Republican senator Burton Wheeler and Socialist congressman Vito Marcantino also expressed displeasure with the FBI's conduct.

Faced with mounting criticism, Hoover looked to newly appointed Attorney General Robert Jackson for support. Jackson only slowly came to his Bureau chief's defense. He disapproved of the FBI arrests of Spanish Civil War veterans and dropped all charges against the Lincoln Brigade members, noting that it was foolish to reawaken the animosities of the Spanish Civil War. J. Edgar Hoover sent his assistant director, Edward Tamm, to seek Jackson's public approval of the Bureau's activities. The Attorney General balked, telling Tamm that he "had been very dubious of Mr. Hoover's policies in operating the Bureau when he became Attorney General." Jackson noted that he had been told stories by Frank Murphy that the Bureau maintained investigative files on many government officials in Washington. Tamm denied these charges.[68]

Hoover expressed a willingness to resign if the Attorney General was unhappy with the administration of the FBI. Jackson refused this offer. Assistant Secretary of State Berle applauded the Attorney General's decision, noting that "Hoover on the loose would probably let out a good many things which would not be good politics for Jackson—or for that matter anyone else."[69]

On March 1, 1940, Jackson met with Tamm. The Attorney General agreed to release a statement showing that a schism had not developed between himself and Hoover. Jackson suggested that his statement include an admission that the Bureau and its directors had made errors in the past, but were nonetheless committed to civil liberties. Tamm disagreed with this approach. He humbly informed Jackson "that the official activities of the Bureau were generally so carefully planned and executed that the possibility of human error was eliminated by careful procedure."[70] On March 2, Jackson sent a letter to Senator Norris regarding the Bureau's handling of the Spanish Civil War veterans. The Attorney General wrote that after a review of the facts he had "found nothing to justify any charge of misconduct against the FBI."[71] Norris expressed dissatisfaction with the report. Jackson then called for Henry Schweinhaut, of the Civil Liberties Division of the Justice Department, to further investigate the case. Schweinhaut again found that the Bureau had acted properly.

Jackson also defended Hoover against others worried by the Bureau's expanding powers. He wrote private letters to Roger Baldwin and Arthur Garfield Hays of the American Civil Liberties Union defending the FBI. Jackson justified Hoover's reestablishment of the General Intelligence Division of the Bureau, noting that the government's obligation to remain tolerant of extremist groups did not necessarily require that it remain ignorant as well. In correspondence with Hays, the Attorney General asked why liberals sought "systematically to discredit, often with the use of untruth, the Federal Bureau of Investigation," and added that the "FBI was far more closely circumscribed in its activities than many local police or prosecuting organizations have been."[72]

Hoover claimed that the attacks directed against him were part of a Communist/Nazi Fifth Column conspiracy. Friendly reporters in the Hearst press wrote stories emphasizing the same point. Indeed, the *Daily Worker* and the *New Masses* gleefully ripped the Bureau and Hoover. However, the attacks on the FBI and its director were hardly the result of a totalitarian conspiracy. Instead they reflected the concerns of a wide spectrum of Americans who feared that in fighting dictatorship, the nation came dangerously close to adopting dictatorial methods. Concerns about the growth of FBI power were raised into 1941. However, after America's entry into the war such criticisms became less frequent. Certainly, the widespread public fear of Fifth Column activity helped limit attacks on the creation of a more powerful FBI.

The FBI and the Dies Committee

Throughout the last half of 1940, HUAC chairman Martin Dies repeatedly attacked President Roosevelt and the FBI for failing to offer the nation adequate protection from the Fifth Column.[73] Dies pulled few punches in his assault on the Bureau. He warned Chicagoans that 20,000 Fifth Columnists were active in their city and that the menace ". . . was not understood by some of the novices sent on investigations by the Federal Bureau of Investigation."[74] In May 1940, Dies suggested the creation of a Home Defense Council to handle intelligence matters. (The principal aim of this suggestion was to put representatives of the Dies committee on a joint board with representatives from the FBI, MID, and ONI.) Hoover called on Attorney General Jackson to denounce the proposal as unnecessary and to advise the HUAC chairman to pass to the FBI any intelligence he possessed regarding the Fifth Column. Hoover predicted that Dies's constant suggestions that "nothing is being done to protect the internal defenses of the country . . . will give momentum to the so-called Fifth Column hysteria."[75]

On October 2, Dies sent a telegram to the White House expressing his desire to work with the executive office in order to head off an impending Axis sabotage campaign. He warned that the entire national defense effort was in jeopardy and he registered discontent with America's overall counterintelligence effort: "I do not believe that adequate steps are now being taken or that government agencies understand the technique and strategy being employed by agents of Stalin, Hitler, Mussolini, and Japan in the United States." Moreover, the HUAC chairman stated that he possessed the names of large numbers of German sympathizers residing in the Los Angeles region who were working in "aircraft industries and other industries vital to national defense." Dies argued that the nation needed to develop a systematic and agreeable program of coordination among the government's counter-Fifth Column agencies in order to get "real results." He also requested that the President lend Department of Justice attorneys and investigators to his committee.[76] FDR rejected Dies's request for Justice Department assistance, noting that the FBI was already overburdened and could not assign its agents to HUAC. Roosevelt ignored Dies's suggestion that HUAC be more fully integrated into the White House's counterespionage program.[77]

When a series of explosions occurred at several defense plants and a strike was staged at the Vultee aircraft corporation in November 1940, Dies blamed foreign subversion. He claimed to have explicitly warned government officials that such developments were in the offing, and he predicted a new wave of sabotage.

On November 20, the Texas Democrat upstaged the administration when his House committee released a White Paper on Nazi and fascist activities in New York and Chicago. Documents which Dies's investigators had collected in raids on Italian and German organizations in New York and Chicago formed the basis of HUAC's report. The White Paper cited numerous unneutral actions committed by diplomatic representatives of Hitler and Mussolini's regimes. The study also demonstrated that Manfred Zapp's Transocean News Service was a vehicle for the transmission of German propaganda rather than a private journalistic enterprise.

The director believed that HUAC's claim to possess inside information about enemy subversion was pure malarkey. When Dies began his autumn attacks on the FBI, Hoover suggested that the Attorney General call a grand jury to examine HUAC's evidence. Such an approach would force the Texas representative to "lay his cards on the table." The director resented Dies's amateur sleuthing and his encroachments on Bureau turf.[78] Historian Kenneth O'Reilly has shown that immediately after Dies's release of the White Paper, the FBI encouraged friendly contacts in the press and radio to attack HUAC. The Bureau succeeded in planting many negative stories. On November 24, Attorney General Jackson supplemented these attacks when he scored Dies for undermining public confidence in the G-men.[79]

Late in November 1940, Dies again contacted the President. He lectured FDR on the administration's "inexcusable" failure to bring about the necessary coordination of the State Department, the Justice Department, and the Dies committee in "ferreting out Fifth Column activities and agents in this country." Dies cautioned against "childish rivalries" and informed the President that the Congress had an important part to play in combating the Fifth Column. Dies observed that HUAC was "the only agency of government that can obtain records under subpoena, expose Fifth Column activities and require suspected persons to testify under oath."[80]

Franklin Roosevelt sent a firm rejoinder to Dies. Roosevelt warmly endorsed cooperation between HUAC and the administration, but he added that the constitutional responsiblity for counterespionage work lay in the executive branch of government. The President needled the publicity hungry Dies by commenting that countersubversion was handicapped "by premature disclosure of facts or of suppositions to the public, or by hasty seizure of evidence, . . . or by the giving of immunities to witnesses before congressional committees as to matters revealed by their own testimony."[81] On November 29, 1940, FDR held a face-to-face meeting with the HUAC chairman. Dies requested to be kept up to date on the FBI's various investigations. FDR refused. He justified his action by challenging the discretion of Congress: "You can't tell any congressional committee anything in secret. The Press has it in 12 hours. I don't know an exception to the case." The President used the meeting to lecture Dies on the danger of harming innocent people through unfounded accusations. Roosevelt noted that "it is awfully hard . . . for the word of acquittal to catch up with the charge which is not proven." At the end of the conference Dies protested that the tension between his committee and the Justice Department was the result of a misunderstanding. Roosevelt told the HUAC chairman to meet with the Attorney

General. On December 10, HUAC member Jerry Voorhis met with Robert Jackson and reached a cooperative arrangement with the administration.[82] After this point Dies sought to avoid confrontations with the Federal Bureau of Investigation, though he occasionally attacked the Attorney General.

J. Edgar Hoover and the Fifth Column

Hoover believed that the success of his agency depended upon citizen support and cooperation. He thus developed a remarkably effective public relations department, in which he took a lively interest. The FBI cultivated numerous contacts with friendly members of the newspaper, radio, and film industries. This access to the media allowed the Bureau to publicize its triumphs and to respond, either overtly or covertly, to its critics.

Hoover tried to convince the public that his agency was aloof from everyday politics and dedicated only to combating individuals, ideas, and organizations which undermined Americanism. The Bureau publicity department tried to portray its agents as well-educated, clean-cut professionals; the kind of respectable middle-class figures who would gladly lend a lawnmower to a neighbor or volunteer to coach the local sandlot baseball team. Seizing on the G-men's pious image, Martin Dies sneered that Hoover's agents were a bunch of overgrown boy scouts.[83]

Hoover also worked to make the public see the Bureau as an extension of his own personality. He controlled the release of all information to the press, personally announced FBI triumphs, and tried to keep other agents out of the media spotlight. By the late thirties, Hoover had been transformed into a folk hero. He retained this standing among Americans until the turbulence of the sixties. In 1964, humorist Art Buchwald satirized the apotheosis of Hoover in a column which claimed that the FBI chief was a mythical person invented by the editors of the *Reader's Digest*.[84]

The tremendous admiration and trust which Americans had for Hoover during the World War II era left him in a position to influence greatly public attitudes toward the Axis Trojan Horse. From 1940 to 1942, Hoover helped excite national fears by stressing the dangers posed by internal enemies. However, he also took steps which prevented Fifth Column hysteria from getting out of control.

The director realized that an overly lurid account of the spy menace might send the populace into a panic, causing internal confusion and domestic discord. National hysteria would impede effective counterespionage work and undermine home-front morale. In fact, if Hoover should be perceived as initiating a witch-hunt, then the Bureau risked disgrace and the loss of both political and popular support. On the other hand, a too cheery presentation of the problem might prevent the Bureau from doing its job. The FBI was a small organization functioning in a geographically large nation with a heterogenous population. Given such factors, the director believed effective counterintelligence work demanded public cooperation, and such cooperation called for an alert and slightly anxious citizenry.

Furthermore, if Hoover did not appear to be taking the Axis Fifth Column seriously, then any enemy success might be blamed on a slumbering FBI. Apocalyptic rhetoric in some ways insulated the Bureau against criticism. By claiming the country had let the Trojan Horse menace get out of hand, the G-men could absolve themselves from an occasional enemy success. Better yet, the FBI could take credit for a job well done if there were no spectacular Fifth Column victories.

Keeping the Fifth Column problem on the minds of voters and Congress also helped to assure that the FBI received adequate funding and manpower. In his appearances before the House Appropriations Committee, Hoover repeatedly complained that he needed more resources to face the Fifth Column threat. In January of 1940, the director told Congress that a lack of manpower meant that 1,847 cases, or "41 percent of national defense matters," were unassigned. Six months later he testified that 1,554 national defense cases were unattended. In February 1941, the chair of the House Appropriations Committee complained that the Bureau had only completed surveys of a fraction of America's industrial plants. Hoover explained that his agents already worked twelve hours a day, six days a week. He added that his agents were so shorthanded that 48,864 national defense matters had gone unassigned. Congress responded to the FBI's request for greater funding. In fiscal year 1937 the Bureau's annual budget was $6 million; in 1946, the figure rose to $28 million.[85]

Prior to World War II, when Hoover had been faced with subversion he had tended to fan the flame of popular hysteria. While an assistant to Attorney General A. Mitchell Palmer, Hoover produced reports on the Red Scare which Palmer claimed were so frightening that they gave him "the creeps."[86] The alarmist tone which Hoover adopted toward the Fifth Column was in line with his usual approach toward the FBI's adversaries.

During the course of the Bureau's "War Against Crime," the director employed many of the rhetorical tactics on which he would later rely while fighting Axis Fifth Columnists. One of these tactics was to suggest that the very foundations of the republic were under attack. Throughout the thirties Hoover claimed that an army of criminals, "the Huns and Vandals of a modern era," besieged the nation. He warned that one in 25 Americans was inclined toward criminality, and "if this tremendous body of evil-doers could be welded into a unit of conquest, America would fall before it in not a month, not in a day, but in a few hours." The director observed that the standing army of crime in the U.S. was twice as large as the nation's armed forces. In April of 1936 Hoover informed a meeting of the Daughters of the American Revolution that the enemy had fully penetrated the nation: "Crime lives next door to you. Crime often plays bridge with you. Crime dances with your sons and daughters. It is ever present."[87]

Hoover blamed lawlessness on the public. He cautioned that America's citizenry had to support law enforcement more energetically, otherwise the criminals would take control of society. The United States needed "a rebirth of vigilance and the casting out of lethargy which has brought this nation to a maximum of 1,500,000 serious crimes per year." For Hoover it was axiomatic that "crime thrives, violence and murder rage, only in that country, state, or nation where the moral fiber and resistance are weak." Whether fighting gangsters in the thirties, Fifth Columnists in the forties, or Communist agents in the fifties, the director harped on the theme that a decline in public virtue and the rise of private vice invited national disaster.

In the wake of the Rumrich espionage case in 1938, Hoover began to include frequent allusions in his speeches and writings to the threat of foreign subversion. At first he linked this problem with the government's war against crime. Both gangsters and foreign agents were "in a state of revolt against the American way." The two groups had formed an unholy alliance, as "the representative of gangster governments finds a fertile field for his recruits in the underworld."[88] Hoover noted that both political dictators and members of the criminal underworld "deal in avarice, in greed, in the lust for power and blood purges."[89]

The director's rhetoric shrewdly linked gangsters and "gangster nations." The "War Against Crime" had been a showcase success for the FBI. By underscoring similarities between anti-crime work and counterespionage, Hoover suggested that his agency was well suited to lead a national crusade against the Fifth Column. This approach also allowed him to suggest that his enlarged Bureau merely performed the same function it always had, thus reassuring citizens that no American OGPU or Gestapo was being created.

Hoover sought to persuade the public that his bureaucracy was not an octopus grasping for more and more power. In his speeches he noted that a direct order from President Roosevelt had resulted in the expansion of FBI duties. Hoover also claimed that military intelligence and naval intelligence had both asked the Bureau to take on greater responsibility for counterespionage work. The director made a concerted effort to show Americans that more and more responsibility was being thrust upon a passive FBI.[90]

When he talked about the Fifth Column in the period between 1940 and 1942, the director made shocking and potentially explosive statements. He told citizens that "never in our history has our national security been menaced as it is today."[91] "Renegades" and "termites" were everywhere seeking to weaken the structures of democracy; these "emissaries from totalitarian governments" hoped to "undermine our nationalism and to implant their doctrines of hate." Hoover claimed subversive forces had "penetrated every realm of society seeking allies in our schools, our churches, and our civic organizations."[92] The danger of un-American activities "was real and not imaginary."[93] In October 1940, Hoover told graduates of the FBI National Police Academy that a great challenge faced law enforcement:

> That there is a Fifth Column which has already started to march is an acknowledged reality. That it menaces America is an established fact. A Fifth Column of destruction following in the wake of confusion, weakening the sinews of a nation and paralyzing it with fear can be met only by the nation-wide enforcement of all law enforcement.[94]

How was Hoover to explain such a crisis? Clearly he could not blame the FBI, nor would it have been possible for him to point a finger of accusation at the White House. Ultimately, the director argued that the Fifth Column was caused by the same problem which allowed for widespread crime: namely, the indifference of the American people. Hoover claimed that the nation had become soft and flabby: "With our minds engrossed in materialistic and selfish pursuits we have allowed thousands of espousers of alien hate and foreign isms to enter our communities, our neighborhoods, our homes, our factories and even our governmental agencies."[95]

Hoover's speeches and writings were alarming. He repeatedly warned America that "Fifth Column methods have permeated into every walk of life."[96] However, by rooting the cause of the threat in public indifference and gullibility, the Bureau chief suggested an easy solution to the problem. All that was needed was a little more alertness on the part of the citizenry. Hoover noted that in the past, the republic's citizens had rallied to protect their democratic form of government, and he expressed confidence that Americans would do so now. However, the stakes were quite high: "Gullibility must cease [for] too much trustful innocence may be repaid by a stab in the back." Confidence in victory should be tempered by a recognition that the country faced "a resourceful and ruthless foe."[97]

Hoover assured the public that his own organization was prepared for any Fifth Column offensive. The director bragged of his Bureau's advanced scientific laboratory and of the sophisticated training his agents received at the FBI National Academy. He also informed the public of the cooperation which existed between local and federal law enforcement. Such cooperation meant that the government could release "a veritable army of highly trained men against the emissaries of any nation which seeks to pry too deeply into our affairs."[98] Thanks to the work of the FBI "the foundations of an impregnable America have been well laid."[99] The rest of the job depended upon the public acting as "listening posts" for the Bureau. If the citizenry did this, the home front would remain secure.

Hoover's effort to jolt a drowsy American public into action was tempered by his desire to discourage national hysteria. He wanted to avoid the mistakes of the First World War when the actions of the American Protective League had discredited the Bureau of Investigation. Therefore, Hoover insisted on a narrowly defined counterintelligence role for the public. He believed citizen activity "should be limited to passing on to the proper officials all questions of facts or rumors which may come one's way."[100] Hoover explained that amateur spybusters might disrupt ongoing FBI operations. For example, if the Bureau had already penetrated a particular German espionage ring, an overeager citizen performing independent detective work might unknowingly flush the quarry and upset months of FBI sleuthing. The director also noted the danger which both unfounded gossip and vigilante actions could cause for domestic unity and morale. One of the major objectives of the Fifth Columnists was to set neighbor against neighbor. Thus, the most sincere patriot might be turned into a dupe for America's enemies by passing along divisive hearsay or by participating in mob action. Hoover told the Daughters of the American Revolution of his fears along these lines:

> I must remind you that in times like these, there is a great danger of misguided efforts on the part of zealous groups of individuals who are the victims of those motivated by a desire to further their own selfish end. Let me warn you against the patriotic racketeer; the only things lower are the vipers of alien isms whose poisonous fangs are fatal.[101]

Hoover cautioned that America must "remain watchful and vigilant, but, at the same time, sensible and calm."[102] Though the country might be in a state of crisis, this was "no time for hysteria, wild rumors or hair trigger prejudices."[103] Hoover believed that the centralization of counterintelligence within the FBI would prevent the sort of excesses which had occurred during World War I.

Nothing helped to quell national jitters more effectively than repeated demonstrations of the FBI's mastery over Axis Fifth Columnists. The G-men skillfully thwarted Germany's pitiable efforts at clandestine warfare. Hoover saw to it that the Bureau's victories over spies and saboteurs received plenty of press coverage. A widely publicized FBI capture of German saboteurs in the summer of 1942 went a long way toward dispelling spy mania.

Richard Powers has focused on responsible aspects of Bureau activity in dealing with the Fifth Column threat and credits the director with preventing public panic. It is true that Hoover both spoke out against hysteria and forcefully controlled Axis subversion. However, he also injected overblown and careless language in many of his public messages. Hence, pulp fiction magazines regularly reprinted the latest statement from the director alongside their tales of Nazi intrigue, finding in Hoover's excesses material compatible with alarmist spy stories.

By 1943, Hoover began to declare victory over the Fifth Column. He noted that now the real dangers to America were the Sixth and Seventh columns. The Bureau Chief identified the Sixth Column as "unwitting accomplices" of the Axis who undermined Allied unity by passing on rumors. The Seventh Column, which Hoover called "the most destructive home front enemy," was carelessness.[104] The Bureau continued to issue warnings against complacency and even occasionally suggested impending landings by enemy saboteurs. However, the FBI's releases adopted a tone of confidence and self-satisfaction. By 1944, when Hoover discussed the Axis Fifth Column, he did so with the pride of a man who feels he has done his job well. News stories began appearing with such headlines as "Hoover Tells How FBI Erased Fifth Column."[105] In early October 1944, Hoover informed listeners of CBS radio that "our Axis undercover enemies have been met and completely defeated."[106]

If the Nazi Trojan Horse had been defeated, the country still had to worry about Communism. From the early thirties through the course of World War II, Hoover noted that the Fifth Column threat included both Communists and the Bundsmen. Both were proponents of alien ideologies which relied upon "slimy racketeering" and "revolution-inciting ways" in order to undermine Americanism.[107] Both isms espoused "a way of life, a fanatical worship of materialism, destruction, and the blacking out of decency."[108]

Even after the Soviets had joined the war against Hitler, the director remained wary of Communist subversion. Hoover issued hundreds of reports to the White House on the Red menace, and the Bureau's monthly reports on domestic security devoted more pages to Communism than to any other threat.

As the war wound down, Hoover's principal domestic worry was Communism. In 1944, Colonel Donovan proposed an exchange of missions between the OSS and the NKVD (the People's Commissariat for Internal Affairs). An OSS station would be set up in Moscow and an NKVD station in Washington, D.C. Hoover quickly moved to block such a step, fearing the establishment in America of a legalized Soviet spy nest. In the middle of 1944, the very same time as he was declaring victory over Nazi Fifth Columnists, the director warned graduates of Holy Cross College that Communists posed behind a dozen fronts and "have endeavored to infiltrate practically every strata of life." Hoover had no difficulties praising the Russian people and their war effort, but he made it clear that "when it comes to governmental systems we prefer our own American way, and do not want the Communists in this country to undermine our democracy or any of our institutions."[109] A private FBI estimate drawn up in 1944 concluded that almost one million Americans were knowingly and unknowingly tied to Communist-front activity.[110]

President Franklin Roosevelt eventually came to believe that his top G-man spent too much time investigating Fifth Columnists of the left. In May 1942, the Attorney General informed Hoover of FDR's concern. The director complained that the President "must have been misinformed," and he proceeded to reel off the numerous investigations which the Bureau had conducted into the activities of right-wing groups and individuals. Hoover concluded that his agency had "properly evaluated" the relative danger of pro-Axis and pro-Communist activities.[111] While Hoover spent most of his life grossly misreading the actual menace posed by Communist subversion, his view that Soviet agents constituted a greater threat to U.S. security than did German agents appears to have been accurate. By 1942, the Bureau had disabled the minor German Fifth Column activity which did exist in America. The director could be fairly confident of this fact thanks to evidence revealed by the interrogation of captured Nazi spies, the Bureau's penetration of Nazi spy efforts in the United States, and the failure of the Nazis to reap any detectable victories from Fifth Column work. On the other hand, during the course of World War II, the Soviets made the United States a major target of their espionage work (for example, Soviet espionage successes at the Los Alamos plant far surpassed anything the Germans accomplished during the war).[112]

From 1940 to 1942, the head of the FBI, like FDR, heightened fears of a dangerous Fifth Column, yet also took steps to see that the panic remained contained. He managed in his own speeches and writings to be both horrifying and reassuring. Hoover scolded the American people for allowing the Trojan Horse to penetrate the nation; at the same time he expressed confidence that the nation would respond to the ongoing emergency. He spoke out on the importance of protecting civil liberties, yet he also denounced the way the Constitution was used by subversive agents "just as John Dillinger used a steel vest."[113] He noted that there were more spies in America than at any time since World War I, but he added that the country had never been better prepared to combat espionage. Hoover's public comments on the Fifth Column doubtlessly heightened popular fears of home front treachery. It would have been only natural for citizens to focus on the more frightening aspects of his rhetoric, especially at the height of America's Trojan Horse scare. Nonetheless, Hoover prevented spy mania from manifesting itself in the destructive way that it had during the First World War.

Conclusion

After 1942, Fifth Column fears subsided dramatically. The White House, FBI, Congress, and the media all sharply curtailed the issuance of warnings about hidden Axis enemies. Nonetheless, an attenuated interest in the Nazi Trojan Horse lingered. The Justice Department sought to prosecute criminally a number of far-right extremists through the course of World War II. The primary government case, *U.S. v. McWilliams*, ended in a mistrial with the defendants consistently revealing themselves as pathetic lunatics rather than the sinister vanguard of a Nazi Trojan Horse.[1]

In 1943, John Roy Carlson (Avedis Derounian) published *Under Cover*, an exposé of native fascism. Carlson's book rose to first place on the nonfiction best-sellers list for 1943 and fourth place for 1944.[2] On the radio, newsmen such as Walter Winchell and entertainment programs like *The FBI in Peace and War* frequently dealt with the homefront battle against pro-Hitler Fifth Columnists.[3] From 1943 to 1945 Hollywood produced numerous features on the Axis spy menace, albeit far fewer than during the early part of the war.[4]

In the decades following World War II, novelists and filmmakers stubbornly clung to Nazi villains. Unreformed refugees from the Third Reich became stock characters in postwar suspense thrillers. In Hitchcock's film *Notorious*, former followers of Hitler seek to develop nuclear weapons. In the *Odessa File* (a novel written by Frederick Forsythe and turned into a film by Columbia studios), ex-S.S. officers plot to supply Egypt with guided missiles armed with biological weapons. In *The Boys from Brazil* (a novel written by Ira Levin and filmed by ITC pictures), Joseph

Mengele attempts to clone hundreds of young Hitlers. Numerous other literary and cinematic works helped keep the idea of a pro-Hitler Fifth Column alive in the popular imagination (for example, *The Stranger, The Quiller Memorandum, The Marathon Man, The Salzburg Connection, The Holcroft Covenant*).

Real-life Nazis also managed to win attention for themselves in post-war America. In 1958, George Lincoln Rockwell created the American Nazi Party. Rockwell's followers wore Nazi uniforms, saluted the swastika, denounced Jews, backed the mass deportation of African-Americans, and urged an end to democratic government. The tiny extremist group (active membership never exceeded 100 members) sought media coverage by resorting to publicity stunts. On one occasion Rockwell supporters paraded around the White House with signs reading "Save Ike from the Kikes." At another time the Nazis disrupted a civil rights rally by appearing in gorilla costumes. Despite such repellent antics, Rockwell's followers did not stimulate much concern from the press or the government.[5]

In 1967 Rockwell was assassinated. Shortly thereafter his organization splintered into several different factions. One fragment, the National Socialist Party of America, made national headlines in the late seventies. Frank Collin, the group's leader, planned a rally in Skokie, Illinois, a suburb of Chicago. The site for the Nazi demonstration proved especially provocative as the town had a significant Jewish population, including a number of Holocaust survivors. Officials in Skokie attempted to employ local ordinances to keep the Nazis out of their community. The American Civil Liberties Union believed an important First Amendment issue was at stake and sued on behalf of Collin and his followers. The Nazis won their case, but they opted not to march in Skokie. Instead they staged two rallies in Chicago, one at the Federal Plaza and the other at Marquette Park. The Skokie case became a cause célèbre, sparking nationwide debates on the degree to which the Constitution protected hate speech.

In the eighties, the Aryan Nation, a neo-Nazi movement based in Idaho, forced its way into the public consciousness. Law enforcement authorities linked some of the group's former members to the murder of Denver radio talk-show host Alan Berg and to several armed robberies.[6] In recent years other far-right zealots—skinheads, survivalists, and Larouchites—have intrigued the public and the mass media. Yet the nation's interest in domestic fascists hardly signifies a Fifth Column panic. Extremists earned coverage for breaking the law, for raising constitutional issues, or for behaving in bizarre and hence newsworthy ways. Few believed that these fringe elements actually threatened to bring down the republic. In the postwar period no outside power existed to aid America's far-right fanatics as there had been in the thirties and forties.

Toward the Red Scare

Prior to Operation Barbarossa (the Nazi invasion of the USSR), Americans suspected Moscow as well as Berlin of participating in Trojan Horse activities. The Second World War brought a brief period of alliance between the Soviet Union and the United States. The common effort against Hitler improved Stalin's image in the West and helped abate fears of Communist Trojan Horse operations. However, with the end of World War II and the collapse of the Grand Alliance, the American public came to believe once again that the Soviet Union routinely resorted to Trojan Horse techniques. In his Iron Curtain speech delivered in March 1946, Winston Churchill warned the United States that "in a great number of countries, far from the Russian frontiers and throughout the world, Communist fifth columns are established and work in complete unity and absolute obedience to the directions they receive from the Communist center."[7] Churchill offered the consoling opinion that Red Fifth Columns had not yet successfully penetrated the United States or the British Commonwealth. J. Edgar Hoover was less optimistic. In 1947, the FBI chief warned HUAC that America's Communist party represented "a Fifth Column if ever there was one. It is far better organized than were the Nazis in occupied countries prior to their capitulation. . . ."[8] Throughout the late forties dread and suspicion of the Soviet Union grew. Many Americans in and out of government believed that Joseph Stalin aimed at world conquest and that he had already set a Communist Fifth Column force upon the United States. America's Red Scare peaked in 1950 and did not markedly decline until the Army-McCarthy hearings of 1954.

Many of the conditions that helped cultivate the Axis Fifth Column panic contributed to the Red Scare. First, the Cold War with the Soviet Union (combined with a hot war against North Korea and China) left Americans justifiably worried about outside enemies. Second, the exposure of foreign intriguing in the United States confirmed the existence of hidden internal enemies. Finally, large segments of the government and media attested to the reality of a Fifth Column menace.

In 1945, Joseph Stalin issued a public address stating that capitalism and Communism were locked in mortal combat. The Sovietization of Eastern Europe, the triumph of Mao Zedong in China, Moscow's development of a nuclear device, and North Korea's invasion of South Korea all gave testimony to the apparent truth of Stalin's claim. Western democracies understandably expressed alarm at the Soviet Union, viewing it as a hostile and ruthless despotism. For many Americans the successes of Communism seemed partially due to conspiracy and treachery.

Those who believed in a Communist Fifth Column could point to several notorious espionage cases. In 1946, Igor Gouchenko, a Soviet code clerk stationed in Ottawa, Canada, defected to the West. He brought with him documentation which helped unmask widespread Russian nuclear spying. In 1948, ex-Communist Whittaker Chambers told HUAC that several government officials, including former State Department official Alger Hiss, had spied for the Russians. Hiss indignantly denied Communist sympathies, initially claiming he did not even know Chambers. (He later stated that he had known Chambers under a different name.) A celebrated government investigation followed. Charges and countercharges were exchanged. In January 1950, a jury concluded that Hiss had indeed known Chambers and had passed classified documents to him. In 1949 news stories revealed that Justice Department employee Judith Coplon gave secret FBI materials to a Soviet official. Early in 1950 the FBI arrested Harry Gold and David Greenglass for passing atomic secrets to the Soviets. Greenglass told the Bureau that he had been recruited into espionage by his brother-in-law Julius Rosenberg. In July 1950, the government arrested Julius and Ethel Rosenberg. After a highly publicized trial the two were found guilty. In 1953 the couple received the death penalty. While historians still debate the legitimacy of the Hiss and Rosenberg verdicts, the reality of Soviet espionage is beyond dispute.

The government helped inflame popular fears. Congress investigated Moscow's suspected infiltration of labor unions, the film industry, colleges, and universities. Republican legislators especially played up the Communist issue, using it for partisan political gain. GOP leaders denounced the Democrats for "twenty years of treason" and questioned the loyalty of Truman's advisers. Representative Edward Jenner called General George Marshall "a front man for traitors . . . either an unsuspecting or an actual co-conspirator with the most treasonable array of political cutthroats ever turned loose in the Executive branch of Government."[9] Joseph McCarthy, the junior senator from Wisconsin, brought red-baiting to its zenith. Shortly after the conviction of Alger Hiss for perjury, McCarthy began his hunt for Communists within the government.

The Federal Bureau of Investigation played a key part in the Red Scare. Hoover told the President and Congress that Moscow had planted a dangerous Fifth Column inside the United States. He launched a major education campaign designed to alert the public to the danger of homefront Communist agents.

Neither Harry Truman nor Dwight Eisenhower succeeded in calming the nation. In 1947 Truman institutionalized a government loyalty program. The President's actions aimed at preserving national security and at the same time preempting Republican demagoguery on the Communist issue. The loyalty program did not achieve the latter objective. In fact, some scholars have contended that Truman's step inflamed popular paranoia by treating Communist penetration of the government as a serious problem. Eisenhower, while privately disdainful of McCarthy, publicly ac-

knowledged the seriousness of the problem of Communists. In 1953, the
new administration altered the loyalty codes to cover a broader range of
unacceptable activities. Eisenhower subordinates boasted to the press that
they had rooted out thousands of subversive government employees.[10]

The mass media also helped keep the panic going. Many newspaper
editors and reporters expressed scorn for Joseph McCarthy. Nonetheless,
the press gave extensive coverage to McCarthy's accusations and failed
to follow up properly his more outrageous charges. The film industry
churned out over forty features on the Communist menace.[11] Like the
Fifth Column pictures of the thirties and forties, most of the anti-Red
productions were low budget quickies. The Communist Trojan Horse
also became an important theme for radio shows, comic books, and pulp
novels of the period. In fact, long after the McCarthy era had passed,
many works of popular culture still based their story lines on the idea
of a Red Fifth Column.

The Red Scare was the last of a series of national hysterias that
wracked America between 1914 and 1954. The panics affecting the
United States during World War I, World War II, and the Cold War
served a useful therapeutic function. The notion of a Fifth Column
helped Americans to rationalize their rejection of regional isolation in
favor of global involvement.

In particular, the Second World War experience significantly eroded
isolationist sentiment. The apparent exposure of a Nazi Trojan Horse
suggested that a foreign policy of non-involvement was cowardly, dangerous, naive, and unpatriotic. Historian Wayne Cole has written that
by the end of the war "isolationists were identified with Hitler, fascism,
totalitarianism, anti-Semitism, and even treason."[12] After the defeat of
the Axis powers, internationalists still worried about a revival of isolation. Indeed, the nation's rapid demobilization and initial caution on
matters of foreign aid hinted at the possibility of United States retreat
from world affairs. However, the Axis Fifth Column scare so profoundly
shook the country's long-held faith in Washington's "Great Rule"
against entangling alliances that isolationism had little chance to succeed
in postwar America. Moreover, the emergence of a new totalitarian enemy and a new Trojan Horse panic made internationalism's victory inevitable.

Fear of Hitler's Fifth Column produced major changes in the area of
national security as well as in international relations and popular culture.
The fight against Nazi espionage led to a close intelligence liaison between the United States and Britain. The intelligence organizations of
both countries maintained their special relationship into the postwar period. The United States developed its own Fifth Column weapon during
World War II in the OSS. Following the creation of the Central Intelligence Agency in 1947 the nation retained an ability to mount overseas
black operations during peace time. The Fifth Column scare produced

an expansion of the FBI's jurisdiction, personnel, and budget. Hoover's successes against his Nazi adversaries ensured that the Bureau retained control of domestic counterintelligence long after Hitler's fall. In the prewar period, anxiety over Brown and Red subversion caused Congress to establish the House Un-American Activities Committee and to pass legislation such as the Smith Act. The Fifth Column scare also had a powerful affect on American culture, inspiring a flood of films, comic books, pulp novels, and radio shows from 1938 to 1942. Most of these productions lacked genuine artistic merit and now retain interest only as period pieces. Nonetheless, the panic has had lasting cultural signficance, for it gave birth to a sub-genre of suspense stories that focus on the fiendish plottings of Nazis or ex-Nazis. Because we still enjoy such productions as *Indiana Jones and the Last Crusade* and *The Boys from Brazil* for their entertainment value, it is easy to underestimate the fear that inspired the original stories about hidden Axis agents. The Fifth Column panic profoundly influenced American diplomacy, politics, and culture in the late thirties and early forties. Indeed, it is impossible to understand the period without acknowledging the pervasive nature of the scare.

In the forty years since the Army-McCarry hearings, the United States has experienced no national panic comparable to the Red Scare. What explains the nation's apparent recent immunity to such phenomena? The assassinations of several prominent public figures, repeated acts of anti-American terrorism, and wars against Vietnam and Iraq would seem to offer the requisite occasions to ignite a popular panic. William Freehling contends that alongside the conspiratorial strain in American culture there has also existed "a counterconspiratorial tradition, the resistance to believe in a plot and the inclination to draw back from unsubstantiated delusions." Freehling posits that the scope of disapproval regarding McCarthy may have left the nation only with "its countervailing anticonspiratorial tradition fully intact."[13] Indeed, the historical lessons of Cold War hysteria have served to make those who speak of hidden plots and insidious foes suspect as un-American themselves. Since the early seventies, America's relations with its superpower rivals have been placed on a more stable basis, diminishing the perceived menace of foreign-launched conspiracies against the republic. While worries about dangers from outside rivals persist, as when, for instance, buildings in New York City are blown up by Middle Eastern terrorists, or bought by Japanese investors, no current external adversary appears as menacing as Stalin's Soviet Union or Hitler's Germany did to an earlier generation of Americans. Throughout this study of the Fifth Column scare I have emphasized the coalescence of forces needed to stir the public to a full-scale panic. Without continuing evidence of a plot and without simultaneous reinforcement from politicians, law enforcement, and the media, conspiracy theories tend to lose their hold over the public rather quickly. America's experience with the Axis Fifth Column points out not only the slender evidence needed to start a scare, but the unusual circumstances required to sustain one. Without a blend of self-interested, idealistic, and opportunistic motives at work within individual persons, agencies, public institutions, and private businesses, reinforcing one another's representations of imminent peril, panics are sure to be evanescent.

NOTES

Preface

1. Louis De Jong, *The German Fifth Column in the Second World War* (Chicago: Univ. of Chicago Press, 1956).

2. Richard Steele, "Franklin D. Roosevelt and His Foreign Policy Critics," *Political Science Quarterly* 94 (Spring, 1979); 15–32; Leo Ribuffo, *The Old Christian Right: The Protestant Far Right from the Great Depression to the Cold War* (Philadelphia: Temple Univ. Press, 1983); Geoffrey Smith, *To Save a Nation: American Countersubversives, the New Deal, and the Coming of World War II* (New York: Basic Books, 1973); Wayne Cole, *Roosevelt and the Isolationists 1932–1945* (Lincoln: Univ. of Nebraska Press, 1983); Richard Gid Powers, *Secrecy and Power: The Life of J. Edgar Hoover* (New York: Free Press, 1987); Bradley Smith, *Shadow Warriors: O.S.S. and the Origins of the C.I.A.* (New York: Basic Books, 1983).

3. Robert K. Murray, *Red Scare: A Study of National Hysteria, 1919–1920* (Minneapolis: Univ. of Minnesota Press, 19550; Richard Fried, *Nightmare in Red: The McCarthy Era in Perspective* (New York: Oxford Univ. Press, 1990).

Introduction

1. De Jong's study remains the most comprehensive treatment of the Fifth Column scare's international impact. Louis De Jong, *The German Fifth Column in the Second World War* (Chicago: Univ. of Chicago Press, 1956).

2. Bernard Bailyn, *The Ideological Origins of the American Revolution* (Cambridge, Mass.: Harvard Univ. Press, 1967); Richard Hofstadter, *The Paranoid Style in American Politics* (New York: Knopf, 1965), 3–40; and David Brion Davis, "Some Themes of Counter–Subversion: An Analysis of Anti-Masonic, Anti-Catholic, and Anti-Mormon Literature," *Mississippi Valley Historical Review* 47 (Sept. 1960): 205–24; and David Brion Davis, *The Fear of Conspiracy: Images of Un-American Subversion from the Revolution to the Present* (Ithaca: Cornell Univ. Press, 1971).

3. For example, FBI director Hoover wrote the following memo to Assistant Secretary of State Berle: "Information of a confidential character has been received to the effect that for some time the Nazis have been exploiting the "Jewish refugee" problem for the purposes of espionage and other subversive activities in the Western Hemisphere." J. E. Hoover to A. Berle, April 29, 1941, RG 59 862.20210/474 in National Archives and Records Service (hereafter NARS), Washington, DC.

4. *Time*, June 3, 1940, p. 12.

5. "There Are Signs of Nazi Fifth Columns Everywhere," *Life*, June 17, 1940, p. 10.

6. "Without mentioning any names do you think there are fifth columnists in this community?" Yes 48%, No 26%, No Opinion 26%: Survey 204-K, 8/27/40, released Sept. 15, 1940, in *The Gallup Poll: Public Opinion 1935–1971*, 3 vols. (New York: Random House, 1972), 1 (1935–48): 241.

7. Hoover to Attorney General Jackson, Box 92, Attorney General National Defense Matters in Robert Jackson Papers, Library of Congress, Washington, D.C.

8. Letter to Secretary of State Cordell Hull, Oct. 9, 1941, RG 59 862.20211/3272, NARS.

9. Letter to Secretary of War Cordell Hull, undated (received Dec. 3, 1941), RG 59 800.20211/632, NARS.

Chapter One. Prelude to the Fifth Column Scare

1. Woodrow Wilson, "An Address to a Joint Session of Congress," April 2, 1917, in *The Papers of Woodrow Wilson*, Arthur S. Link, ed., 64 vols. (Princeton, N.J.: Princeton Univ. Press), 41: 525. Before giving his war address Wilson was supplied with a background report on German espionage by Secretary of State Robert Lansing. Lansing to Wilson, "Improper Activities of German Officials in the United States," March 30, 1917, in the Woodrow Wilson papers, microfilm reel 383, series 5A, frames 428–436.

2. Woodrow Wilson to Robert Lansing, Dec. 5, 1915, 701.6211/327.5, RG 59, NARS.

3. Henry Landau, *The Enemy Within: The Inside Story of German Sabotage in America* (New York: G. P. Putnam's Sons, 1937), 10–17.

4. On Goltz see Landau, 18–19; on Bopp see ibid., 23–28; on Horn see Jules Witcover, *Sabotage at Black Tom: Imperial Germany's Secret War in America 1914–1917* (Chapel Hill, N.C.: Algonquin Books, 1989), 68–69.

5. On Rintelen see Barbara Tuchman, *The Zimmermann Telegram* (New York: Macmillan, 1958), 66–87, and Witcover, 83–101. Rintelen wrote two potboiler memoir accounts of his espionage exploits: see Captain Franz von Rintelen, *The Dark Invader* (London: Lovat Dickson, 1933), and Rintelen, *The Dark Invader Returns* (London: Dickson and Thompson, 1935).

6. Landau, 38–41; also see Thomas Tunney, *Throttled! The Detection of the German and Anarchist Bomb Plotters* (Boston: Small, Maynard, 1919), 143–55.

7. Landau, 36.

8. Figures are drawn from Witcover, 24.

9. For lengthy discussions of Black Tom and Kingsland see Landau, *The Enemy Within*, and Witcover, *Sabotage at Black Tom*.

10. William McAdoo, *The Crowded Years* (Boston: Houghton Mifflin, 1931), 325–27.

11. German Ambassador to Secretary of State, Aug. 18, 1915, *Foreign Relations of the United States* (hereafter *FRUS*) 1915 supplement, p. 929. (Washington, D.C.: Government Printing Office, 1928).

12. Constantin Dumba to Baron Burian, Austro-Hungarian Minister for Foreign Affairs, quoted in telegram from U.S. ambassador in London Walter Hines Page to Secretary of State Robert Lansing, Washington, D.C., Sept. 1, 1915, RG59 701.6311/141, National Archives and Records Service (hereafter NARS), Washington, D.C.

13. Enclosure 1, translation, Hungarian memorandum enclosed in the letter from Austro-Hungarian Ambassador Dumba to Austro-Hungarian Minister of Foreign Affairs, *FRUS*, 1915 supplement, pp. 937–38.

14. "I always say to these idiotic Yankees that they should shut their mouths. . . ." Enclosure 5, translation, German Military Attaché to his wife, undated, *FRUS*, 1915 supplement, p. 939.

15. *Selections from Papers Found in the Possession of Captain von Papen, Late German Military Attaché at Washington, Falmouth, Jan. 2 and 3, Presented to Both Houses of Parliament by Command of His Majesty* (London: Harrisons and Sons, 1916), OG1024 box 280, NARS.

16. For an in-depth discussion of British naval intelligence during the First World War, see Patrick Beesly, *Room 40: British Naval Intelligence, 1914–1918* (London: Hamilton, 1982).

17. Zimmermann claimed to be surprised by the American reaction to his proposed alliance with Mexico. Since the alliance was only to go in effect if the U.S. and Germany were at war, Zimmermann believed there was nothing unneutral about his policies. For more details on the entire affair, see Friedrich Katz, *The Secret War in Mexico: Europe, the United States and the Mexican Revolution* (Chicago: Univ. of Chicago Press, 1981), 350–78, and Tuchman, *Zimmermann Telegram*.

18. For a memoir of the workings of the Bohemian National Alliance, see Emmanuel Voska, *Spy and Counterspy* (New York: Doubleday, Doran, 1940).

19. Walter Hines Page to Woodrow Wilson, Sept. 10, 1917, in Link, ed., *Papers of Woodrow Wilson*, 44: 182.

20. W. B. Fowler, *British-American Relations 1917–1918: The Role of Sir William Wiseman* (Princeton: Princeton Univ. Press, 1969).

21. Tuchman, 75.

22. Clifton James Child, *The German-Americans in Politics 1914–1917* (Madison: Univ. of Wisconsin Press, 1939), 98–102. Links between LeQeuex and British intelligence are dealt with extensively in Christopher Andrew, *Her Majesty's Secret Service: The Making of the British Intelligence Community* (New York: Viking, 1986), 37–56.

23. Ambassador Gerard to Woodrow Wilson, Jan. 24, 1915, in *The Intimate Papers of Colonel House*, Charles Seymour, ed., 4 vols. (Boston: Houghton Mifflin, 1926), 4: 356. James Gerard, *My Four Years in Germany* (New York: Grosset and Dunlap, 1917), 173; and Tuchman, 113.

24. E. M. House to Woodrow Wilson, Aug. 23, 1915, and Woodrow

Wilson to Edith Bolling Galt, Aug. 24, 1915, in Link, ed., *Papers of Woodrow Wilson* 34: 309.

25. Carl Wittke, *German-Americans and the World War (With Special Emphasis on Ohio's German-Language Press* (Columbus: Ohio State Archaeological and Historical Society, 1936), 23.

26. Ibid., 172–79.

27. The most detailed account of the German–American Alliance is Clifton James Child, *The German-Americans in Politics 1914–1917* (Madison: Univ. of Wisconsin Press, 1939).

28. See, for example, Woodrow Wilson, "An Address to the Daughters of the American Revolution," Oct. 11, 1915, in Link, ed., *Papers of Woodrow Wilson*, 35: 51.

29. Woodrow Wilson, "An Annual Message on the State of the Union," December 7, 1915, in ibid., 35: 306.

30. Woodrow Wilson, "A Flag Day Address," June 14, 1917, in ibid., 42: 499.

31. On the Creel committee see James Mock and Cedric Larson, *Words That Won the War* (Princeton, N.J.: Princeton Univ. Press, 1939), and Stephen Vaughn, *Holding Fast the Inner Lines: Democracy, Nationalism, and the Committee on Public Information* (Chapel Hill: Univ. of North Carolina Press, 1980).

32. Mock and Larson, 20, 42.

33. Material quoted from pamphlets is described in Vaughn, 78–81.

34. O'Brian quoted in William Chafee, *Freedom of Speech in War Time* (Cambridge, Mass.: Harvard Univ. Press, 1954), 70.

35. These examples were found in Wittke, 184–86, and Frederick Luebke, *Bonds of Loyalty: German-Americans and World War I* (Dekalb: Northern Illinois Univ. Press, 1974), 247–48.

36. Wittke, 163–96.

37. The standard history of the American Protective League is Joan Jensen, *The Price of Vigilance* (Chicago: Rand McNally, 1968).

38. For a full discussion of the Prager lynching, see Luebke, 3–24, and Donald R. Hickey, "The Prager Affair: A Study in Wartime Hysteria," *Journal of the Illinois State Historical Society* 62 (Summer 1969): 117–34.

39. For a discussion of the links which American policymakers saw between German and Soviet authoritarianism during World War I, see Daniel Smith, "Authoritarianism and American Policy Makers in Two World Wars," *Pacific Historical Review* 43, no. 3 (Aug. 1974): 303–10.

40. Hans Trefousse, "Failure of German Intelligence in the United States, 1933–1945," *Mississippi Valley Historical Review* 42 (June 1955): 92.

41. "The example of 1917 shows that American public opinion was incited to war far less by German submarine warfare than by alleged and actual cases of sabotage." Chargé d'Affaires in the United States to the Foreign Minister, May 21, 1940, in *Documents on German Foreign Policy 1918–1945*, series D 9 (London: Her Majesty's Stationary Office, 1956), 399.

42. Botticher Resenberg embassy U.S. to Foreign Ministry, May 24, 1940, in *Documents on German Foreign Policy 1918–1945*, 425.

43. Arthur Schlesinger, Jr., *The Age of Roosevelt*, vol. 1: *The Crisis of the Old Order* (Boston: Houghton Mifflin, 1957), 353.

Chapter Two. Dangerous Demagogues, Men on Horseback, and Native Fascists

1. Excellent discussions of the "fascist" scare are available in Geoffrey Smith, *To Save a Nation: American Countersubversives, the New Deal, and the Coming of World War II* (New York: Basic Books, 1973), 66–69 and Arthur Schlesinger, Jr., *The Age of Roosevelt*, vol. 3: *The Politics of Upheaval* (Boston: Houghton Mifflin, 1960), 69–95.

2. J. B. Matthews and R. E. Shallcross, "Must America Go Fascist?," *Harper's* 169 (June, 1934): 1–15; Stuart Chase, "New Deal for America: Road of the Fascists," *New Republic*, July 13, 1932, pp. 225–26; E. M. Hugh-Jones, "Little Nest of Fascists," *New Republic*, May 30, 1934, pp. 68–70; "The Great Fascist Plot," *New Republic*, Dec. 5, 1934, pp. 87–89; Hugh Tigner, "Will America Go Fascist?," *Christian Century*, May 2, 1934, pp. 592–94; Raymond Gram Swing, "Patriotism Dons the Black Shirt," *Nation*, April 10, 1935, pp. 409–11; Carey McWilliams, "Hollywood Plays with Fascism," *Nation*, May 29, 1935, pp. 623–24; Amy Schechter, "Fascism in Pennsylvania," *Nation*, June 19, 1935, pp. 713–14, Tigner, "Will America Go Fascist?," 592–94; "They're at It Again: Outlook for Fascism in the United States," *Commonweal*, March 9, 1934, pp. 509–10.

3. Travis Hoke, *Shirts! A Survey of the New Shirted Organizations in the U.S. Seeking a Fascist Dictatorship* (New York, 1934); Carmen Haider, *Do We Want Fascism?* (New York: John Day, 1934); Norman Thomas, *The Choice Before Us* (New York: Macmillan, 1934); Raymond Gram Swing, *Forerunners of American Fascism* (New York: Julian Messner, 1935).

4. Anonymous, *The President Vanishes* (New York: Farrar, 1934); Andre Sennwald, "The President Vanishes," *New York Times*, Dec. 8, 1934, p. 18.

5. Sinclair Lewis, *It Can't Happen Here* (Garden City, N.Y.: Doubleday, Doran, 1935), 458.

6. Breen quoted in "Hays Gets Blame for Film Ban," *Publishers' Weekly*, Feb. 29, 1935, p. 988.

7. "Berlin and Rome Hail 'Ban' on Lewis Film," *New York Times*, Feb. 27, 1935, p. 21.

8. Lewis quoted in "Lewis Says Hays Bans Film of Book," *New York Times*, Feb. 16, 1935, p. 1.

9. "Hays Gets Blame for Film Ban," *Publishers' Weekly*, Feb. 29, 1935, p. 988.

10. Alice Payne Hackett and James Henry Burke, *80 Years of Best Sellers 1895–1975* (New York: R. P. Bowker, 1977), 121.

11. "WPA, Lewis and Co.," *Time*, Nov. 9, 1936, p. 21.

12. "Fascism: Nightmarish History That Hasn't Even Happened Yet," *Newsweek*, Oct. 26, 1935, p. 38.

13. "Buzz and Antibuzz," *Time*, Oct. 28, 1935, p. 73.

14. J. Donald Adams, "America Under the Iron Heel," *New York Times*, Oct. 20, 1935, sec. 6, p. 1.

15. Benjamin Stolberg, "Sinclair Lewis Faces Fascism in the U.S." *New York Herald Tribune*, Oct. 20, 1935, sec. 7, p. 2.

16. Clifton Fadiman, "Red Lewis," *New Yorker*, Oct. 26, 1935, pp. 83–84. Elmer Davis echoed Fadiman's concern about United States vulnerability to

fascism: "Brethren, it could happen here—not in 1936, perhaps; but sooner than anybody might think, if the hard times go on." Elmer Davis, "Ode to Liberty," *Saturday Review of Literature*, Oct. 19, 1935, p. 5.

17. S. J. Woolf, "It Won't Happen Here, Lewis Believes," *New York Times*, Oct. 4, 1936, sec. 7, pp. 3, 25. Other skeptical views of Lewis's story include Robert Morss Lovett, "Mr. Lewis Says It Can," *New Republic*, Nov. 6, 1935, pp. 366–67, and "It Can't Happen Here," *Commonweal*, Nov. 13, 1936, p. 76.

18. There are many outstanding discussions of Long's career and significance. I have used T. Harry Williams, *Huey Long* (New York: Alfred A. Knopf, 1969); Alan Brinkley, *Voices of Protest: Huey Long, Father Coughlin, and the Great Depression* (New York: Alfred A. Knopf, 1982); Arthur Schlesinger, Jr., *The Politics of Upheaval* (Boston: Houghton Mifflin, 1969); and Smith, *To Save a Nation.*

19. Brinkley, 9.

20. Williams, 635–40.

21. Ibid., 813.

22. For material on Father Coughlin I have relied on Smith, *To Save a Nation*; Brinkley, *Voices of Protest*; Schlesinger, *Politics of Upheaval*; Sheldon Marcus, *Father Coughlin, The Tumultuous Life of the Priest of the Little Flower* (Boston: Little, Brown, 1973); and David H. Bennett, *Demagogues in the Depression: American Radicals and the Union Party, 1932–1936* (Brunswick, N.J.: Rutgers Univ. Press, 1969).

23. 40 million in 23 different states in Marcus, 34.

24. Schlesinger, 23.

25. On National Union for Social Justice, see Marcus, 71–100. Alan Brinkley focuses on the lack of organizational structure in the NUSJ in *Voices of Protest*, 186–92.

26. Ohio and Pennsylvania results in Marcus, 111.

27. Bennett, 190.

28. Schlesinger, 36; three and one-half million drawn from Bennett, 173.

29. Brinkley, 256–257, and Bennett, 230, 239.

30. The best discussions of Smith's career are available in Glen Jeansonne, *Gerald L. K. Smith: Minister of Hate* (New Haven, Conn.: Yale Univ. Press, 1988), and Leo Ribuffo, *The Old Christian Right* (Philadelphia, Pa.: Temple Univ. Press, 1983).

31. Factors behind the collapse of the Union campaign are discussed in Bennett, 201–13.

32. Brinkley, 266, Ronald Bayor, *Neighbors in Conflict: The Irish, Germans, Jews, and Italians of New York City, 1929–1941*, (2nd ed.: Urbana, Ill.: Univ. of Illinois Press, 1988), 97–104.

33. Donald Strong, *Organized Anti-Semitism in America: The Rise of Group Prejudice during the Decade 1930–1940* (Washington, D.C.: American Council on Public Affairs, 1941), 63–69.

34. Robert Lewis Taylor, "A Reporter at Large: The Kampf of Joe McWilliams," *New Yorker*, Aug. 24, 1940, p. 33.

35. McWilliams quoted in ibid., 39.

36. Roosevelt to Attorney General Robert Jackson, June 10, 1940, in OF4008 folder entitled Joseph McWilliams, Franklin Delano Roosevelt Library (hereafter FDRL), Hyde Park, New York.

37. Bennett, 279–82; Strong, 57–70.

38. On NAB code see Marcus, 176–77.

39. Winrod's political activities are discussed in Ribuffo, 80–127.

40. Ibid., 119.

41 On Winrod's election campaign see ibid., 119–24.

42. Stanley High, "Star Spangled Fascists," *Saturday Evening Post*, May 27, 1939, p. 70.

43. Ribuffo, 125.

44. Material on the Khaki Shirts is based on Nathaniel Weyl, "The Khaki Shirt—American Fascists," *New Republic*, Sept. 21, 1932, pp. 145–46; John Nicholas Beffel, "Murder and the Khaki Shirts," *Nation*, Nov. 29, 1933, p. 620; "Khaki Shirt 'Invaders' Halted at District Line," *Washington Post*, Oct. 13, 1933, p. 1; "Police Smash Khaki Shirts as Smith Flees," *Philadelphia Evening Bulletin*, Oct. 12, 1933, p. 1, 5; "Art Smith Pleads Guilty in Perjury Case," *New York Times*, April 14, 1934, p. 5.

45. For a summary of Butler, French, and Maguire's testimony see House Un-American Affairs Committee, *Investigation of Un-American Activities, Nazi Propaganda*, 73rd Cong., 2nd sess. (Washington, D.C.: Government Printing Office, 1934), 1–12. French quoted on p. 5. A brief scholarly treatment of the affair is available in Hans Schmidt, *Maverick Marine: General Smedley D. Butler and the Contradictions of American Military History* (Lexington: Univ. of Kentucky Press, 1987), 223–32; a book-length account without footnotes is available in Jules Archer, *The Plot to Seize the White House* (New York: Hawthorn Books, 1973).

46. Congressional testimony on the alleged plot is available in *Investigation of Un-American Propaganda Activities in the United States, Hearings*, 76th Cong., 1st sess., v. 5 (Washington, D.C.: Government Printing Office, 1939).

47. Testimony of James Campbell, May 18, 1939, in ibid., 3281.

48. Testimony of George Van Horn Moseley, May 31, 1939, in ibid., 3579.

49. This quote is from a speech made by Moseley in Philadelphia on March 28, 1939. Moseley admitted having made these comments at the Dies hearings. Testimony of George Van Horn Moseley, May 31, 1939, in ibid., 3584.

50. See, for example, Stanley High, "Star Spangled Fascists," *Saturday Evening Post*, May 27, 1939, p. 70; Roy Tozier, "Moseley of the Fifth Column," *New Republic*, June 7, 1939, pp. 119–21.

51. A brief discussion of Moseley's activities is available in Morris Schonbach, *Native American Fascism during the 1930s and 1940s: A Study of Its Roots, Its Growth and Its Decline* (New York: Garland, 1985), 236–43, 280–81. See also Robert Edwin Herzstein, *Roosevelt and Hitler: Prelude to War* (New York: Paragon House, 1989), 262–70.

52. The major works on Nazi organizations in America prior to World War II include Sander Diamond, *The Nazi Movement in the United States 1924–1941* (Ithaca, N.Y.: Cornell Univ. Press, 1974); Joachim Remak, " 'Friends of the New Germany': The Bund and German-American Relations," *Journal of Modern History* 29 (March 1957): 38–41; Leland V. Bell, *In Hitler's Shadow: The Anatomy of American Nazism* (Port Washington, N.Y.: Kennikat Press, 1973); and Bell, "The Failure of Nazism in America: The German American Bund, 1936–1941," *Political Science Quarterly* 85 (Dec. 1970): 585–99. On

German policy in America, see Alton Frye, *Nazi Germany and the American Hemisphere 1933–1941* (New Haven, Conn.: Yale Univ. Press, 1967).

53. On Spanknobel's activities see Diamond, 113–27.

54. Bell says 10,000 members in FONG in 1935 (Bell, 15); Diamond estimates 5000 to 6000 members (Diamond, 146).

55. On Dickstein's exaggeration of FONG's size and activities, see Diamond, 162, 169.

56. Special House Committee on Investigation of Nazi and Other Propaganda, 74th Cong., 1st sess., House Report 153(A) (Washington: Government Printing Office, 1935).

57. 60 percent drawn from Bell, 15.

58. See Bell, "The Failure of Nazism in America," 585–99, for a brief summary of the Bund's history.

59. Diamond, 301.

60. William Mueller, "Hitler Speaks, the Bund Obeys," *Look*, Oct. 10, 1939, p. 16.

61. Bell, 57–59.

62. Diamond, 324; Bell, 85–87.

63. Bell, 104.

64. On the collapse of the Bund, see Bell, *In Hitler's Shadow*, 93–106.

65. Excellent treatments of Pelley are available in Ribuffo, 25–79, and Smith, 53–65.

66. Justice Department interest in Pelley was spurred on by President Roosevelt, who expressed concern about Silver Shirt activities. See, for example, Franklin Roosevelt to Attorney General, April 21, 1939, OF3206 folder entitled Liberation in FDRL and Franklin Roosevelt to J. Edgar Hoover, Jan. 21, 1942, in PSF Justice Dept. file folder entitled J. Edgar Hoover 1941–1944, FDRL.

67. David M. Chalmers, *Hooded Americanism: The First Century of the Ku Klux Klan 1865–1965* (Garden City, N.Y.: Doubleday, 1965), 322–23.

68. Effinger quoted in Morris Janowitz, "Black Legions on the March," in *America in Crisis*, Daniel Aaron, ed. (New York: Alfred A. Knopf, 1952), 306.

69. For more information on Deatherage see O. John Rogge, *The Official German Report: Nazi Penetration 1924–1942, Pan-Arabism 1939–Today* (New York: Thomas Yoseloff, 1961), 195–202.

70. Material on Christians in J. Edgar Hoover to Stephen Early, Oct. 15, 1941, Memorandum Re: George Christians in OF Crusaders for Economic Liberty, FDRL.

71. Brief discussions of Sanctuary, True, and Edmondson's activities are available in Strong, 79–82, 124–31, and Rogge, 202–12.

72. Harold Lavine, "Fifth Column 'Literature.'" *Saturday Review of Literature*, Sept. 14, 1940, p. 3.

Chapter Three. The Opening Alarm: The Rumrich Spy Case

1. William Fulton, "Indict Hitler's U.S. Spy Ring," *Chicago Tribune*, June 21, 1938, p. 1.

2. "Nazi Spy Epidemic," *Newsweek*, June 13, 1938, p. 9.

3. Hanson Baldwin, "A Spy Thriller—in Real Life," *New York Times*, June 26, 1938, sec. IV, p. 7.

4. The ensuing discussion of the facts of the spy case is drawn from Ladislas Farago, *The Game of the Foxes: The Untold Story of German Espionage in the United States and Great Britain during World War II* (New York: David McKay, 1971); William Breuer, *Hitler's Undercover War: The Nazi's Espionage Invasion of the U.S.A.* (New York: St. Martin's Press, 1989); Leon Turrou, *Nazi Spies in America* (New York: Random House, 1938); "German Espionage Case in the United States," undated report in Robert Vansittart papers, Churchill College, Cambridge University; J. Edgar Hoover to Admiral Sidney Soeurs, Feb. 20, 1946, FBI report, "Espionage/World War II Summary," serial 332, v. 1, file #65–37193 available through FBI; and contemporary press accounts.

5. FBI report, "Espionage/World War II Summary," 11.

6. Farago, 19–35.

7. FBI report, "Espionage/World War II Summary," 44.

8. Turrou, 7.

9. See, for example, "Spy Business," *Time*, Nov. 14, 1938, p. 19, and Baldwin, "A Spy Thriller—in Real Life."

10. "German Espionage Case in the United States," p. 4.

11. On Germany's alleged plans for the passports, see FBI report, "Espionage/World War II summary," 28.

12. Ibid., 28, 42.

13. Ibid., 18.

14. "German Espionage Case in the United States," 1–2.

15. The FBI summary report claimed Rumrich pretended to be Hull. However, accounts by Turrou, Farago, and the contemporary press hold that the German spy only used the name of Edward Weston. FBI report, "Espionage/World War II Summary," 32; Turrou, 47; Farago, 63.

16. On Rumrich, see FBI report, "Espionage/World War II Summary," 33–34; Breuer 58–76; Farago, 61–76; and Turrou, 16–79.

17. "German Espionage Case in the United States," 4–5.

18. Turrou quoted in Breuer, 85.

19. Hardy quoted in Turrou, 264.

20. "Two Nazi Officials Indicted as U.S. Spy Ring Heads," *Washington Post*, June 21, 1938, p. 4.

21. "4 High-Ranking Nazis Names as Spy 'Brains,'" *Washington Post*, June 23 1938, p. 1; "Snoop, Look and Listen," *Time*, July 4, 1938, p. 9; P. E. Foxworth to J. Edgar Hoover, Nov. 21, 1938, File#67–6600–319 available from the FBI on request.

22. Advertisement, *New York Post*, June 22, 1938, pp. 12–13.

23. J. Edgar Hoover to the Assistant to the Attorney General Joseph B. Keenan, June 24, 1938, file #67–6600–211, FBI.

24. Leon Turrou confidentiality oath, signed Nov. 13, 1935, FBI file #67–6600–147.

25. "Snoop, Look and Listen."

26. Ibid.

27. "Turrou and Hoover Clash on Writings," *New York Post*, July 1, 1938, pp. 1, 22; "Hoover Jealous Turrou Declares," *New York Times*, July 1, 1938, p. 28.

28. Robert Horton, "Hoover's Income as G-Man Author Nears Six Figures," *New York World Telegram*, July 2, 1938, p. 3.

29. "4 High-Ranking Nazis Named as Spy 'Brains,' " 3.

30. Stern quoted in "Turrou's Spy Story Barred in Press," *New York Times*, June 23, 1938, p. 1.

31. J. David Stern to President Roosevelt, June 23, 1938, President's Personal File (hereafter PPF), J. David Stern 1933–39, at Franklin Delano Roosevelt Library, Hyde Park, New York (hereafter FDRL).

32. Roosevelt quoted in "President Urges Fund to Fight Spies," *New York Times*, June 25, 1938, p. 1.

33. Franklin Roosevelt to J. David Stern, June 24, 1938, PPF 1039, J. David Stern 1933–39, FDRL.

34. E. A. Tamm to Hoover, Oct. 12, 1938, FBI file #67–6600–294, pp. 2, 9, and E. A. Tamm to Hoover, Oct. 13, 1938, FBI file #67–6600–285.

35. E. A. Tamm memorandum for the file, Oct. 11, 1938, FBI file #67–6600–340, and E. A. Tamm memorandum for the file, March 1, 1939, FBI file #67–6600–360; J. Edgar Hoover to the Attorney General, March 8, 1939, FBI file #67–6600–367.

36. "Turrou Accused by Spy Witness," *New York Times*, Nov. 15, 1938, p. 7.

37. "Voss Says Agents Forced Spy Story," *New York Times*, Nov. 16, 1938, p. 10.

38. "Shooting Threat Told at Spy Trial," *New York Times*, Nov. 2, 1938, p. 16.

39. "Griebl Deposition Read at Spy Trial," *New York Times*, Nov. 10, 1938, p. 10.

40. In his instructions to the jury Judge Knox admitted that Rumrich was "an unmitigated liar," but he added that "a liar . . . can on occasion speak truth." Knox quoted in "Jury Convicts Two as Nazi Spies Here; Third Awaits Fate" *New York Times*, Nov. 30, 1938, p. 1. On coverage of Rumrich testimony, see "Rumrich Admits He Used Narcotics," *New York Times*, Nov. 18, 1939, p. 4.

41. "Griebl Described as an Informer," *New York Times*, Nov. 4, 1938, p. 9.

42. "Witness's Story Hits at Turrou," *New York Times*, Nov. 16, 1938, p. 10.

43. P. E. Foxworth to E. A. Tamm, Nov. 15, 1938, FBI file #67–6600–313.

44. Ibid.

45. Hoover marginal note on P. E. Foxworth to Hoover, Nov. 18, 1938, FBI file #67–6600–342.

46. P. E. Foxworth to E. A. Tamm, Nov. 23, 1938, FBI file #67–6600–320.

47. E. A. Tamm to J. E. Hoover, Oct. 12, 1938, FBI file #67–6600–294, p. 8.

48. Judge John Knox's comments, Dec. 2, 1938, from the stenographer's minutes, United States District Court, Southern District of New York, *United States of America v. Otto Voss et al.* in "Confessions of a Nazi Spy" file, box 2247, Warner Brothers Archives (hereafter WBA), University of Southern California, Los Angeles, p. 3.

49. Felix Belair, "Roosevelt Plans Nation-wide Drive on Foreign Spies," *New York Times*, Oct. 8, 1938, p. 1.

50. "Roosevelt Starts Big Drive on Spies," *New York Times*, Dec. 10, 1938, p. 1.

51. "Wages of Sin," *Time*, Dec. 12, 1938, p. 27, and "Suspect Found Guilty as Spy," *Los Angeles Times*, Dec. 1, 1938, p. 2.

52. Tom Tracy quoted in "Snoop, Look and Listen."

53. Grzesinski quoted in "Reich Spy System Seen as the Best," *New York Times*, June 22, 1938, p. 2.

54. Rintelen quoted in "Dark Invader," *New York Times*, Nov. 13, 1938, sec. IV, p. 2.

55. Turrou, 12, 297.

56. Harry Warner testimony in Propaganda in Motion Pictures, Hearings before a Subcommittee of Interstate Commerce, United States Senate, 1941–42, 77th Cong., lst sess., p. 344.

57. Roy J. Obringer to Jack Warner and Hal Wallis, undated, in "Confessions of a Nazi Spy" file, box 2247, WBA.

58. Jack Warner, *My First Hundred Years in Hollywood* (New York: Random House, 1964), 224.

59. John Davis, "Notes on Warner Brothers Foreign Policy, 1918–1948," *Velvet Light Trap* 17 (Winter 1978): 19–31.

60. Warner, 249.

61. Edward G. Robinson to Hal Wallis, Oct. 20, 1938, in "Confessions of a Nazi Spy" folder, Edward G. Robinson Collection, University of Southern California, Los Angeles.

62. Many cast members were part of Hollywood's émigré community, a fact which contributed to their anti-Nazi views. See Eric J. Sandeen, "Confessions of a Nazi Spy and the German-American Bund," *American Studies* 20 (Fall 1979): 73, and Clayton R. Koppes and Gregory D. Black, *Hollywood Goes to War: How Politics, Profits, and Propaganda Shaped World War II Movies* (New York: Free Press, 1987), 27.

63. Robert Taplinger to Hal Wallis, Feb. 28, 1939, in "Confessions of a Nazi Spy" file, box 2247, WBA.

64. Names were changed in order to avoid an invasion of privacy suit. Morris Ebenstein to Hal Wallis, Jan. 4, 1939, "Confessions of a Nazi Spy" file, box 2247, WBA.

65. R. J. Obringer wrote to Hal Wallis that "anyone who sees the picture and is at all familiar with the recent spy trial will recognize the situation and the circumstances." The *Washington Post* review of Warner's film observed that there was "no attempt to disguise any of the characters." R. J. Obringer to Hal Wallis, Feb. 28, 1939, "Confessions of a Nazi Spy" file, box 2247, WBA, and Nathan B. Bell, "Confessions of a Nazi Spy, Earle, Exposes Work of Espionage Ring," *Washington Post*, May 27, 1939, p. 6.

66. Final Script, "Confessions of a Nazi Spy," Jan. 27, 1939, in "Confessions of a Nazi Spy" file, box 2257, WBA, 54, 57–59, 146–47.

67. Ibid., 27–29.

68. Ibid., 27–29.

69. Ibid., 151–53.

70. J. E. Hoover to Clyde Tolson, April 20, 1939, FBI file #67–6600–387.

71. L. B. Nichols Memorandum for Mr. Tolson, June 13, 1939, FBI file #61–7560–7669.

72. R. J. Untreiner, Special Agent to the Director, July 19, 1939, FBI file #61–7560–1721.

73. J. D. Swenson Special Agent, Report Re German Activities in the United States, Oct. 10, 1939, FBI file #61–7560–3022.

74. Posters in Warner Brothers Press Book, and Arthur Cornelius, Jr., Special Agent, June 5, 1940, FBI file #61–7560–9590x1.

75. Hoover to Clyde Tolson, June 8, 1939, FBI file #62–15068–70x.

76. Typed addendum by Hoover on Memorandum from Clyde Tolson for the Director, Nov. 10, 1939, FBI file #80–7–7346x1.

77. Attorney General Frank Murphy to Will Hays, June 20, 1939, FBI file #80–7–1286x2.

78. "Statement of Purpose" enclosed in Will Hays to Attorney General Frank Murphy, Oct. 27, 1939, FBI file #80–7–1338.

79. L. B. Nichols Memorandum for Mr. Tolson, June 13, 1939, FBI file #61–7560–7669.

80. Warner, 262 (document available at Academy Library, Beverly Hills, CA).

81. Thomsen quoted in "Objects to Spy Film," *New York Times*, June 7, 1939, p. 26.

82. Consul General Wiedemann to State Secretary Weizsacker, July 9, 1939, in *Documents on German Foreign Policy 1918–1945*, series D 6 (London: Her Majesty's Stationary Office, 1956), 896.

83. "Tempestuous Career of 'Nazi Spy,' " *New York Times*, June 2, 1940, Section IX, p. 4. This document was kindly supplied to me by Mr. Tim Naftali, who came upon it while researching his study of OSS counterintelligence. Statement by General Major Lahousen in RG226/109/51, National Archives and Records Services, Washington, D.C.

84. Kate Cameron, "Spy Film at Strand Is Bold and Exciting," *New York Daily News*, April 29, 1939, p. 24; Mae Tinee, "Movie Exposes Work of Hitler Stooges in U.S." *Chicago Tribune*, May 28, 1939, sec. VII, p. 4; Edwin Schallert, "Vigorous Film Document of Nazi-ism in America Shown," *Los Angeles Times*, April 28, 1939, p. 12; and Frank Nugent, "The Warners Make Faces at Hitler in *Confessions of a Nazi Spy*," *New York Times*, April 29, 1939, p. 13.

85. "Confessions of a Nazi Spy," *Variety*, May 3, 1939, p. 16.

86. Jack Warner to Franklin Roosevelt, April 28, 1939, Official File 73, Motion Picture Industry, box 4, FDRL.

87. Harry Warner quoted in Propaganda in Motion Pictures, Hearings before a Subcommittee of the Committe on Interstate Congress, United States Senate, 1941–42, 77th Cong., 1st sess. pp. 344–345.

88. Russell Earl Shain, *An Analysis of Motion Pictures about War Released by the American Film Industry, 1939–1970* (New York: Arno Press, 1976), 61.

Chapter Four. Italy, the Soviet Union, and Japan

1. Material on Orson Welles's *War of the Worlds* broadcast was drawn from Hadley Cantril, *The Invasion from Mars: A Study in Psychological Panic* (Princeton, N.J.: Princeton Univ. Press, 1982), and Charles Jackson, "The Night the Martians Came," in *The Aspirin Age*, Isabel Leighton, ed. (New York: Simon

and Schuster, 1948), 431–43. CBS announcements in Cantril, 43; "tidal wave of terror" on 3; popular responses to the scare on 47 and 87–185.

2. Charlie McCarthy quote in Cantril, x; social scientist poll in Cantril, 209; Times, Telegram, and Broun quoted in Jackson, 441–42.

3. "Borers from Within," *New Orleans States*, April 16, 1940, in *What America Thinks* (Chicago: What America Thinks, 1941), 1009.

4. On the Italian Fifth Column see John Diggins, *Mussolini and Fascism: The View from America* (Princeton, N.J.: Princeton Univ. Press, 1972). Poll figures in Diggins, 325.

5. "The War of Nerves: Hitler's Helper," *Fortune*, Nov. 1940, pp. 85–87.

6. "Lay Off the Italians," *Colliers*, Aug. 3, 1940, p. 54.

7. Martin Dies, *The Trojan Horse in America* (New York: Arno Press, 1977), 336.

8. Roosevelt quoted in Francis Biddle, *In Brief Authority* (Garden City, N.Y.: Doubleday, 1962), 207.

9. Federal Bureau of Investigation, General Intelligence Survey, March 1942, report #2076, box 15, OF10B, Franklin Delano Roosevelt Library (hereafter FDRL), Hyde Park, New York.

10. Diggins, 400.

11. See Thomas R. Maddux, "Red Fascism, Brown Bolshevism: The American Image of Totalitarianism in the 1930s," *The Historian* 40 (Nov. 1977): 85–103, and Les K. Adler and Thomas G. Patterson, "Red Fascism: The Merger of Nazi Germany and Soviet Russia in the American Image of Totalitarianism, 1930's–1950's," *American Historical Review* 75 (April 1970): 1046–64.

12. Maddux, 85–92; Adler and Paterson, 1047–49.

13. Lyons quoted in Maddux, 97.

14. Roper Poll, in *Fortune Magazine*, July 1940, p. 54.

15. Maurice Isserman, *Which Side Were You On? The American Communist Party during the Second World War* (Middletown, Conn.: Wesleyan Univ. Press, 1982), 69–71.

16. Krivitsky's articles include "Stalin's Hand in Spain," *Saturday Evening Post*, April 15, 1939, pp. 5–7, 115–122; "Why Stalin Shot His Generals," ibid., April 22, 1939, 16–17, 71–74, 76–77; "Stalin Appeases Hitler," ibid., April 29, 1939, pp. 12–13, 84–89; "My Flight from Stalin," ibid., Aug. 5, 1939, pp. 7–8, 73–74, 76–80; "When Stalin Counterfeited Dollars," ibid., September 30, 1939, pp. 8–9, 80–84; and "Great Red Father," ibid., Nov. 4, 1939, pp. 12–13.

17. Walter Krivitsky, *In Stalin's Secret Service* (New York: Harper and Brothers, 1939), 72.

18. Frank Kluckhorn, "Reports Red Spies in Our Army, Navy," *New York Times*, Oct. 12, 1939, p. 1.

19. "General Krivitsky Found Dead: Suicide Finding Questioned," *New York Times*, Feb. 11, 1941, p. 1, and "Finding Is Delayed in Krivitsky Death," *New York Times*, Feb. 12, 1941, p. 22.

20. Jan Valtin, "Out of the Night," abridged version in *Reader's Digest*, March 1941, pp. 125–68, and "Out of the Night," abridged version in *Life*, Feb. 24, 1941, pp. 82–86, 88, 91–92, 95–99; March 3, 1941, pp. 94–98.

21. "Speaking of Crime," *Time*, Feb. 17, 1941, p. 20, and "The Year in Books," *Time*, Dec. 15, 1941, p. 108.

22. Valtin's revelations of his activities in America helped to land him in trouble with immigration authorities. The U.S. Board of Immigration announced in 1942 that Valtin would be returned to Germany after the war. The Immigration Board charged the ex-Communist with entering the country illegally after a prior arrest and deportation; he was also accused of perjury. In 1943, Valtin was released from Ellis Island and told to report to his draft board in New York. He was eventually sent to the Pacific, where he earned a bronze star for his service in the Philippines. "Valtin Arrested for Deportation," *New York Times*, Nov. 25, 1942, p. 1; "Jan Valtin Gets Order to Report to Camp Upton," *New York Times*, Aug. 12, 1943, p. 8; "Jan Valtin Is Cited," *New York Times*, July 17, 1945, p. 11.

23. "Valtin Says Nazis Plot U.S. Civil War," *New York Times*, May 27, 1941, p. 11; "Valtin Says Reds Try to Cut War Aid," *New York Times*, May 28, 1941, p. 15.

24. There are many excellent works on the Dies committee's anti-Communist activities, see, for example, Aug. Ogden, *The Dies Committee* (Washington, D.C.: Catholic Univ. Press, 1945); Walter Goodman, *The Committee: The Extraordinary Career of the House Un–American Activites Committee* (New York.: Farrar, Straus and Giroux), 24–166; Kenneth O'Reilly, *Hoover and the Un-Americans: The FBI, HUAC and the Red Menace* (Philadephia: Temple Univ. Press, 1983).

25. See Goodman: on 2,850 Communists, p. 75; on Perkins, pp. 47–48; on WPA writers, p. 44.

26. Anti-Communist congressional legislation is discussed in Issermen, 68–69.

27. Attorney General Robert Jackson to FDR, April 29, 1941, folder "AG Wiretapping Controversy," box 94, in the Papers of Robert Jackson, Library of Congress, Washington, D.C.

28. John McCloy to Robert Jackson, May 19, 1941, in folder "AG Wiretappi g Controversy," box 94, in the Papers of Robert Jackson.

29. Henry Stimson and Frank Knox to Franklin Roosevelt, May 29, 1941, box 10, OF10B, FDRL.

30. Franklin Roosevelt to Henry Stimson and Frank Knox, June 4, 1941, box 10, OF10B, FDRL.

31. Isserman, 96–100

32. Stanley High, "We Are Already Invaded," *Reader's Digest*, July 1941, p. 122.

33. Browder quoted in "Radicals," *Time*, June 10, 1940, p. 21.

34. Max Eastman, "Stalin's American Power," *Reader's Digest*, Dec. 1941, p. 39.

35. The internment of the Japanese which resulted from fears of a Tokyo–directed Fifth Column has received considerable scholarly attention. In particular, I have used *Personal Justice Denied, Report of the Commission on Wartime Relocation and Internment of Civilians* (hereafter CWRIC) (Washington, D.C.: Government Printing Office, 1982); Peter Irons, *Justice at War* (New York: Oxford Univ. Press, 1983); Morton Grodzins, *Americans Betrayed: Politics and the*

Japanese Evacuation (Chicago: Univ. of Chicago Press, 1949); and Jacobus tenBroek et al., *Prejudice, War and the Constitution* (Los Angeles: Univ. of California Press, 1968).

36. Hallett Abend, " 'So Sorry for You': Japanese Espionage Used to Be Funny—But No More," *Reader's Digest*, March 4, 1939, p. 7.

37. FBI report, "Espionage/World War II Summary," 91.

38. Jeffrey Dorwart, *Conflict of Duty: The U.S. Navy's Intelligence Dilemma, 1919–1945* (Annapolis, Md.: Naval Institute Press, 1983), 67.

39. "Spy Scare," *Literary Digest*, July 25, 1936, p. 5.

40. "Spies: Two Arrests and Biggest Postwar Scare Resurrect the Bogey of International Complications," *Newsweek*, July 25, 1936, p. 11.

41. On the Tachibana case see FBI report, "Espionage/World War II Summary," 141–45; "Secret Agent," *Time*, June 23, 1941, p. 17; and "Japan Navy Officer Held in Spy Plot," *Los Angeles Times*, p. 1; Bob Kumamoto, "The Search for Spies: American Counterintelligence and the Japanese American Community 1931–1942," *Amerasia Journal* no. 6 (Fall 1979): 55–56; Ken Ringle, Jr., "What Did You Do Before the War, Dad?," *Washington Post Magazine*, Dec. 6, 1981, pp. 54–62.

42. CWRIC, 54.

43. tenBroek et al., 101.

44. Kumamoto, "The Search for Spies," 58–67.

45. John Franklin Carter to Franklin Roosevelt, Oct. 22, 1941, cover note to C. B. Munson, memorandum concerning Japanese situation on the West Coast, PSF, John Franklin Carter, box 122, FDRL.

46. C.B. Munson to Grace Tully, undated, PSF, John Franklin Carter, box 122, FDRL.

47. On these rumors see CWRIC, 65.

48. Frank Knox quoted in tenBroek et al., 70. For various newspaper headlines see ibid.

49. Summary cabinet meeting, Dec. 19, 1941, box 1, Francis Biddle Papers, FDRL, 20.

50. Hoover quoted in Irons, 27.

51. Dept. of Justice quoted in CWRIC, 88.

52. Memorandum, "Luncheon Conference with the President," Feb. 7, 1942, in folder entitled Franklin Roosevelt, box 2, Francis Biddle Papers, FDRL.

53. On February 3, 1942, Hoover wrote the Attorney General that the "necessity for mass evacuation is based primarily upon public and political pressure rather than on factual data." Hoover quoted in CWRIC, 73.

54. "News and Views by John B. Hughes," Jan. 5, 1942, transcript of nationally broadcast report on Mutual Broadcasting Network in microfilm documents of the CWRIC, reel 8, box 8, frames 8707–17.

55. Walter Lippmann, "The Fifth Column on the Coast," *Washington Post*, Feb. 12, 1942, in documents of CWRIC, reel 2, box 2, frame 1401.

56. Pegler and McClemore quoted in tenBroek et al., 85–86, 75.

57. See Grodzins, 380–84.

58. Ford quoted in CWRIC, 84.

59. Dies, Rankin, Stewart: see tenBroek et al. 86–88.

60. On the attitude of West Coast politicians, see Grodzins, 92–148.

61. On various organizations pressuring for internment, see ibid., 19–61.
62. Irons, 64–68.
63. Internment figures in Irons, 73.
64. This discussion of the end of exclusion is based on material in CWRIC, 213–43.
65. Mark Gayn, "Prelude to Treachery," *Reader's Digest*, April 1942, p. 11.
66. Grodzins, 60.

Chapter Five. Great Britain and the Fifth Column

1. Winston Churchill, *The Second World War*, 6 vols. (Boston: Houghton Mifflin, 1950), 3 (1950): 606, 608.
2. David Reynolds, *The Creation of the Anglo-American Alliance 1937–41: A Study in Competitive Cooperation* (London: Europa, 1981), 78–80, 286–89. See also David Reynolds, "Lord Lothian and Anglo-American Relations, 1939–40," in *Transactions of the American Philosophical Society* 73, pt. 2 (1983): 9–14.
3. Lord Lothian to Viscount Halifax, sent Sept. 28, 1939, Foreign Office (hereafter FO) 371 22389, file 7052, document 7053, reel 22.
4. For example, Lothian accepted a proposal to create a new British service in New York City which supplied "hot" news to American press and radio commentators. Nonetheless, he continued to maintain FO supervision of Ministry of Information work in the U.S.. British Publicity in the United States Proposals for Reorganization and Development, July 1940, FO 371 A4025/26/45, reel 5, pp. 179–95.
5. Lord Lothian to Foreign Office, June 8, 1940, FO 371, A3197/26/45, reel 4, pp. 264–65.
6. Martin Gilbert, *Winston S. Churchill*, 8 vols. (London: Heinemenn, 1976), 5: 849
7. Emery Reves, "British Political Action in America," Prem 4/25/7, p. 389, Public Record Office (hereafter PRO). Kew, England.
8. Duff Cooper to Winston Churchill, July 12, 1940, Prem 4/25/7, p. 381, PRO.
9. Frank Pick, Director General Ministry of Information, "Propaganda in Latin America," Aug. 20, 1940, Prem 4/25/7, p. 365, PRO.
10. Churchill to Minister of Information Duff Cooper, Aug. 25, 1940, Prem 4/25/7, p. 360, PRO.
11. Emery Reves to Winston Churchill, Dec. 20, 1940, Prem 4/25/7, p. 357, PRO.
12. For more details on Stephenson's life, see H. Montgomery Hyde, *Room 3603: The Story of British Intelligence in New York during World War II* (New York: Farrar, Straus, 1962) and Anthony Cave Brown, *"C": The Secret Life of Sir Stewart Graham Menzies, Spymaster to Winston Churchill* (New York: Macmillan, 1987), 195.
13. Hyde, 3.
14. Ibid., 73–74, 88–90.

15. The British were thus using the American press in the pre-WWII period in much the same way as they had in the years 1914–17. American Assistant Secretary of State Adolf Berle noted in a memorandum to Undersecretary of State Sumner Welles that he believed that the British "use the *New York Herald Tribune* as the means of publication, much the same as they used the *Providence Journal* in the world war." Berle to Welles, Sept. 27, 1941, in Berle Diary, 8 reels (Washington, D.C., National Archives and Records Service, 1978), reel 3, p. 0421.

16. For all material quoted on Morrell, see Earl Morrell, New York, S.O. 1 Organisation, July 10, 1941, FO 898 Political Warfare Executive, file 103, PRO. For a discussion of the efforts of the Friends of Democracy organization to depict America First as a front for a Nazi Fifth Column, see Wayne Cole, *America First: The Battle Against Intervention, 1940–41* (Madison: Univ. of Wisconsin Press, 1953), 109–12.

17. The British hired Donald Downes, an American citizen, to gather dirt on isolationist groups and to monitor several German consulates. See Robin Winks, *Cloak and Gown: Scholars in America's Secret War* (London: Collins Harvill, 1987), 166–69.

18. For a detailed account of two attempts by BSC to pass on disinformation regarding Latin America to the White House, see Francis MacDonnell, "The Search for a Second Zimmermann Telegram: Franklin Roosevelt, British Security Coordination, and the Latin-American Front," *International Journal of Intelligence and Counterintelligence* (Winter 1990): 487–505, and John F. Bratzel and Leslie B. Rout, "FDR and the 'Secret Map,'" *Wilson Quarterly 9* (New Year's, 1985): 167–73.

19. H. Montgomery Hyde, *Secret Intelligence Agent* (London: Constable, 1982), 153–59.

20. Memorandum, Assistant Secretary of State Adolf Berle, July 7, 1941, RG 59, 824.00, Revolutions, NARS.

21. Memorandum of conversation between Mr. Spruille Braden and A. A. Berle, Jr., May 7, 1942, in Berle Diary, reel 4, p. 0150.

22. Memorandum to Secretary of State, Sept. 5, 1941, in Berle Diary, reel 3, p. 0308.

23. In the same speech FDR also warned the public that the U.S. government had acquired a document which showed the Nazis "plan to abolish all existing religion—Catholic, Protestant, Mohammedan, Hindu, Buddhist, and Jewish alike." Franklin Delano Roosevelt, "Navy and Total Defense Day Address," Oct. 27, 1941, in *The Public Papers of Franklin D. Roosevelt*, Samuel I. Rosenman, ed., 13 vols. (New York: Harper and Row, 1950), 10: 439–40.

24. FDR Press Conference #779, Oct. 28, 1941 in *Complete Presidential Press Conferences of Franklin D. Roosevelt*, 25 vols. (New York: Da Capo Press, 1972), 18: 264.

25. Anthony Cave Brown notes other incidents of the British apparently "crying wolf" over the problem of Nazi penetration in Latin America. For example, in May of 1940 Stephenson spread rumors that J. Edgar Hoover believed that the Axis was working to create an army of fascist Spaniards in Mexico. Hoover found out about this and denied having ever said such a thing. Another case of dubious British intelligence passed on to the Americans involved the

alleged sighting of a German raider off the Dutch Guiana coast. Berle was suspicious of the British report, which may in fact have simply been a device to encourage occupation of the area by Allied troops. For more on both of these cases see Anthony Cave Brown's biography of Sir Stewart Menzies. In addition to documentary evidence Brown's book draws valuable information from an interview with Stephenson. Brown, pp. 264–65, 367.

26. Assistant Secretary of State Berle to Undersecretary of State Sumner Welles, March 31, 1941, RG59 841.20211/23, NARS.

27. Ibid.

28. The best discussion of Berle's life is to be found in Jordan Schwarz, *Liberal: Adolf A. Berle and the Vision of an American Era* (New York: Macmillan, 1987).

29. "I believe that this should be taken up with the President before action is taken. With his authority, however, I think we should indicate to the British Embassy that we should be glad to see these activities at once curtailed to the actual and necessary operations of protecting British ships and British munitions; that even these activities should be undertaken only in conjunction with and after previous authorization by the FBI (unless the President directs some other method of authentication).

"I have in mind, of course, that should anything go wrong at any time the State Department would probably be called upon to explain why it permitted violation of American laws and was complaisant about an obvious breach of diplomatic obligation. Were this to occur, and a Senate investigation should follow, we should be on very dubious ground if we have not taken appropriate steps." Assistant Secretary of State A. A. Berle to Undersecretary of State Sumner Welles, March 31, 1941, RG59 841.20211/23, NARS.

30. Baron Stackleberg, Foreign Manager to *Financial News* in London to Foreign Office, Sept. 11, 1940 FO371 A5091/5091/45, microfilm reel 23, p. 348.

31. Diary entry for Oct. 15, 1940, in Berle Diary, reel 2, p. 0966.

32. Berle memorandum to FDR regarding registration of foreign agents, Feb. 5, 1942, in Berle Diary, reel 3, p. 1119.

33. Assistant Secretary of State A. A. Berle to Undersecretary of State Sumner Welles, March 31, 1941, RG59 841.20211/23, NARS.

34. Diary entry, March 4, 1940, Berle Diary, reel 2, p. 0393.

35. Victor Perowne, marginal comments on letter from Baron Stackleberg, Foreign Manager to Financial News in London, to Foreign Office, Sept. 11, 1940, FO371 A5091/5091/45, reel 23, p. 368.

36. Memorandum of conversation, Attorney General Biddle, British Ambassador Halifax, British Minister Sir R. Campbell, FBI Director Hoover, and Mr. A. A. Berle, Jr., March 5, 1942, in Berle Diary, reel 3, pp. 1227–29, and memorandum of conversation, Lord Halifax, Sir Ronald Campbell, Attorney General Biddle, and Mr. A. A. Berle, Jr., March 10, 1942, in ibid., 1239–46.

37. Report of the Joint Intelligence Committee, May 2, 1940, and Chiefs of Staff meeting, May 4, 1940, quoted in Peter and Leni Gillman, *"Collar the Lot!": How Britain Interned Its Wartime Refugees* (London: Quartet Books, 1980), 85, 88.

38. For an excellent discussion of British internment policy, see Gillman and Gillman, *"Collar the Lot!."* Statistics on internment in John M. Blum, *V*

Was for Victory: Politics and American Culture during World War II (New York: Harcourt, Brace Jovanovich, 1976), p. 170.

39. Lothian to Foreign Office, July 18, 1940, FO371 3542/90/45, reel 8, p. 205.

40. William Donovan and Edgar Ansel Mowrer, "Germans Said to Spend Vast Sums Abroad to Pave Way for Conquest," *New York Times*, Aug. 23, 1940, p. 5.

41. Frank Knox, foreword to article entitled "U.S. Survey of Hitler's Conquests Reveals '5th Column' Spearhead," *New York Times*, Aug. 20, 1940, p. 6.

42. The British ambassador, however, did not believe that these articles "caused any stir." Lothian also rejected Knox's prefatory claim "that they contain the results of Messrs. Donovan and Mowrer's 'careful study, made with every source available.' " Lothian to Halifax, Aug. 26, 1940, FO371 A4153/90/45, reel 8, p. 221.

43. Joseph Kennedy to Secretary of State Cordell Hull, Aug. 1, 1940, RG59 841.00 N/10, NARS.

44. Janet Adam Smith, *A Biography of John Buchan* (Boston: Little, Brown, 1965), see esp. 193–217.

45. John Buchan, *Mr. Standfast*, in *The Four Adventures of Richard Hanney* (Boston: David R. Godine, 1988), 361.

46. Hitchcock deleted much of the content of Buchan's spy story and emphasized the action/adventure components of the tale. Nonetheless, the director did focus on the ability of Professor Jordan, the anti-British agent in the film, to dupe his neighbors into believing that he was a respectable citizen.

47. Sam P. Simone, *Hitchcock as Activist: Politics and the War Films* (Ann Arbor: Univ. of Michigan Press, 1982), 27.

48. François Truffaut, *Hitchcock* (New York: Simon and Schuster, 1984), 146.

49. *Saboteur*, 1942 Permission to quote from Universal Studios. (Transcription of exchanges is available in Simone.)

50. Both of these men also make interesting case studies because of their direct links to British governmental propaganda agencies (Hitchcock directed two short films for the British Ministry of Information during the war). Donald Spoto, *The Life of Alfred Hitchcock: The Dark Side of Genius* (London: Collins, 1983), 270–71.

Chapter Six. The Fifth Column in Europe

1. Newspaper clipping, "Anderson, S.C. Enacts Its Fall to Fifth Column," *New York Herald Tribune*, July 12, 1941, p. 1; Mrs. T. Nellis to Franklin Roosevelt, White House folder 1941, box 5, Lowell Mellett papers, FDRL.

2. Information on Nazi Fifth Column operations has been drawn from Donald McKale, *The Swastika Outside Germany* (Kent, Ohio: Kent State Univ. Press, 1977); Alton Frye, *Nazi Germany and the Western Hemisphere 1933–1941* (New Haven, Conn.: Yale Univ. Press, 1967); Arthur Smith, Jr., *The Deutschtum of Nazi Germany and the United States* (The Hague: Martinus Ni-

jhoff, 1965); David Kahn, *Hitler's Spies: German Military Intelligence in World War II* (New York: Macmillan, 1978); Michael Geyer, "National Socialist Germany: The Politics of Information," in Ernest May, ed., *Knowing One's Enemies: Intelligence Assessment Before the Two World Wars* (Princeton, N.J.: Princeton Univ. Press, 1986); and MacAlister Brown, "The Third Reich's Mobilization of the German Fifth Columns in Eastern Europe," *Journal of Central European Affairs* 19 (July 1959): 128–48.

3. Frye, 20–31.

4. Kahn, 54–56, 69.

5. Ibid., 47, 56–63; Geyer, 317–21.

6. On the VDA and DAI, see Frye, 16–18, and Smith, 1–25.

7. My discussion of the Anschluss has drawn from the work of Bruce F. Pauley, *Hitler and the Forgotten Nazis: A History of Austrian National Socialism* (Chapel Hill: Univ. of North Carolina Press, 1981), 197–215; Alfred D. Low, *The Anschluss Movement, 1931–1938, and the Great Powers* (New York: Columbia Univ. Press, 1985), 399–406.

8. Low, xii–xiii.

9. Pauley, xiv.

10. Ronald Smelser, *The Sudetan Problem 1933–1938: Volkstumspolitik and the Formulation of Nazi Foreign Policy* (Middletown, Conn.: Wesleyan Univ. Press, 1975), 210–42;, Telford Taylor, *Munich: The Price of Peace* (Garden City, N.Y.: Doubleday, 1979), 745, 800–801.

11. On Hitler's "divide and conquer" tactics in the rump Czech state, see Donald Cameron Watt, *How War Came: The Immediate Origins of the Second World War, 1938–1939* (New York: Pantheon, 1989), 145–56.

12. Material on Poland is principally drawn from Louis De Jong, *The German Fifth Column in the Second World War*, C. M. Geyl, trans. (Chicago: Univ. of Chicago Press, 1956), 39–53, 147–57.

13. Saul Padover, "Unser Amerika" condensed from the *Forum* in *Reader's Digest*, (Jan. 1939), p. 3.

14. Stowe quoted in De Jong, 63.

15. On Norway, see ibid., 58–64, 167–81.

16. "Tale of Two Brothers," *Time*, April 22, 1940, p. 23.

17. "Norway Betrayed," *Indianapolis Times*, April 16, 1940, in *What America Thinks* (Chicago: What America Thinks, 1941), 1007.

18. "Norway's Betrayal," *St. Louis Post-Dispatch*, April 16, 1940, in *What America Thinks*, 1011.

19. "More 'Trojan Horses'? It Could Happen Here: Military Authorities See Some Parallels in America to Tactics Used for Nazi Invasion of Norway," *U.S. News and World Report*, April 26, 1940, p. 12.

20. Paul Hayes, *Quisling: The Career and Political Ideas of Vidkun Quisling, 1887–1945* (London: David and Charles, 1971), 165–209.

21. Telford Taylor, *The March of Conquest: The German Victories in Western Europe, 1940* (New York: Simon and Schuster, 1958) 82–84, 90.

22. Taylor, 187–205.

23. De Jong, 66–77.

24. Ibid., 78–94.

25. "They Were Impregnable," *Buffalo Courier & Express*, May 31, 1940, in *What America Thinks*, 1209.

26. "Nazi Netherlands," *Newsweek*, May 27, 1940, p. 22.

27. "Treachery," *Flint Journal*, June 25, 1940, in *What America Thinks*, 1355.

28. "Significance," *Newsweek*, May 20, 1940, p. 22.

29. "Let's Be Logical," *Atlanta Constitution*, June 15, 1940, p. 6. A similar editorial is "The Enemy Behind," *New York Herald*, June 19, 1940, p. 24.

30. M. W. Fodor, "The Blitzkrieg in the Low Countries," *Foreign Affairs*, 19 (Oct. 1940): 205.

31. Tolischus quoted in Otto Tolischus, *They Wanted War* (New York: Reynal and Hitchcock, 1940), 61, and Otto Tolischus, "How Hitler Made Ready: The Fifth Column," in *New York Times Magazine*, June 16, 1940, pp. 3–4, 17.

32. Some of Rauschning's works included: Herman von Rauschning, "Hitler Could Not Stop," *Foreign Affairs*, 18 (Oct. 1939): 1–12; *The Revolution of Nihilism: Warning to the West* (New York: Alliance Book Corp., 1939) (this book was synopsized in the November 1939 issue of *Reader's Digest*); *The Voice of Destruction* (New York: G. P. Putnam's Sons, 1940); and *The Redemption of Democracy: The Coming Atlantic Empire* (New York: Literary Guild of America, 1941).

33. Hitler quoted in Rauschning, *The Voice of Destruction*, 4, 8, 10; Goebbels quoted on 71.

34. Albert Grzesinski, a less prominent defector than Rauschning, also denounced Hitler's Fifth Column. Grzesinski was a former chief of the Prussian police. In the December 1940 issue of *Reader's Digest* he claimed that Nazi Trojan Horse activity in the U.S. would entail "confusing broadcasts, destruction of factories and disruption of railroads, stalling of battleships and breakdown of army equipment." Albert Grzesinski, "Hitler's Branch Offices, U.S.A.," *Reader's Digest*, Dec. 1940, p. 32.

35. Leland Stowe, *No Other Road to Freedom* (New York: Alfred A. Knopf, 1941), 362, 374.

36. Edmond Taylor, "Yes, We Have Fifth Columnists," *Reader's Digest*, Oct. 1940, p. 41.

37. William Bullitt to Cordell Hull, May 17, 1940, 740.0011/3 115(7/8) RG 59, NARS.

38. Diary entry, Aug. 1, 1940, in Henry Stimson Diaries, reel 6, frame 53.

39. William Bullitt, "America Is in Danger," speech delivered to the American Philosophical Society in Philadelphia, Aug. 18, 1940, in *Vital Speeches of the Day*, Sept. 1, 1940, p. 684.

40. A. G. Kirk to ONI Chief Walter Anderson, May 14, 1940, box 2, personal papers of A. G. Kirk, p. 69, Naval Operational Archives Branch, Washington, D.C.

41. Kirk to Anderson, June 11, 1940, box 2, p. 78, Naval Operational Archives Branch, Washington, D.C.

42. Brigadier General Sherman Miles to Chief of Staff George Marshall, Feb. 1, 1941, box 1644, 2657–C–314, RG 165, NARS.

43. FDR and his cabinet's response to events in Europe will be discussed more fully in a subsequent chapter.

44. "Asserts Lindbergh Aids 'Fifth Column,'" *New York Times*, May 23, 1940, p. 1.

45. Roper poll, in *Fortune*, July 1940, p. 54.

46. "Fifth Columns," *Newsweek*, May 27, 1940, p. 36.

47. "Erie County American Legion Along New York Frontier," *New York Times*, June 5, 1940, p. 15.

48. "Fifth Columns," p. 35.

49. "Navajos Vote Defense Aid," *New York Times*, June 6, 1940, p. 14.

50. "We Want No 5th Column," *Chicago Tribune*, June 16, 1940, p. 20.

51. "The War of Nerves: U.S. Front," *Fortune Magazine*, Oct. 1940, p. 47.

52. "National News," *Time*, June 3, 1940, p. 13.

53. News reports claimed that the Hobo convention drew 1,000,000 delegates. "People," *Time*, June 10, 1940, p. 70. Also see "King Jeff's Court," *Newsweek*, May 27, 1940, p. 37.

54. "Grange Demands Curb on Imports," Nov. 22, 1940, *New York Times*, p. 25; "Defense Program Backed by Porters," *New York Times*, Sept. 19, 1940; Anne Peterson, "Women Urged to Be Guardians," *New York Times*, Oct. 6, 1940, sec. II, p. 4; Henry Krueger (Lions International) to Jennings Randolph, June 10, 1940, 76th Cong., 3rd sess., *Appendix to the Congressional Record*, 86:16: 3810–11.

55. "Dark Doings," *Time*, July 15, 1940, pp. 46–47. Former Attorney General Homer Cummings discussed the possibility of working on an anti-Fifth Column radio show to be produced by Phillips H. Lord, Inc. Homer Cummings to Stephen Early, Aug. 7 and 20, 1940, and Stephen Early to Homer Cummings, Aug. 13, 1940, all in OF136, box 3, FDRL.

56. Hitler quoted in "Mississippi Frontier," *Time*, June 24, 1940, p. 38.

Chapter Seven. Keeping the Panic Alive: German Propaganda, Espionage, and Sabotage in the United States

1. See, for example, "Nazi Propaganda in America: Hitler has a Pre-tested Plan for the Conquest of America. Will It Work?," *Look*, Dec. 31, 1940, pp. 12–15.

2. *Report on the Axis Front Movement in the United States*, 78th Cong., 1st sess., Appendix Part VII (Washington, D.C.: Government Printing Office, 1943), 13.

3. Statistics on *Facts in Review* drawn from Niel Johnson, *George Sylvester Viereck* (Urbana: Univ. of Illinois Press, 1972), 215.

4. *Report on the Axis Front Movement*, 14–18.

5. The principle congressional investigation of these groups is in *A Preliminary Digest and Report on the Un-American Activities of Various Nazi Organizations and Individuals in the United States, Including Diplomatic and Consular Agents of the German Government*, 76th Cong., 3rd sess., Appendix Part II (Washington, D.C.: Government Printing Office, 1940).

6. Ibid., 18–21, 26–30.

7. An excellent scholarly account of Viereck's pro-German activities during the thirties and forties is available in Johnson, 171–250.

8. O. John Rogge, *The Official German Report, Nazi Penetration 1924–1942, Pan Arabism 1939–Today* (New York: Thomas Yoseloff, 1961), 160–64.

9. "Viereck Indicted and Seized Here as German Agent," *New York Times*, Oct. 9, 1941, pp. 1, 4; "Viereck Held Accused of Using Frank," *Wash-*

ington Post, Oct. 9, 1941, pp. 1, 6; "Viereck Held Guilty, Faces Two to Six Years in Jail," *Washington Post*, Oct. 11, 1941, pp. 1, 4.

10. For scathing indictments of Germany's espionage activities in the United States, see Thomas Etzold, "The (F)utility Factor: German Information Gathering in the United States, 1933–1941," *Military Affairs* 39 (April 1975): 77–82, and Hans Trefousse, "Failure of German Intelligence in the United States, 1935–1945," *Mississippi Valley Historical Review* 42 (June 1955): 84–100.

11. Etzold, 79.

12. Ladislas Farago, *The Game of the Foxes: The Untold Story of German Espionage in the United States and Great Britain during World War II* (New York: David McKay, 1971), 371–75.

13. FBI report, "Espionage/World War II Summary," Serial 332, v. 1, file #65-3713, pp. 236–37; Farago, 540.

14. Names of contacts are cited in Farago; names are classified in FBI report.

15. Farago, 541–43.

16. FBI report, "Espionage/World War II Summary," 348.

17. On hotel search see Farago, 452.

18. Ludwig's orders quoted in Farago, 497.

19. On Ludwig's intelligence-gathering see FBI report, "Espionage/World War II Summary," 373–76.

20. "Death Toll Is 42 in Powder Blast," *New York Times*, Sept. 14, 1940, p. 1; "Another Black Tom?" *New York Times*, Sept. 15, 1940, sec. V, p. 5.

21. Dies quoted in "Dies Sees More Blasts," *New York TImes*, Nov. 13, 1940, p. 4.

22. Thomas quoted in "3 Powder Plants Blow Up in East," *New York Times*, Nov. 13, 1940, p. 3.

23. Jackson quoted in Conference Propaganda Committee, Nov. 28, 1940, box 247, Harold Ickes Papers, Library of Congress, pp. 13–14.

24. J. Edgar Hoover to Lowell Mellett, FBI Report Re Wythe Williams, Dec. 5, 1940, in FBI folder, box 3, Lowell Mellett Papers, FDRL.

25. These rumors are noted in "Report of the Committee on Naval Affairs on the Capsizing of the U.S.S. 'Lafayette,' Formerly the T.E.L. Normandie," House of Representatives, 77th Cong., 2nd sess., p. 21.

26. John Franklin Carter Report on Public Opinion in New York Re "Normandie" Fire, Feb. 11, 1942, in box 122, PSF, John Franklin Carter, FDRL.

27. J. Edgar Hoover to Watson, Feb. 26, 1942, report 1185, box 15, OF10B, FDRL.

28. See "Investigation of the Fire and Capsizing of the U.S.S. Lafayette (Normadie), May 27, 1942, 77th Cong., 2nd sess., "Report of the Committee on Naval Affairs on the Capsizing of the U.S.S. 'Lafayette,' Formerly the T.E.L. Normandie."

29. Two recent monographs on the submarine battle off the U.S. coast include Michael Gannon, *Operation Drumbeat: The Dramatic Story of Germany's First U-Boat Attacks Along the American Coast in World War II* (New York: Harper and Row, 1990), and Homer Hickam, *Torpedo Junction: U-Boat War Off America's East Coast, 1942* (Annapolis, Md.: Naval Institute Press, 1989).

30. The literature on Operation Pastorius is extensive. The FBI has made available many of its files on the saboteurs, as well as a 261-page case summary

in George John Dasch (file "Eight Nazi Saboteurs"), FBI Reading Room, J. Edgar Hoover Building, Washington D.C. A book-length account of the affair is offered by Eugene Rachlis, *They Came to Kill* (New York: Random House, 1961). Two articles on the case are W. A. Swanberg, "The Spies Who Came in from the Sea," *American Heritage* 21 (April 1970): 66–69, 87–91, and Leon Prior, "The Nazi Invasion of Florida!," *Florida Historical Quarterly* 49 (Oct. 1970): 129–39.

31. Seven of the eight saboteurs were involved with the German-American Bund before the war.

32. J. Edgar Hoover to McIntyre, June 22, 1942, report 2192, box 16, OF10B, FDRL.

33. Statement by J. Edgar Hoover, July 2, 1942, in FBI files, George John Dasch file #98–10288–487 in FBI reading room.

34. Franklin Roosevelt to Attorney General Francis Biddle, June 30, 1942, Justice Department 1938–44, PSF 76, FDRL.

35. This operation is discussed in David Kahn, *Hitler's Spies: German Military Intelligence in World War II* (New York: Macmillan, 1978), 3–26.

36. The first issue of Captain America is available in Jules Feiffer, *The Great Comic Book Heroes* (New York: Dial Press, 1965). Quote is on 167.

37. "Superman," *Washington Post*, March 10, 1942, p. 28.

38. See "Little Orphan Annie" strips running from April to July, 1940, in the *Atlanta Constitution* for story on Fifth Column kidnapping.

39. See Harold Lavine and James Wechsler, *War Propaganda and the United States* (New Haven, Conn: Yale Univ. Press, 1940), 277.

40. Von Reichenstein quoted in Emile Tepperman, "The Suicide Squad's Private War," *Ace G-Man Stories*, Dec. 1941, pp. 37–38, in Pulp Fiction Collection, Library of Congress, Washington, D.C. Hoover speech, "Turn on the Heat," in *Ace G-Man Stories*, April 1940, p. 4, Pulp Fiction Collection.

41. Peter Paige, ". . . And God Won't Tell," *Black Mask*, July 1940, pp. 49–67, and C. P. Donnel, Jr., "Conspiracy in Sunlight," *Black Mask*, March 1943, in Rare Book Room, Library of Congress.

42. Charles Strong, "Blitzkrieg in 1520," *Thrilling Adventures*, Sept., 1940, p. 80; Pegleg quoted in Clay Perry, "Patterns in Pine," *Thrilling Adventures*, Feb. 1941, p. 47; Henry Lewis, "Death Ray," *Startling Stories*, Nov. 1942, pp. 114–16; and Norman A. Daniels, "Speak of the Devil," *Startling Stories*, March 1943, pp. 15, all in Pulp Fiction Collection.

43. Larry Langman and David Ebner, eds., *Encyclopedia of American Spy Films* (New York: Garland, 1990), xii.

Chapter Eight. Franklin Roosevelt and the Fifth Column

1. For FDR's reactions to the Rumrich trial, see FDR Press Conference #469, June 24, 1938, in *Complete Presidential Press Conferences of Franklin D. Roosevelt*, 25 vols. (New York: Da Capo Press, 1972), 11; 488–89; press conference #489, Oct. 7, 1938, in ibid., vol. 12: 151; and press conference #507, Dec. 9, 1938, in ibid., 12: 288–90.

2. Statement of the President, Sept. 6, 1939, in "The Development of FBI Domestic Investigations," Senate Select Committee, *Final Report*, book III, 94th Cong., 2nd sess., report no. 94–755, serial 13133–5, p. 404.

3. Press conference #577, Sept. 8, 1939, in *Press Conferences of FDR*, 14: 55.

4. Franklin Roosevelt, Message to Congress Asking Additional Appropriations for National Defense, May 16, 1940, in *The Public Papers of Franklin D. Roosevelt*, Samuel I. Rosenman, ed., 13 vols. (New York: Harper and Row, 1950), 9: 198.

5. Press Conference #646, May 24, 1940, in *Press Conferences of FDR*, 15: 380–81.

6. Franklin Roosevelt, Fireside Chat on National Defense, May 26, 1940, in *Public Papers of FDR*, 9: 238.

7. Press conference #647A, May 30, 1940, in *Press Conferences of FDR*, 15: 420–21.

8. Press conference #649A, June 5, 1940, in ibid., 15: 482–83.

9. Franklin Roosevelt, Fireside Chat on National Security, Dec. 29, 1940, in the *Public Papers of FDR*, 9: 639.

10. Franklin Roosevelt, Address at Annual Dinner of White House Correspondents Association, March 15, 1941, in the *Public Papers of FDR*, 10: 62–63.

11. Other examples of Roosevelt speaking out on the problems of domestic espionage and subversion can be found in Franklin Roosevelt, Address on Hemisphere Defense, Oct. 12, 1940, in *Public Papers of FDR*, 9: 462; Annual Message to the Congress, Jan. 6, 1941, in *Public Papers of FDR*, 9, pp. 665–66; Radio Address to Jackson Day Dinners, March 29, 1941, in *Public Papers of FDR*, 10: 86; Radio Address Announcing the Proclamation of an Unlimited National Emergency, May 27, 1941, in *Public Papers of FDR*, 10:. 191; Fireside Chat to the Nation, Sept. 11, 1941, in *Public Papers of FDR*, 10: 387; Address to the Congress on the State of the Union, Jan. 6, 1942, in *Public Papers of FDR*, 11: 39; Fireside Chat on the Progress of the War, Feb. 23, 1942, in *Public Papers of FDR*, 11: 105, 112, 114; and Address to the New York Herald Tribune Forum, March 17, 1942, in *Public Papers of FDR*, 11: 485.

12. See Press Conference #747, June 6, 1941, in *Press Conferences of FDR*, 17: 382–87.

13. Franklin Roosevelt, Acceptance of Third Term, July 19, 1940, in *Papers of FDR*, 9: 302.

14. There are several excellent scholarly accounts of FDR's attempts to brand the isolationists as Nazi dupes. See, for example, Richard Steele, "Franklin D. Roosevelt and His Foreign Policy Critics," *Political Science Quarterly* 9 (Spring 1979): 15–32, and Wayne Cole, *Roosevelt and the Isolationists 1932–1945* (Lincoln: Univ. of Nebraska Press, 1983).

15. Press conference #738, April 25, 1941, in *Press Conferences of FDR*, 17: 293.

16. FDR to Henry Stimson, May 21, 1940, PSF War Dept., in folder marked Henry Stimson 1940, box 106, Franklin Delano Roosevelt Library, Hyde Park, New York (hereafter FDRL).

17. Henry Morgenthau Presidential Diaries, 2 reels (Frederick, Md.: University Publications of America, 1981), May 20, 1940, book 3, reel 1, frame 0562.

18. On Lindbergh in the Pacific, see Wayne Cole, *Charles A. Lindbergh*

and the Battle Against American Intervention in World War II (New York: Harcourt Brace Jovanovich, 1974), 223.

19. Geoffrey Smith, *To Save a Nation*, and Smith, "Isolationism, the Devil and the Advent of the Second World War: Variations on a Theme," *International History Review* 4 (1982): 54–89.

20. "The Fifth Column Strikes," *Chicago Tribune*, June 2, 1940, p. 11; Lloyd Wendt, "We Spy," *Chicago Tribune*, Graphic section, June 23, 1940, p. 2; Captain M. M. Corpening, "Why Did Hit Wait 8 Months? Writer Explains," *Chicago Tribune*, June 1, 1940, p. 2.

21. Wayne Cole, *America First: The Battle Against Intervention, 1940–1941* (Madison: Univ. of Wisconsin Press, 1953), 119–27.

22. Chargé d'Affaires in United States to Foreign Minister, Aug. 7, 1940, in *Documents on German Foreign Policy 1918–1945*, series D 10, 14 vols. (London: Her Majesty's Stationary Office), 10: 427, and Chargé d'Affaires to Foreign Minister, Sept. 1, 1940, in ibid., 11: 2.

23. Roosevelt to the Attorney General, Nov. 17, 1941, PSF Justice Department 1938–44, box 76, FDRL.

24. Walter Stratton Anderson, Columbia Oral History Project, Part 3 of 4, p. 230, Columbia University, New York.

25. Memorandum for J. Edgar Hoover, May 21, 1940, OF10B, box 10, FDRL; Hoover to Stephen Early, FBI report #112, June 4, 1940, OF10B, box 11, FDRL; and Summary of Lunch with FDR, Aug. 12, 1942, in folder entitled Domestic Propaganda, box 2, Francis Biddle Papers, FDRL.

26. Roosevelt to Hoover, April 3, 1942, PSF 77, in folder entitled J. Edgar Hoover, FDRL.

27. See, for example, FDR to Hoover, Jan. 21, 1942, in PSF Justice Department, box 57, FDRL

28. Robert Jackson to Major General Edwin M. Watson, April 15, 1941, PSF Justice Department 1938–44, box 76; FDRL, Description of Cabinet Meeting, March 20, 1942, box 1, in Francis Biddle Papers, p. 43, FDRL; and Stephen Early to FDR, March 20, 1942, PSF Justice Department 1938–44, box 76, FDRL.

29. See these fears expressed in Chief of Naval Operations, "Report German Intelligence Activity in the United States and Countermeasures," Jan. 24, 1942, p. 15, 862.20211, RG 59, NARS.

30. Hoover to Watson, Feb. 11, 1940, FBI report #33, box 11, OF10B, FDRL; Hoover to Watson, May 28, 1941, FBI report #792, box 13, OF10B, FDRL; and Hoover to Mcintyre, June 22, 1942, FBI report #2192A, box 16, OF10B, FDRL.

31. John Franklin Carter to Franklin Roosevelt, confidential report on organized labor, Dec. 31, 1941, PSF John Franklin Carter, Jan.–Feb. 1942, box 122, FDRL.

32. C. B. Munson to John Franklin Carter, Jan. 9, 1942, PSF John Franklin Carter, Jan.–Feb. 1942, box 122, FDRL; John Franklin Carter to Franklin Roosevelt, "Progress Report on Combatting Axis Fifth Column Among Citizens," Jan. 19, 1942, PSF John Franklin Carter, Jan.–Feb. 1942, box 122, FDRL.

33. Carter, "Progress Report on Combatting Axis Fifth Column Among Citizens."

34. Franklin Roosevelt, Fireside Chat, Oct. 12, 1942, in *Public Papers of FDR*, 11: 418.

35. Hoover to Berle, enclosure entitled "General Intelligence Survey in the United States," July 1942, 800.20211/924, RG 59, in NARS.

36. Broadcast interview in "National Defense Series," by Office of Government Reports, Sept. 11, 1940, in box 40, p. 3, Jackson papers, LC.

37. There are many excellent accounts of the formation and operation of various wartime morale organizations. Richard Steele has written extensively on the subject. See Steele, *Propaganda in an Open Society: The Roosevelt Administration and the Media 1933–1941* (Westport, Conn.: Greenwood, 1985); "Preparing the Public for War: Efforts to Establish a National Propaganda Agency, 1940–1941," *American Historical Review*, 75 (June 1970): 1640–53; and "The Great Debate: Roosevelt, the Media, and the Coming of the War, 1940–1941," *Journal of American History* 71 (June 1984): 69–92. Other works which were useful in writing this chapter include: David Lloyd Jones, "The U.S. Office of War Information and American Public Opinion During World War II, 1939–1945" (Ph.D. dissertation, State University of New York at Binghamton, 1976); Sydney Stahl Weinberg, "Wartime Propaganda in a Democracy: America's Twentieth Century Information Agencies" (Ph.D. dissertation, Columbia University, 1969); Weinberg, "What to Tell America: The Quarrel in the Office of War Information" *Journal of American History* 60 (June 1968): 73–89; Lamar MacKay, "Domestic Operations of the Office of War Information," (Ph.D. dissertation, University of Wisconsin, 1966); and Alan Winkler, *The Politics of Propaganda: The Office of War Information, 1942–1945* (New Haven: Yale Univ. Press, 1978).

38. Harold Ickes to Franklin Roosevelt, April 28, 1941, Office of Government Reports Folder, box 15, in Lowell Mellett papers, FDRL.

39. Ickes quoted in Wayne Cole, *Roosevelt and the Isolationists 1932–1945* (Lincoln: Univ. of Nebraska Press, 1983), 461.

40. For an account of the public's distrust of propaganda in the thirties, see Weinberg, "Wartime Propaganda in a Democracy," "The Propaganda Bogey," 88–138.

41. On early proposals for improving public morale see Steele, "Preparing the Public for War," 1641. Brownlow briefly describes meetings in Conference Committee on Propaganda, Nov. 18, 1940, box 247, in Harold Ickes Papers, Library of Congress, pp. 1–3.

42. Diary entry, Nov. 9, 1940 in *The Secret Diary of Harold Ickes*, 3 vols. (New York: Simon and Schuster, 1954), 3: 368. For confirming report see diary entry, Nov. 8, 1940, in Henry Stimson Diary, reel 6, vol. 31, frame 116.

43. Stimson was the ranking member of the committee, but he asked Ickes to run the meetings. Diary entry for Nov. 9, 1940, *Ickes Diary*, 3: 368.

44. Conference Propaganda Committee, Nov. 13, 1940, box 247, in Harold Ickes Papers, Library of Congress, pp. 3, 21.

45. Harold Ickes to Franklin Roosevelt, Nov. 28, 1940, in OF1661A Fifth Column, FDRL.

46. Harold Ickes to Franklin Roosevelt, Nov. 28, 1940, OF 1661A, FDRL, and Franklin Roosevelt to Harold Ickes, March 3, 1941, OF 1661A, FDRL.

47. On Lowell Mellett and the OGR see Mackay, 11–13; Weinberg, "War-

time Propaganda in a Democracy," 125–26; Jones, 49–57; and especially Steele, *Propaganda in an Open Society*, 74, 90–91.

48. Diary entry for March 1, 1941, in *Ickes Diary*, 3: 444–45.

49. On Ickes's request for the report, see Ickes to Mellett, Feb. 20, 1941, in Secretary of the Interior File, National Morale Committee folder 2, box 379, Ickes Papers, LC.

50. Francis Biddle to Harold Ickes, March 3, 1941, Secretary of the Interior File, National Morale Committee folder 3, box 379, Ickes Papers, LC.

51. Harold Ickes to Lowell Mellett, March 18, 1941, Secretary of the Interior File, National Morale Committee folder 3, Ickes Papers, LC.

52. Harold Ickes to Franklin Roosevelt, March 6, 1941, OF1661A, FDRL.

53. Entry for May 10, 1941, *Ickes Diary*, 3: 511.

54. Horton's unit is discussed in MacKay, 21–30.

55. Steele, "Preparing the Public for War," 1642.

56. Entry for April 17, 1941, Stimson Diary, v. 33, reel 6, p. 170, Yale University Library, New Haven.

57. Entry for April 20, 1941, *Ickes Diary*, 3: 484.

58. Conversation, Harold Ickes and Henry Morgenthau, Jr., April 11, 1941, book 388, in Henry Morgenthau diary, FDRL.

59. Harold Ickes to Franklin Roosevelt, April 30, 1941, OCD folder April/July 1941, box 1, OF4422, FDRL.

60. Franklin Roosevelt to Lowell Mellett, May 19, 1941, Charles Lindbergh folder 1930–41, OF92, FDRL.

61. Executive Order Establishing the Office of Civilian Defense, May 20, 1941, OCD folder April–July 1941, box 1, OF4422, FDRL.

62. Entry for May 25, 1941, *Ickes Diary*, 3: 518–19.

63. Harold Ickes to Franklin Roosevelt, Sept. 17, 1941, Secretary of the Interior File, National Morale Committee, folder 4, box 379, Ickes Papers, LC; conference with the President, May 29, 1941, in container 3, Harold Smith Papers, FDRL.

64. George Marshall to Franklin Roosevelt, Sept. 6, 1941, and Franklin Roosevelt to George Marshall, Sept. 23, 1941, both in PSF War Department, George Marshall folder, box 106, FDRL.

65. MacLeish quoted in Archibald MacLeish to Franklin Roosevelt, undated, Office of Facts and Figures 1941 folder, box 1, OF4619, FDRL.

66. Ibid.

67. Krock quoted in Weinberg, "Wartime Propaganda in a Democracy," 126.

68. *Divide and Conquer*, OWI—Office of Facts and Figures folder, box 1, OF5015, pp. 4, 12.

69. Winkler, 26–28, 76–78, 123–36, 148; Thomas Troy, *Donovan and the CIA: A History of the Establishment of the Central Intelligence Agency* (Frederick, Md.: University Publications of America, 1981), 179–208; and Bradley Smith, *The Shadow Warriors: O.S.S. and the Origins of the C.I.A.* (New York: Basic Books, 1983), 165–67; and Charles Ameringer, *U.S. Foreign Intelligence: The Secret Side of American History* (Lexington, Mass.: Lexington Books, 1990).

70. These causes of OWI's difficulties are fully explained in Weinberg, "What to Tell America." Davis quoted in ibid., 89.

71. Winkler, 105.

72. On posters, see Jones, 252–57.

73. For a full-length scholarly study of the Bureau of Motion Pictures, see Clayton Koopes and Gregory Black, *Hollywood Goes to War: How Politics, Profits, and Propaganda Shaped World War II Movies* (New York: Free Press, 1987), and also Koopes and Black, "What to Show the World: The Office of War Information and Hollywood 1942–1944," *Journal of American History* 64 (June 1977): 87–104.

74. Thomas Brady, "OWI Criticizes Hollywood's War Films," *New York Times*, Sept. 13, 1942, sec. VIII, p. 3.

75. Russell Shain, *An Analysis of Motion Pictures About War Released by the American Film Industry, 1939–1945* (New York: Arno Press, 1976), 61.

76. There were a number of other reasons which explain Roosevelt's lack of enthusiasm for propaganda. Historian Richard Steele has argued that the White House believed that a morale agency would arouse congressional and popular opposition, might repeat excesses of the Creel committee, and would become increasingly unnecessary as America was drawn more and more into the war. Steele persuasively argues that FDR's ultimate backing for OCD and OFF "was really designed more to still the demands of the interventionists than to effect a revolution in public opinion." Steele, "Preparing the Public for War," 1653.

77. Steele, "Franklin D. Roosevelt and His Foreign Policy Critics," 15–32; Leo Ribuffo, *The Old Christian Right: The Protestant Far Right from the Great Depression to the Cold War* (Philadelphia: Temple Univ. Press, 1983), 215; Arthur Schlesinger, Jr., "A Comment on Roosevelt and His Foreign Policy Critics," *Political Science Quarterly* 94 (Spring 1979): 33.

78. Norman Rich, *Hitler's War Aims: The Establishment of the New Order* (New York: W. W. Norton, 1974), 416–20; Gerhard Weinberg, *World in the Balance: Behind the Scenes of World War II* (Hanover, N.H.: Univ. Press of New England, 1981); and James Compton, *The Swastika and the Eagle* (Boston: Houghton Mifflin, 1967), 258.

79. See, for example, Cole, *Roosevelt and the Isolationists*, 465–67, and Michele Flynn Stenehjem, *An American First: John T. Flynn and the American First Committee* (New Rochelle: Arlington House, 1976), 35.

Chapter Nine. J. Edgar Hoover versus the Nazis

1. Athan Theoharis and John Stuart Cox, *The Boss: J. Edgar Hoover and the Great American Inquisition* (Philadelphia: Temple Univ. Press, 1988), 157.

2. The best history of the American Protective League is Joan Jenson, *The Price of Vigilance* (Chicago: Rand McNally, 1968).

3. Specific numbers from New York area raids are drawn from Don Whitehead, *The FBI Story* (New York: Random House, 1956), 38.

4. Johnson and *New York World* quoted in ibid., 38.

5. The best treatment of the Red Scare is Robert K. Murray, *Red Scare: A Study of National Hysteria, 1919–1920* (Minneapolis: Univ. of Minnesota Press, 1955).

6. Theoharis and Cox, 56–57.

7. Richard Gid Powers, *Secrecy and Power: The Life of J. Edgar Hoover* (New York: Free Press, 1987), 104.

8. Murray, 249–251.

9. Material for my discussion of the FBI's activities during the Red Scare is largely drawn from the accounts available in Murray, *Red Scare*; Powers, *Secrecy and Power*, 56–129; and Theoharis, 51–70.

10. During the First World War Burns's detective agency agreed to spy for the British on the Germans, and to spy for the Germans on the British. Burns was also involved in stacking a jury against Senator John Mitchell of Oregon in a land fraud case. Eugene Lewis, *Public Entrepreneurship: Toward a Theory of Bureaucratic Political Power* (Bloomington: Indiana Univ. Press, 1980), 102, and Whitehead, 18.

11. For more on Bureau scandals of the Harding period, see Kenneth O'Reilly, *Hoover and the Un-Americans: The FBI, HUAC, and the Red Menace* (Philadelphia: Temple Univ. Press, 1983), 17–19.

12. See Whitehead, 68, and O'Reilly, 18.

13. Stone quoted in Theoharis and Cox, 85.

14. Powers, *Secrecy and Power*, 303.

15. On the FBI's growth during the thirties, see, especially Kenneth O'Reilly, "A New Deal for the FBI: The Roosevelt Administration, Crime Control, and National Security," *Journal of American History* 69, no. 3 (Dec. 1982): 638–58. The best account of Bureau publicity and Hoover's rise to folk-hero status is in Richard Powers, *G-Men: Hoover's FBI in American Popular Culture* (Carbondale: Southern Illinois Univ. Press, 1983).

16. Hoover memorandum to Franklin Roosevelt, Aug. 24, 1936, in "The Development of FBI Domestic Intelligence Investigations," U.S. Senate, Select Committee to Study Governmental Operations with Respect to Intelligence Activities, *Final Report*, book III, 94th Cong., 2nd sess., report no. 94–755, serial 13133–5, p. 394.

17. Confidential Memorandum by J. Edgar Hoover, Aug. 24, 1936, in Hoover O&C files, file #61–7559–49, sec. 136, FBI Reading Room, Washington, D.C.

18. Confidential memorandum by J. Edgar Hoover, Aug. 24, 1936, in Hoover O&C files, section 136, file #61–7559–49, and confidential memorandum by J. Edgar Hoover, Aug. 25, 1936, Hoover O&C files, section 136, file #61–7559–49, both in FBI reading room. Hull quoted in Whitehead, 158.

19. Hoover to Franklin Roosevelt, Oct. 20, 1938, in U.S. Senate, Select Committee to Study Governmental Operations with Respect to Intelligence Activities, 392.

20. For a description of counterintelligence work in 1938, see James Clement Dunn to George Messersmith, Oct. 11, 1938, 800.20211 Esp. 1/12, RG 59, National Archives and Records Service (hereafter NARS), Washington, D.C.

21. James Clement Dunn to Sumner Welles, Dec. 21, 1938, 800.20211 Esp. 2/12, RG 59, NARS.

22. The decline of the State Department as the coordinator of America's intelligence agencies is a central theme of Rhodri Jeffreys-Jones, *American Espionage: From Secret Service to CIA* (New York: Macmillan, 1977), 42–55, 157–61.

23. Messersmith's biographer omits discussion of his work as coordinator of intelligence. He focuses instead on Messersmith's other reponsibilities as Assistant Secretary of State. Jesse Stiller, *George S. Messersmith: Diplomat of Democracy* (Chapel Hill: Univ. of North Carolina Press, 1987).

24. Memorandum of conversation of George Messersmith, Attorney General Frank Murphy, FBI Director Hoover, Colonel Smith, MID, and Admiral Holmes, ONI, May 4, 1939, 800.20211 Esp./5 RG59, NARS.

25. George Messersmith memorandum, May 9, 1939, 800.20211 Esp./7 RG 59, NARS.

26. Fletcher Warren to George Messersmith, March 24, 1939, 800.20211 Esp. 11/12, RG 59, NARS.

27. Attorney General Frank Murphy to Franklin Roosevelt, June 17, 1939, box 10, OF10B, Franklin Delano Roosevelt Library (hereafter FDRL), Hyde Park, New York.

28. Franklin Roosevelt to Secretary of State Hull, June 26, 1939, 800.20211 Esp./14, RG59, NARS.

29. George Messersmith to Fletcher Warren, Sept. 14, 1939, 800.20211 Esp./19, RG59, NARS.

30. Franklin Roosevelt to Secretary of State, Secretary of War, Attorney General, Secretary of the Treasury, Secretary of Commerce, Secretary of the Navy, and Postmaster General, June 26, 1939, box 10, OF10B, FDRL.

31. Statement of the President, Sept. 6, 1939, in "The Development of FBI Domestic Intelligence Investigations," U.S. Senate, Select Committee to Study Governmental Operations with Respect to Intelligence Activities, 404.

32. Statement of Attorney General Frank Murphy, Sept. 6, 1939, over the Fox-Movietone News, in folder entitled Attorney General, Subversive Activities and Investigations, box 93, Robert Jackson Papers, LC.

33. Proposal for Coordination of FBI, MID, ONI, June 5, 1940, in folder marked Delimitation Agreement, box 5, ONI Op–16, RG38, NARS.

34. 360 agents from Powers, 252.

35. For accounts of the Hoover/Miles feud, see Bruce Bidwell, *History of the Military Intelligence Division, Department of the Army General Staff: 1775–1941* (Frederick, Md.: Univ. Publications of America, 1986), 398–403, and Thomas Troy, *Donovan and the CIA: A History of the Establishment of the Central Intelligence Agency* (Washington, D.C.: CIA, 1981), 46–47. On FBI/ONI relations, see Jeffrey Dorwart, *Conflict of Duty: The U.S. Navy's Intelligence Dilemma, 1919–1945* (Annapolis, Md.: Naval Institute Press, 1983), 117–22, 152–53, 199–201, and Theoharis, 184.

36. Counter-Fifth Column plan, enclosure in J. Edgar Hoover to Henry Morgenthau, July 30, 1940, Morgenthau diary, book 287, pp. 339–43, FDRL.

37. Ibid., 339.

38. J. Edgar Hoover to Robert Jackson, date unknown, in folder entitled coordinated FBI, Military Intelligence, Naval Intelligence Program, box 93, Robert Jackson papers, LC.

39. J. Edgar Hoover to General Watson, Oct. 29, 1940, FBI report #415, box 12, OF10B, FDRL.

40. Hoover to Watson, Oct. 29, 1940, FBI report #415, box 12, OF10B, FDRL. Another example of Hoover reassuring the White House on the effect-

iveness of intelligence coordination is Hoover to Watson, Nov. 25, 1940, report #489, box 12, OF10B, FDRL.

41. Diary entry, Oct. 14, 1940, Stimson Diary, v. 31, reel 6, p. 53, Yale University Library, New Haven.

42. Diary entry, Feb. 12, 1941, Stimson Diary, v. 33, reel 6, p. 25.

43. Diary entry, Feb. 13, 1941, Stimson Diary, v. 33, reel 6, pp. 27–28.

44. Diary entry, Feb. 5, 1941, Berle Diary, reel 2, frame 1125.

45. Diary entry, Feb. 12, 1941, Berle Diary, reel 2, frame 1140.

46. Diary entry, Feb. 7, 1941, Berle Diary, reel 2, frame 1132.

47. Figure of 65 percent drawn from Historical Narrative of the District Intelligence Office, Third Naval District, Sept. 1, 1939–Aug. 14, 1945, p. 2, at Naval History Division, Operational Archives, Washington, D.C.

48. J. Edgar Hoover to Robert Jackson, Feb. 3, 1941, folder entitled Attorney General, Subversive Activities and Investigations, box 93, Robert Jackson Papers, LC, and J. Edgar Hoover to Robert Jackson, Feb. 5, 1941, in ibid.

49. The best treatment of the Roosevelt/Astor relationship is in Jeffrey M. Dorwart, "The Roosevelt-Astor Espionage Ring," *New York History* 62 (July 1981): 307–22.

50. Franklin Roosevelt to William Vincent Astor, March 19, 1941, Astor file, PSF 116, FDRL.

51. William Vincent Astor to Franklin Roosevelt, June 7, 1940, Astor file, PSF 116, FDRL.

52. Troy, 51

53. J. Edgar Hoover to Edwin Watson, June 2, 1941, FBI report #796A, box 13, OF10B, FDRL.

54. Letter Donovan to Knox, April 26, 1941, in Appendix A, Troy, 417.

55. Ibid., 417.

56. Executive Order Designating a Coordinator of Information, July 11, 1941, in Appendix C, Troy, 423.

57. Confidential directive of the President, issued Dec. 1941, to the Government Departments and Agencies Concerned, box 5, ONI Directors file, RG39, NARS.

58. Anthony Cave Brown, *The Last Hero: Wild Bill Donovan* (New York: Random House, 1982), 285.

59. Troy, 252–260.

60. Bradley Smith, *The Shadow Warriors: O.S.S. and the Origins of the C.I.A.* (New York: Basic Books, 1982), 36–42, 160, 164, 447–49.

61. *Milwaukee Journal* quoted in "American OGPU," *New Republic*, Feb. 19, 1940, p. 230.

62. Hoover before subcommittee of House Appropriations Committee, Nov. 30, 1939, Hearings on Emergency Supplemental Appropriations Bill for 1940, quoted in Max Lowenthal, *The Federal Bureau of Investigation* (New York: William Sloane Associates, 1950), 304–5.

63. "Civil Liberties," *New Republic*, Feb. 17, 1941, p. 250.

64. "Investigate the American OGPU," *New Republic*, March 11, 1940, p. 330.

65. Editorial clipping, *Philadelphia Inquirer*, March 1, 1940, in folder entitled Attorney General, Subversive Activities and Investigations, box 93, Robert Jackson Papers, LC.

66. On Miami raids, see Lowenthal, 420.

67. Norris quoted in ibid., 400.

68. Tamm for File, Feb. 29, 1940; Hoover to Jackson, Feb. 26, 1940; and Tamm for File, Feb. 27, 1940, Smear Campaign, part 1, Nichols O&C files, FBI reading room.

69. Entry for March 4, 1940, in Berle Diary, reel 2, frame 00393.

70. Tamm to Hoover, March 1, 1940, Smear Campaign, part 1, Nicols O&C Files, FBI reading room.

71. Jackson quoted in "Jackson Clears FBI in Recruiting Case," *New York Times*, March 2, 1940, p. 30.

72. Robert Jackson to Roger Baldwin, April 6, 1940, and Robert Jackson to Arthur Garfield Hays, March 8, 1941, both in folder entitled Attorney General Subversive Activities and Investigations, box 93, Robert Jackson papers, LC.

73. The dispute between Dies and Hoover has been treated most fully in Kenneth O'Reilly, "The Roosevelt Administration and Legislative–Executive Conflict: The FBI vs. the Dies Committee," *Congress and the Presidency* 10 (Spring 1983): 79–93, and O'Reilly, *Hoover and the Un–Americans: The FBI, HUAC, and the Red Menace* (Philadelphia: Temple Univ. Press, 1983).

74. Dies quoted in "20,000 Chicago Fifth Columnists," *Chicago Tribune*, June 16, 1940, p. 16.

75. J. Edgar Hoover to Robert Jackson, June 2, 1940, folder entitled Attorney General HUAC folder 1, box 89, Jackson papers, LC.

76. Martin Dies to Franklin Roosevelt, Oct. 2, 1940, in folder entitled Dies Committee 1940–41, OF320, FDRL.

77. Franklin Roosevelt to Martin Dies, Oct. 9, 1940, folder entitled Dies Committee 1940–41, OF320, FDRL.

78. J. Edgar Hoover to Robert Jackson, Oct. 21, 1940, Hoover O&C files, sec. 59

79. On the Bureau's media campaign against Dies, see Kenneth O'Reilly, "The Roosevelt Administration and Legislative-Executive Conflict," 85–86.

80. Martin Dies to Franklin Roosevelt, Nov. 25, 1940, folder entitled Dies Committee 1940–41, OF320, FDRL.

81. Franklin Roosevelt to Martin Dies, Nov. 26, 1940, folder entitled Dies Committee 1940–41, OF320, FDRL.

82. Transcript, President Roosevelt's conference with representative Martin Dies, Nov. 29, 1940, folder entitled Dies Committee 1940–41, OF320, FDRL.

83. Dies quoted in O'Reilly, "The Roosevelt Administration and Legislative-Executive Conflict," 82.

84. Buchwald anecdote drawn from Powers, *Secrecy and Power*, 285

85. Hoover's testimony before Congress drawn from Lowenthal, 420–22.

86. Palmer quoted in Powers, *Secrecy and Power*, 109.

87. J. Edgar Hoover, "Patriotism and the War Against Crime," address delivered before the Daughters of the American Revolution, Washington, D.C., April 23, 1936, from the Office of Congressional and Public Affairs (hereafter OCPA), FBI, pp. 2, 10. In a radio address broadcast in June 1936, Hoover noted that "the standing military and naval forces of the United States constitute about 250,000 armed men, but did you realize that the criminal standing army of

America consists of twice that number—a whole half-million of armed thugs, murderers, thieves, firebugs, assassins, robbers, and hold-up men?" J. Edgar Hoover radio address, June 22, 1936, OCPA.

88. J. Edgar Hoover, "The Test of Citizenship," address delivered before the Daughters of the American Revolution, Washington, D.C., April 18, 1940, in *Vital Speeches of the Day*, vol. 6, no. 14, p. 441.

89. J. Edgar Hoover, "The Call of Americanism," address delivered to the Michigan Bankers Association, Grand Rapids, Michigan, June 19, 1940, p. 4, OCPA.

90. For example, see, Hoover, "The Test of Citizenship," and Hoover, "Protect America," address delivered at the Federal-State Conference on Law Enforcement Problems of National Defense, Washington, D.C., Aug. 5, 1940, p. 4, OCPA.

91. Hoover, "The Call of Americanism," 1–2.

92. J. Edgar Hoover, "The Test of Americanism," address delivered to the American Legion, Boston, Sept. 23, 1940, p. 1, OCPA.

93. Hoover, "The Call of Americanism," 2.

94. Address by J. Edgar Hoover to the National Police Academy, Washington, D.C., Oct. 5, 1940, quoted in Lowenthal, 360.

95. J. Edgar Hoover, "Your Future Task," address at the University of the South, Sewanee, Tennessee, June 9, 1941, p. 3, OCPA.

96. J. Edgar Hoover, "An Adventure in Public Service," address delivered at Drake University, Des Moines, Iowa, June 3, 1940, through the Mutual Broadcasting Network, OCPA.

97. Hoover, "Protect America," 4, 5.

98. J. Edgar Hoover with Courtney Ryley Cooper, "Stamping Out Spies," *American Magazine* (Jan. 1940): 83.

99. J. Edgar Hoover, "Guarding the Ramparts of Freedom," *American Foreign Service Journal* 18, no. 9 (Sept. 1941): 534.

100. Hoover and Cooper, "Stamping Out Spies," *American Magazine* (Jan. 1940): 84.

101. Hoover, "The Test of Citizenship," 441.

102. J. Edgar Hoover, address at Notre Dame University, South Bend, Indiana, May 10, 1942, p. 4, OCPA.

103. J. Edgar Hoover and Courney Ryley Cooper, "Stamping Out Spies," *American Magazine* (Jan. 1940): 83.

104. J. Edgar Hoover, "Our Merciless Home Front Enemies," *Saturday Evening Post*, Sept. 25, 1943, p. 3.

105. J. Edgar Hoover, "Hoover Tells How FBI Erased Fifth Column," Aug. 27, 1944, clipping from an unidentified newspaper, OCPA.

106. J. Edgar Hoover, statement on the radio program, "Victory F.O.B.," CBS, Oct. 7, 1944, p. 1.

107. J. Edgar Hoover, speech before the International Association of Chiefs of Police at Milwaukee, Sept. 1940, quoted in Lowenthal, 359.

108. Hoover, "An Adventure in Public Service," 3.

109. J. Edgar Hoover, "A Graduate's Responsibility," address at Holy Cross College, Worcester, Massachusetts, June 29, 1944, p. 4.

110. "The Development of FBI Domestic Intelligence Investigations," in U.S.

Senate, Select Committee to Study Governmental Operations with Respect to Intelligence Activities, 412.

111. Memorandum, Attorney General Biddle to J. Edgar Hoover, May 29, 1942, in Hoover O&C Files, sec. 136, 66–65–00–101332, and memorandum, J. Edgar Hoover to Attorney General Biddle, June 1, 1942, in Hoover O&C Files, sec. 136, 66–65–00–101332, exhibit 2.

112. Christopher Andrew and Oleg Gordievsky, *KGB: The Inside Story of Its Foreign Operations from Lenin to Gorbachev* (New York: HarperCollins, 1990), 281.

113. Hoover, "The Call of Americanism," 5.

Conclusion

1. See Ribuffo, *The Old Christian Right: The Protestant Far Right from the Great Depression to the Cold War* (Philadelphia, Pa: Temple Univ. Press, 1983), 198–215, for a detailed account of the case.

2. Alice Payne Hackett and James Henry Burke, *Eighty Years of Best Sellers 1895–1975* (New York: R. R. Bowker, 1977), 135, 137.

3. The FBI monitored Winchell's weekly broadcasts. Summaries of many of his radio programs are available at the FBI Reading Room in files titled Walter Winchell #62–31615, J. Edgar Hoover Building, Washington, D.C. On the FBI in peace and war see Richard Gid Powers, *G-Men: Hoover's FBI in American Popular Culture* (Carbondale: Southern Illinois Univ. Press, 1983), 221–22.

4. Russell Earl Shain, *An Analysis of Motion Pictures About War Released by the American Film Industry 1939–1970* (New York: Arno Press, 1976), 61.

5. *Committee on Un-American Activities Annual Report for the Year 1967*, 90th Cong., 2nd sess., report #1935 (Washington, D.C: Government Printing Office, 1968), 75–78; "Der Tag," *Newsweek*, Sept. 4, 1967, p. 31. For general treatments on Rockwell, see Jerry Bornstein, *The Neo-Nazis: The Threat of the Hitler Cult* (New York: Julian Messner, 1986), 55–67, and Leland Bell, *In Hitler's Shadow: The Anatomy of American Nazism* (Port Washington, N.Y.: Kennikat Press, 1973), 109–23.

6. Bornstein, 68–92.

7. Winston Churchill, speech delivered March 5, 1946, at Westminster College, Fulton, Missouri, in *Churchill Speaks: Winston Churchill in Peace and War*, Robert Rhodes James, ed. (New York: Chelsea House, 1980), 882–83.

8. Hoover quoted in Richard Gid Powers, *Secrecy and Power: The Life of J. Edgar Hoover* (New York: Free Press, 1987), 288.

9. Jenner quoted in Robert Griffith, *The Politics of Fear: Joseph R. McCarthy and the Senate* (Lexington: Univ. of Kentucky Press, 1970), 115–16.

10. Richard Fried, *Nightmare in Red: The McCarthy Era in Perspective* (New York: Oxford Univ. Press, 1990), 68–73, 133–35.

11. Fried, 78.

12. Wayne Cole, *Roosevelt and the Isolationists* (Lincoln: Univ. of Nebraska Press, 1983), 530.

13. William Freehling, "Conspiracy and Conspiracy Theories," *Encyclopedia of American Political History*, vol. 1 (New York: Charles Scribner's Sons, 1984), 368, 374.

BIBLIOGRAPHY

Archives

Franklin Delano Roosevelt Presidential Library

Adolf A. Berle Papers, Diary
Francis Biddle Papers, Diary
Wayne Coy Papers
Harry Hopkins Papers
Lowell Mellett Papers
Henry Morgenthau Papers
Franklin Delano Roosevelt Papers, President's Personal File, President's Secretary File, President's Official File
Samuel Rosenman Papers
Harold Smith Papers

National Archives and Records Administration, Washington, D.C

U.S. Department of State, General Records of the Department of State, Decimal File, Record Group 59
U.S. Navy Department, Records of Office of Chief of Naval Operations, Office of Naval Intelligence, Record Group 38
U.S. War Department, Records of the General and Special Staffs, Record Group 165

Naval Historical Center, Washington, D.C

Alan Kirk Papers

Library of Congress

Thomas Gregory Papers
Harold Ickes Papers

Robert Jackson Papers
Frank Knox Papers
Pulp Fiction Collection

Federal Bureau of Investigation, Washington, D.C

Confessions of a Nazi Spy file (through FOIA)
Courtney Ryley Cooper file
George Dasch file (Nazi Saboteurs file)
Espionage/World War II Summary (through FOIA)
Files related to William Stephenson and British Security Coordination (through
    FOIA)
J. Edgar Hoover O&C files
Walter Krivitsky file
Louis Nichols O&C files
Westbrook Pegler file
Leon G. Turrou file (through FOIA)
Walter Winchell file

Public Record Office, Kew, England

Foreign Office (FO)
Ministry of Information (INF)
Prime Minister's Office (PREM)

Other University Archives

Confessions of a Nazi Spy file and Edward G. Robinson file at Warner Brothers
    Film Archive, University of Southern California Los Angeles
Homer Cummings Papers, University of Virginia, Charlottesville, Virginia
Interview with Robert Jackson in Columbia University Oral History Project,
    Columbia University, New York City
Robert Sherwood Papers, Houghton Library, Harvard University, Cambridge,
    Mass.
Robert Vansittart Papers, Churchill College, Cambridge University, Cambridge,
    England

Papers on Microfilm

Henry Lewis Stimson Diaries, 9 reels. New Haven, Conn.: Yale University Li-
    brary, 1973
Adolf Berle Diaries 1937-1971, 8 reels. Washington, D.C.: National Archives
    and Records Service, 1978
Presidential Diaries of Henry Morgenthau Jr., 2 reels. Frederick, Md.: University
    Publications of America, 1981
British Foreign Office United States Correspondence 1938–1945, 197 reels. Wil-
    mington, Del.: Scholarly Resources, 1977

Congressional Documents

Personal Justice Denied, Report of the Commission on Wartime Relocation and Internment of Civilians. Washington, D.C.: U.S. Government Printing Office, 1982.

U.S. House, Un-American Affairs Committee, Hearings, Investigation of Nazi Propaganda Activities and Investigation of Certain Other Propaganda Activities, 73 Cong., 2nd sess., pts. 1 and 2.

U.S. House, Un-American Affairs Committee, Report on Investigation of Nazi and Other Propaganda, 74th Cong., 1st sess.

U.S. House, Un-American Activities Committee. Investigation of Un-American Propaganda Activities in the United States. Hearings, 5, 76th Cong. 1st session.

U.S. House, Special Committee on Un-American Activities. Preliminary Report, Totalitarian Propaganda in the United States. Appendix III. 76th Cong., 3rd sess.

U.S. House, Special Committee on Un-American Activities. Preliminary Report, Un-American Activities of Various Nazi Organizations and Individuals in the United States, Including Diplomatic and Consular Agents of the German Government, Appendix II. 76th Cong., 3rd sess.

U.S. House, Committee on Naval Affairs. Report on the Fire and Capsizing of the U.S.S. "Lafayette," Formerly the T.E.L. Normandie, 77th Cong., 2nd sess.

U.S. House, Special Committee on Un-American Activities. Report on Axis Front Movements in the United States, Appendix Part VII. 78th Cong., 1st sess.

U.S. Senate, Committee on Interstate Commerce, Hearings on Propaganda in Motion Pictures, 77th Cong., 1st sess.

U.S. Senate, Committee on Naval Affairs. Report on the Investigation of the Fire and Capsizing of the U.S.S. Lafayette (Normandie), 77th Cong., 2nd sess.

U.S. Senate, Select Committee to Study Governmental Operations with Respect to Intelligence Investigations, Report on the Development of FBI Domestic Intelligence Investigations, Book III. 94th Cong., 2nd sess. pp. 373-558.

Books

Ameringer, Charles. *U.S. Foreign Intelligence: The Secret Side of American History.* Lexington: D.C. Heath, 1990.

Andrew, Christopher. *Her Majesty's Secret Service: The Making of the British Intelligence Community.* New York: Viking, 1986.

—— and Oleg Gordievsky. *KGB: The Inside Story of Its Foreign Operations from Lenin to Gorbachev.* New York: HarperCollins, 1990.

Archer, Jules. *The Plot to Seize the White House.* New York: Hawthorn Books, 1973.

Austwärtiges Amt. *Documents on German Foreign Policy.* Series D, 9 vols. London: Her Majesty's Stationary Office, 1949– .)

Bayor, Ronald. *Neighbors in Conflict: The Irish, Germans, Jews, and Italians of New York City, 1929–1941.* 2nd ed. Urbana: Univ. of Illinois Press, 1988.

Beesly, Patrick. *Room 40: British Naval Intelligence, 1914–1918*. London: Hamilton, 1982.

Bell, Leland. *In Hitler's Shadow: The Anatomy of American Nazism*. Port Washington, N.Y.: Kennikat Press, 1973.

Bennett, David. *Demagogues in the Depression: American Radicals and the Union Party, 1932–1936*, Brunswick, N.J.: Rutgers Univ. Press, 1969.

Biddle, Francis. *In Brief Authority*. Garden City, N.Y.: Doubleday, 1962.

Bidwell, Bruce. *History of the Military Intelligence Division, Department of the Army General Staff: 1775–1941*. Frederick, Md.: University Publications of America, 1986.

Blum, John M. *V Was for Victory: Politics and American Culture During World War II*. New York: Harcourt, Brace Jovanovich, 1976.

Bornstein, Jerry. *The Neo–Nazis: The Threat of the Hitler Cult*. New York: Julian Messner, 1986.

Breur, William. *Hitler's Undercover War: The Nazi's Espionage Invasion of the U.S.A.* New York: St. Martin's Press, 1989.

Brinkley, Alan. *Voices of Protest: Huey Long, Father Coughlin, and the Great Depression*. New York: Alfred A. Knopf, 1982.

Britt, George. *The Fifth Column Is Here*. New York: Wilfred Funk, 1940.

Brown, Anthony Cave. *"C": The Secret Life of Sir Stewart Graham Menzies, Spymaster to Winston Churchill*. New York: Macmillan, 1987.

———. *The Last Hero: Wild Bill Donovan*. New York: Times Books, 1982.

Buchan, John. *The Four Adventures of Richard Hanney*. Boston: David R. Godine, 1988.

Cantril, Hadley. *The Invasion from Mars: A Study in Psychological Panic*. Princeton, N.J.: Princeton Univ. Press, 1982.

Carlson, John Roy [Avedis Deounian]. *Under Cover: My Four Years in the Nazi Underground of America*. New York: Dutton, 1943.

Chadwin, Mark. *The Hawks of World War II*. Chapel Hill: Univ. of North Carolina Press, 1968.

Chalmers, David. *Hooded Americanism: The First Century of the Ku Klux Klan*. Garden City, N.Y.: Doubleday, 1965.

Child, Clifton James. *The German-Americans in Politics 1914–1917*. Madison: Univ. of Wisconsin Press, 1939.

Churchill, Winston. *The Second World War*. Vol. 3. Boston: Houghton Mifflin, 1950.

Cole, Wayne. *America First: The Battle Against Intervention, 1940–1941*. Madison: Univ. of Wisconsin Press, 1953.

———. *Charles A. Lindbergh and the Battle Against American Intervention in World War II*. New York: Harcourt Brace Jovanovich, 1974.

———. *Roosevelt and the Isolationists 1932–1945*. Lincoln: Univ. of Nebraska Press, 1983.

Compton, James. *The Swastika and the Eagle*. Boston: Houghton Mifflin, 1967.

Conn, Stetson, and Byron Fairchild. *The Framework of Hemisphere Defense*. Washington, D.C.: Department of the Army, 1960.

Davis, David Brion. *The Fear of Conspiracy: Images of Un-American Subversion from the Revolution to the Present*. Ithaca, N.Y.: Cornell Univ. Press, 1971.

De Jong, Louis. *The German Fifth Column in the Second World War*. Chicago: Univ. of Chicago Press, 1956.

Diamond, Sander. *The Nazi Movement in the United States 1924–1941*. Ithaca, N.Y.: Cornell Univ. Press, 1974.

Dies, Martin. *The Trojan Horse in America*. New York: Arno Press, 1977.

Diggins, John. *Mussolini and Fascism: The View from America*. Princeton, N.J.: Princeton Univ. Press, 1972.

Dorwart, Jeffrey. *Conflict of Duty: The U.S. Navy's Intelligence Dilemma, 1919–1945*. Annapolis, Md.: Naval Institute Press, 1983.

Farago, Ladislas. *The Game of the Foxes: The Untold Story of German Espionage in the United States and Great Britain During World War II*. New York: David McKay, 1971.

Fine, Sidney. *Frank Murphy: The Washington Years*. Vol. 3. Ann Arbor: Univ. of Michigan, 1984.

Fowler, W. B. *British-American Relations 1917–1918: The Role of Sir William Wiseman*. Princeton, N.J.: Princeton Univ. Press, 1969.

Fried, Richard. *Nightmare in Red: The McCarthy Era in Perspective*. New York: Oxford Univ. Press, 1990.

Frye, Alton. *Nazi Germany and the Western Hemisphere 1933–1941*. New Haven, Conn.: Yale Univ. Press, 1967.

Gerard, James. *My Four Years in Germany*. New York: Grosset and Dunlap, 1917.

Gilbert, Martin. *Winston S. Churchill*. Vol. 5. London: Heinemenn, 1976.

Gillman, Peter and Leni Gillman. *"Collar the Lot!": How Britain Interned Its Wartime Refugees*. London: Quartet Books, 1980.

Goodman, Walter. *The Committee: The Extraordinary Career of the House Un-American Activities Committee*. New York: Farrar, Straus and Giroux, 1968.

Griffith, Robert. *The Politics of Fear: Joseph R. McCarthy and the Senate*. Lexington: Univ. of Kentucky Press, 1970.

Grodzins, Morton. *Americans Betrayed: Politics and the Japanese Evacuation*. Chicago: Univ. of Chicago Press, 1949.

Hayes, Paul. *Quisling: The Career and Political Ideas of Vidkun Quisling, 1887–1945*. Newton Abbott: David and Charles, 1971.

Herzstein, Robert Edwin. *Roosevelt and Hitler: Prelude to War*. New York: Paragon House, 1989.

Hofstadter, Richard. *The Paranoid Style in American Politics*. New York: Knopf, 1965.

Hoke, Henry. *Blackmail*. New York: Reader's Book Service, 1944.

House, Col. Edward. *The Intimate Papers of Colonel House*. Charles Seymour, ed., 4 vols. Boston: Houghton Mifflin, 1926.

Hyde, H. Montgomery. *Room 3603: The Story of British Intelligence in New York during World War II*. New York: Farrar, Straus, 1962.

———. *Secret Intelligence Agent*. London: Constable, 1982.

Ickes, Harold. *The Secret Diaries of Harold Ickes*. 3 vols. New York: Simon and Schuster, 1954.

Irons, Peter. *Justice at War*. New York: Oxford Univ. Press, 1983.

Isserman, Maurice. *Which Side Were You On? The American Communist Party during the Second World War.* Middletown, Conn.: Wesleyan Univ. Press, 1982.

Jeansonne, Glen. *Gerald L. K. Smith: Minister of Hate.* New Haven, Conn.: Yale Univ. Press, 1988.

Jeffreys-Jones, Rhodri. *American Espionage: From Secret Service to CIA.* New York: Macmillan, 1977.

Jenson, Joan. *The Price of Vigilance.* Chicago: Rand McNally, 1968.

Kahn, David. *Hitler's Spies: German Military Intelligence in World War II.* New York: Macmillan, 1978.

Katz, Friedrich. *The Secret War in Mexico: Europe, the United States and the Mexican Revolution.* Chicago: Univ. of Chicago Press, 1981.

Koopes, Clayton, and Gregory Black. *Hollywood Goes to War: How Politics, Profits, and Propaganda Shaped World War II Movies.* New York: Free Press, 1987.

Krivitsky, Walter. *In Stalin's Secret Service.* New York: Harper and Brothers, 1939.

Landau, Henry. *The Enemy Within: The Inside Story of German Sabotage in America.* New York: G. P. Putnam's Sons, 1937.

Lavine, Harold. *Fifth Column in America.* New York: Doubleday, Doran, 1940.

Lewis, Eugene. *Public Entrepreneurship: Toward a Theory of Bureaucratic Political Power.* Bloomington: Indiana Univ. Press, 1980.

Lewis, Sinclair. *It Can't Happen Here.* Garden City, N.Y.: Doubleday, Doran, 1935.

Low, Alfred. *The Anschluss Movement, 1931–1938, and the Great Powers.* New York: Columbia Univ. Press, 1985.

Lowenthal, Max. *The Federal Bureau of Investigation.* New York: William Sloane Associates, 1950.

Luebke, Frederick. *Bonds of Loyalty: German-Americans and World War I.* Dekalb: Northern Illinois Univ. Press, 1974.

McAdoo, William. *The Crowded Years.* Boston: Houghton Mifflin, 1931.

McKale, Donald. *The Swastika Outside Germany.* Kent, Ohio: Kent State Univ. Press, 1977.

Marcus, Sheldon. *Father Coughlin: The Tumultuous Life of the Priest of the Little Flower.* Boston: Little, Brown, 1973.

Mock, James, and Cedric Larson. *Words That Won the War.* Princeton, N.J.: Princeton Univ. Press, 1939.

Ogden, August. *The Dies Committee.* Washington, D.C.: Catholic Univ. Press, 1945.

O'Reilly, Kenneth. *Hoover and the Un-Americans: The FBI, HUAC, and the Red Menace.* Philadephia: Temple Univ. Press, 1983.

Pauley, Bruce. *Hitler and the Forgotten Nazis: A History of Austrian National Socialism.* Chapel Hill: Univ. of North Carolina Press, 1981.

Powers, Richard Gid. *G-Men: Hoover's FBI in American Popular Culture.* Carbondale: Southern Illinois Univ. Press, 1983.

———. *Secrecy and Power: The Life of J. Edgar Hoover.* New York: Free Press, 1987.

Rachlis, Eugene. *They Came to Kill: The Story of Eight Nazi Saboteurs in America.* New York: Random House, 1961.

Rauschning, Herman. *The Redemption of Democracy: The Coming Atlantic Empire.* New York: Literary Guild of America, 1941.

———. *The Revolution of Nihilism: Warning to the West.* New York: Alliance Book Corporation, 1939.

———. *The Voice of Destruction.* New York: G. P. Putnam's Sons, 1940.

Reynolds, David. *The Creation of the Anglo-American Alliance 1937–1941: A Study in Competitive Cooperation.* London: Europa Publications, 1981.

Ribuffo, Leo. *The Old Christian Right: The Protestant Far Right from the Great Depression to the Cold War.* Philadelphia, Pa.: Temple Univ. Press, 1983.

Rich, Norman. *Hitler's War Aims: The Establishment of the New Order.* New York: W. W. Norton, 1974.

Rintelin, Franz. *The Dark Invader.* London: Lovat Dickson, 1933.

———. *The Dark Invader Returns.* London: Dickson and Thompson, 1935.

Rogge, O. John. *The Official German Report: Nazi Penetration 1924–1942, Pan-Arabism 1939–Today.* New York: Thomas Yoseloff, 1961.

Rollins, Richard. *I Find Treason: The Story of an American Anti-Nazi Agent.* New York: William Morrow, 1941.

Roosevelt, Franklin. *Complete Presidential Press Conferences of Franklin D. Roosevelt.* 25 vols. New York: Da Capo Press, 1972.

———. *The Public Papers of Franklin D. Roosevelt.* Samuel I. Rosenman, ed., 13 vols. New York: Harper and Row, 1950.

Rowan, Richard Wilmer. *Secret Agents Against America.* New York: Doubleday, Doran, 1939.

Schlesinger, Arthur Jr. *The Age of Roosevelt: The Politics of Upheaval.* Boston: Houghton Mifflin, 1960.

Schmidt, Hans. *Maverick Marine: General Smedley D. Butler and the Contradictions of American Military History.* Lexington: Univ. of Kentucky Press, 1987.

Schonbach, Morris. *Native American Fascism during the 1930s and 1940s: A Study of Its Roots, Its Growth and Its Decline.* New York: Garland, 1985.

Schwarz, Jordan. *Liberal: Adolf A. Berle and the Vision of an American Era.* New York: Macmillan, 1987.

Shain, Russell Earl. *An Analysis of Motion Pictures About War Released by the American Film Industry, 1939–1970.* New York: Arno Press, 1976.

Simone, Sam P. *Hitchcock as Activist: Politics and the War Films.* Ann Arbor: Univ. of Michigan Press, 1982.

Smelser, Ronald. *The Sudetan Problem 1933–1938: Volkstumspolitik and the Formulation of Nazi Foreign Policy.* Middletown, Conn.: Wesleyan Univ. Press, 1975.

Smith, Arthur. *The Deutschtum of Nazi Germany and the United States.* The Hague: Martinus Nijhoff, 1965.

Smith, Bradley. *Shadow Warriors: O.S.S. and the Origins of the C.I.A.* New York: Basic Books, 1983.

Smith, Geoffrey. *To Save a Nation: American Countersubversives, the New Deal, and the Coming of World War II.* New York: Basic Books, 1973.

Smith, Janet Adam. *A Biography of John Buchan.* Boston: Little, Brown, 1965.

Spoto, Donald. *The Life of Alfred Hitchcock: The Dark Side of Genius.* London: Collins, 1983.

Steele, Richard. *Propaganda in an Open Society: The Roosevelt Administration and the Media 1933–1941*. Westport, Conn.: Greenwood, 1985.

Stenehjem, Michelle. *An American First: John T. Flynn and the America First Committee*. New Rochelle, N.Y.: Arlington House, 1976.

Stiller, Jesse. *George S. Messersmith: Diplomat of Democracy*. Chapel Hill: Univ. of North Carolina Press, 1987.

Stowe, Leland. *No Other Road to Freedom*. New York: Alfred A. Knopf, 1941.

Strong, Donald. *Organized Anti-Semitism in America: The Rise of Group Prejudice During the Decade 1930–1940*. Washington, D.C.: American Council on Public Affairs, 1941.

Taylor, Edmond. *The Strategy of Terror: Europe's Inner Front*. Boston: Houghton Mifflin, 1940.

Taylor, Telford. *The March of Conquest: The German Victories in Western Europe, 1940*. New York: Simon and Schuster, 1958.

———. *Munich: The Price of Peace*. Garden City, N.Y.: Doubleday, 1979.

tenBroek, Jacobus, et al. *Prejudice, War and the Constitution*. Los Angeles: Univ. of California Press, 1968.

Theoharis, Athan, and John Stuart Cox. *The Boss: J. Edgar Hoover and the Great American Inquisition*. Philadephia, Pa.: Temple Univ. Press, 1988.

Torres, Henry. *Campaign of Treachery*. New York: Dodd, Mead, 1942.

Troy, Thomas. *Donovan and the CIA: A History of the Establishment of the Central Intelligence Agency*. Washington, D.C.: CIA, 1981.

Truffaut, Francois. *Hitchcock*. New York: Simon and Schuster, 1984.

Tuchman, Barbara. *The Zimmermann Telegram*. New York: Macmillan, 1958.

Tunney, Thomas. *Throttled! The Detection of the German and Anarchist Bomb Plotters*. Boston: Small, Maynard, 1919.

Turrou, Leon. *Nazi Spies in America*. New York: Random House, 1938.

Vaughn, Stephen. *Holding Fast the Inner Lines: Democracy, Nationalism, and the Committee on Public Information*. Chapel Hill: Univ. of North Carolina Press, 1980.

Voska, Emmanuel. *Spy and Counterspy*. New York: Doubleday, Doran, 1940.

Warner, Jack. *My First Hundred Years in Hollywood*. New York: Random House, 1964.

Watt, Donald Cameron. *How War Came: The Immediate Origins of the Second World War, 1938–1939*. New York: Pantheon, 1989.

Weinberg, Gerhard. *World in the Balance: Behind the Scenes of World War II*. Hanover, N.H.: Univ. of New England Press, 1981.

Welles, Sumner. *Seven Decisions That Shaped History*. New York: Harper, 1951.

Whitehead, Don. *The FBI Story*. New York: Random House, 1956.

Williams, T. Harry. *Huey Long*. New York: Alfred A. Knopf, 1969.

Wilson, Woodrow. *The Papers of Woodrow Wilson*. Arthur Link, ed., 64 vols. Princeton, N.J.: Princeton Univ. Press, 1990.

Winkler, Alan. *The Politics of Propaganda: The Office of War Information, 1942–1945*. New Haven, Conn.: Yale Univ. Press, 1978.

Winks, Robin. *Cloak and Gown: Scholars in America's Secret War*. London: Collins Harvill, 1987.

Witcover, Jules. *Sabotage at Black Tom: Imperial Germany's Secret War in America 1914–1917*. Chapel Hill, N.C.: Algonquin, 1989.

Wittke, Carl. *German-Americans and the World War*. Columbus: Ohio State Archaeological and Historical Society, 1936.

Articles and Dissertations

Adler, Les K., and Thomas G. Patterson. "Red Fascism: The Merger of Nazi Germany and Soviet Russia in the American Image of Totalitarianism, 1930s–1950's." *American Historical Review* 75 (April 1970): 1046–64.

Bratzel, John F., and Leslie B. Rout. "FDR and the 'Secret Map.' " *Wilson Quarterly* 9 (New Years, 1985): 167–73.

Brown, MacAlister. "The Third Reich's Mobilization of the German Fifth Columns in Eastern Europe." *Journal of Central European Affairs* 19 (July 1959): 128–48.

Davis, David Brion. "Some Themes of Counter-Subversion: An Analysis of Anti-Masonic, Anti-Catholic, and Anti-Mormon Literature." *Mississippi Valley Historical Review* 47 (Sept. 1960): 205–24.

Davis, John. "Notes on Warner Brothers Foreign Policy, 1918–1948." *Velvet Light Trap* 17 (Winter 1978): 19–31.

Dorwart, Jeffrey. "The Roosevelt-Astor Espionage Ring." *New York History* 62 (July 1981): 307–22.

"Ex-British Agent Says FDR's Nazi Map Faked." *Foreign Intelligence Literary Scene* 3 (Dec. 1984): 1–3.

Hickey, Donald. "The Prager Affair: A Study in Wartime Hysteria." *Journal of the Illinois State Historical Society* 62 (Summer 1969): 117–34.

"Hyde's Secret Intelligence Agent Awakens in Ernest Cuneo an Old Love." *Foreign Intelligence Literary Scene* 1 (Oct. 1982): 4–6.

Jackson, Charles. "The Night the Martians Came." In *The Aspirin Age*. Isabel Leighton, ed. New York: Simon and Schuster, 1982. Pp. 431–43.

Janowitz, Morris. "Black Legions on the March." *America in Crisis*. Danial Aaron, ed.. New York: Alfred A. Knopf, 1952. Pp. 304–25.

Jones, David Lloyd. "The US Office of War Information and American Public Opinion during World War II, 1939–1945." Ph.D. dissertation, State University of New York at Binghampton, 1976.

Koopes, Clayton, and Gregory Black. "What to Show the World: The Office of War Information and Hollywood 1942–1944." *Journal of American History* 64 (June 1977): 87–104.

Kumamoto, Bob. "The Search for Spies: American Counterintelligence and the Japanese American Community 1931–1942." *Amerasia Journal* (Fall 1979): 45–75.

MacKay, Lamar. "Domestic Operations of the Office of War Information." Ph.D. dissertation, University of Wisconsin at Madison, 1966.

Maddux, Thomas R. "Red Fascism, Brown Bolshevism: The American Image of Totalitarianism in the 1930s." *The Historian* 40 (Nov. 1977): 85–103.

O'Reilly, Kenneth. "A New Deal for the FBI: The Roosevelt Administration, Crime Control, and National Security." *Journal of American History* 69 (Dec. 1982): 638–58.

———. "The Roosevelt Administration and Legislative-Executive Conflict: The FBI vs. the Dies Committee." *Congress and the Presidency* 10 (Spring 1983): 79–93.

Polenberg, Richard. "Franklin Roosevelt and Civil Liberties: The Case of the Dies Committee." *The Historian* 30 (Feb. 1968): 165–79.

Remak, Joachim. "'Friends of the New Germany': The Bund and German-American Relations." *Journal of Modern History* 29 (March 1957): 38–41.

Reynolds, David. "Lord Lothian and Anglo-American Relations, 1939–1940." In *Transactions of the American Philosophical Society* 73, part 2 (1983).

Ringle, Ken. "What Did You Do Before the War, Dad?." *Washington Post Magazine* (Dec. 6, 1981): 54–62.

Sandeen, Eric. "Confessions of a Nazi Spy and the German-American Bund." *American Studies* 20 (Fall 1979): 69–81.

Smith, Daniel. "Authoritarianism and American Policy Makers in Two World Wars." *Pacific Historical Review* 43 (Aug. 1974): 303–23.

Smith, Geoffrey. "Isolationism, the Devil, and the Advent of the Second World War: Variations on a Theme." *International History Review* 4 (Feb. 1982): 55–89.

Stafford, David. "Intrepid: Myth and Reality." *Journal of Contemporary History* (April 1987): 303–17.

Steele, Richard W. "Franklin D. Roosevelt and His Foreign Policy Critics." *Political Science Quarterly* 94 (Spring 1979): 15–32.

———. "The Great Debate: Roosevelt, the Media, and the Coming of the War, 1940-1941." *Journal of American History* 71 (June 1984): 69–92.

———. "Preparing the Public for War: Efforts to Establish a National Propaganda Agency." *American Historical Review* 75 (June 1970): 1640–53.

Theoharis, Athan. "The FBI and the American Legion Contact Program, 1940-1966." *Political Science Quarterly* 100 (Summer 1985): 271–86.

Trefousse, Hans. "Failure of German Intelligence in the United States, 1933-1945." *Mississippi Valley Historical Review* 42 (June 1955): 84–100.

Weinberg, Sydney Stahl. "Wartime Propaganda in a Democracy: America's Twentieth Century Information Agencies." Ph.D. dissertation, Columbia University, 1969.

———. "What to Tell America: The Quarrel in the Office of War Information." *Journal of American History* 55 (June 1968): 73–89.

INDEX

Abraham Lincoln Brigade, 171–74
Abwehr: banned from sabotage in U.S., 27; and *Confessions of a Nazi Spy*, 69; espionage in U.S., 50–54; Fifth Column operations of, 108; in Holland, 115; in Poland, 112; and sabotage in U.S., 131–33; and Sebold case, 127
Adler, Les, 76
Albert, Heinrich, 13, 17
Alien Registration Act, 79
America First, 95, 104, 140
American Civil Liberties Union, 174, 186
American Fellowship Forum, 124–25
American Protective League, 25–26, 159, 181
Anderson, Walter, 140
Anschluss, 109–10
Archibald, J. F. J., 18, 20
Aryan Nation, 186
Astor, William Vincent, 169–70
Auslandsorganisation, 108

Baldwin, Roger, 174
Bell, Leland, 45
Belmonte, J. P., 96
Berg, Alan, 186
Berle, Adolf, 96–99, 168–69, 173
Bernstorff, Joachim, 13, 18
Biddle, Francis, 75, 86–88, 99, 142, 147
Bielaski, A. Bruce, 159
Black Legion, 46
Black Propaganda, 95–96, 124, 154, 171
Black Tom incident: court case, 16–17; fire, 16, 129
Bohemian National Alliance, 19–20
Bopp, Franz, 13–14
Boy-Ed, Karl, 13, 15
The Boys from Brazil, 185
Braden, Spruille, 97
Breen, Joseph, 31, 63, 69

Bridges, Harry, 79, 163
British Joint Intelligence Committee, 100
British Security Coordination, 7, 95–100
Broun, Heywood, 74
Browder, Earl, 81
Brownlow, Louis, 130, 145–46
Buchan, John, 102–3, 105
Bullitt, William, 118–19, 148
Bund, German-American: attacks on New Deal, 44; camps, 44–45; in *Confessions of a Nazi Spy*, 64–66; formation of, 43; investigations of, 44; Madison Square Garden Rally, 42, 45; public fear of, 6–7, 27, 32; sues Warner Bros., 68; suspected of sabotage, 129; in Turrou's book, 62
Bureau of Investigation, 13, 159–63
Burns, William, 162
Butler, Smedley, 32, 41
Byrnes, James, 119

Campbell, James, 42
Canadian Car and Foundry Company, 16
Canaris, Wilhelm, 27, 52, 69, 133
Cantril, Hadley, 73
Captain America, 133–34
Carlson, John Roy, 185
Carter, John Franklin, 85, 131, 141–42
Central Intelligence Agency, 9, 171, 189
Chamberlain, Neville, 91, 111
Chambers, Whittaker, 188
Chicago Tribune, 140
Christian Front, 37–38
Christian Mobilizers, 38
Christians, George, 46–47
Churchill, Winston, 91–95, 187
Cole, Wayne, viii, 96, 189
Collin, Frank, 186
Colombia, 97

Columbia Broadcasting System (CBS), 35, 73–74, 119, 182
Comintern, 78, 81
Committee of One Million, 37
Committee on Public Information: legacy for FDR, 144, 146, 154; organization of, 23–24; publications, 24–25
Confessions of a Nazi Spy, 62–71, 136
Coordinator of Information, 151, 170
Cooper, Duff, 93–94
Coughlin, Charles, 27, 35–39, 40, 140
Council for Democracy, 147
Coy, Wayne, 148
CPUSA (Communist Party of the United States), 77
Creel, George, 23–24, 144, 146
Crusader White Knights, 46–47
Cummings, Homer, 44, 163

Dasch, George, 132–33
Davis, Elmer, 151–52
Deatherage, George, 41–42, 46
The Defender, 39
De Jong, Louis, vii, 4
Deutsches Ausland-Institut, 108
Dennis, Lawrence, 163
DeWitt, John, 86–89
Diamond, Sander, 44
Dickstein, Samuel, 42–44
Dies, Martin: on Communist Fifth Column, 78–79, 81–82; criticism of FBI, 158, 174–77; and FDR, 79, 138, 174–77; on Fifth Column, 6; investigates Bund, 44; on Italian Fifth Column, 75; and Pearl Harbor attack, 88; and U.S. defense plants, 120, 129
Diggins, John, 76
"Divide and Conquer," 4, 111, 150
Dix, John, 60–61
Dollfuss, Engelbert, 110
Donovan, William: cited in OFF pamphlet, 150; and conflict with Hoover, 182; and origins of OSS, 170–71; pursues "strategy of terror," 151; writes about Fifth Column, 101
Dumba, Constantin, 18
Duquesne, Frederick, 127–28

Eastman, Max, 82
Eglin, Henry, 54–55
Eisenhower, Dwight, 188–89
Espionage Act, 25, 98
Europa, 51, 53

Farnsworth, John Semer, 83
Fatherland, 22
Fay, Robert, 15
The F.B.I. in Peace and War, 185
Federal Bureau of Investigation: and alleged violations of civil liberties, 171–

74; and Christian Front, 38; and *Confessions of a Nazi Spy*, 66–69; consequences of Fifth Column for, 190; counter-espionage, 127–129; counter-sabotage, 129–133; and Dies committee, 174–177; estimates German threat, 142; gains power with World War II, 155, 157; and Italian Fifth Column, 76; and Japanese Fifth Column, 82–84; and Japanese internment, 85–87; and Krivitsky, 77; origins of counter-intelligence, 163–64; and OSS, 170–71; proposed creation of "suicide squad," 79; proposed investigation of labor, 80; public statements on Fifth Column, 177–83; relations with State Department, 164–67; role in Fifth Column scare, 6–7; role in post-World War II red scare, 188; Roosevelt annnounces new responsibilities of, 137; and rumors, 141; and Rumrich spy case, 49–50, 55–61; uncovers unauthorized BSC activity, 98–99
Federal Bureau of Investigation National Police Academy, 180
Federal Communications Commission, 73, 86
Fifth Column
  in Austria, 4, 107, 109–10
  in Belgium, 107, 109, 115–17
  blitzkrieg as technique of, vii, 3, 7, 105, 107, 109, 112, 118
  in Bolivia: British falsify Fifth Column plot, 96
  in Canada: German sabotage during World War I, 12
  composition of, 3
  conclusion of, 8, 142–43, 185
  consequences of, 8–9, 189–91
  in Czechoslovakia, 4, 107, 110–11
  in Denmark, 100, 113
  in France, 107, 109, 115–20
  German: agencies of, 108; alleged alliance with Soviet Fifth Column, 76; and blitzkrieg, vii, 3; British heighten U.S. fears of, 95; compared with Japanese Fifth Column, 90; consequences for U.S., 189–90; as depicted in comic books, 133–34; as depicted in motion pictures, 136; as depicted in pulp fiction, 134–36; and espionage in U.S., 126–29; extra-legal FBI action proposed to stop, 80; Hoover announces defeat of, 183; legacy of World War I, 27; propaganda in U.S., 123–26; Roosevelt's fear of, 89, 137–43; sabotage in U.S., 129–33; U.S. Congress acts against, 79

countered by Great Britain: in Ludwig
  spy ring, 128; and intern refugees
  suspected of Fifth Column leanings,
  100; in Rumrich spy case, 54–55;
  World War I in, 17–21,
  93
exploited by Great Britain, 7, 91–105
in Holland, 107, 109, 115–19
Italian, 3, 27, 74–76
Japanese, 3, 27, 74–75, 82–90
in Latin America: and fear of Fifth
  Column, 4; FBI, ONI, MID disputes
  over, 167–69; Great Britain fosters
  fears of Fifth Column in, 92, 95–97,
  105; OSS and FBI disputes over,
  170–71
in Mexico, 12
in Norway, 85, 100, 107, 109, 113–
  14
origins of, 3
phases of, 7–8
in Poland, 4, 107, 109, 112
refugees, 5
Soviet, 3, 26–27, 74–82, 187–90
in Spain, 3
in the United States: domestic fascism,
  29, 32, 42–47; FBI view of threat,
  177–83; German propaganda in,
  123–26; German espionage in, 126–
  29; German sabotage efforts, 129–
  33; mock invasion of Anderson, S.C.,
  107; in popular culture, 133–36;
  result of blitzkrieg in Europe, 109,
  112; Roosevelt on threat of, 137–43;
  vulnerability to, 4–8
Fish, Hamilton, 126
Foreign Correspondent, 103
Forsythe, Frederick, 185
Freehling, William, 190
French, Paul, 41
Fried, Richard, viii
Friedrich der Grosse, 15
Friends of New Germany, 42–43

Gaunt, Guy, 19–20
General Intelligence Division (Bureau of
  Investigation), 160–62; (FBI), 172
German-American Central Alliance, 22
German-Americans, 21–27
The German Fifth Column in the Second
  World War, vii
German Language Press, 22
German Library of Information, 123–25
German Railroads Information Service,
  123–24
Glaser, Erich, 53, 56, 61
"G-Man Oath," 57–58
Goebbels, Joseph, 51, 64–65, 108, 117,
  154
Goltz, Horst, 14, 19

Gouchenko, Igor, 187
Greenmantle, 102
Gregory, Thomas, 25
Griebl, Ignatz, 51–52, 56, 59–60, 64–67,
  71
Grodzins, Morton, 90
Grzesinski, Albert, 61
Gudenberg, Werner, 50, 56, 67

Halifax, Lord, 99
Hall, William, 19–20
Hannay, Richard, 102–3
Hardy, Lamar, 56, 58, 61
Hays, Arthur, 174
Hays, Will, 68
Henlein, Konrad, 110–11
Hess, Rudolf, 42–43
Hiss, Alger, 188
Hitchcock, Alfred, 102–5, 185
Hitler, Adolf: and alleged Fifth Column
  plans for U.S., 117, 121, 123; and
  alleged link to Stalin's Fifth Column, 76;
  and Austria, 109–10; and British fear of
  subversion, 100; and Czechoslovakia,
  111; compared to Stalin, 82; criticizes
  Abwehr, 133; and Fifth Column in
  Europe 107, 118; and lessons of World
  War I, 27, 49; and Norway, 113–14;
  and Poland, 112; U.S. investigates death
  threat against, 163; and world conquest,
  105
Hitler-Stalin pact, 76, 81
Hofmann, Jennie, 56, 59, 60, 61
Hoover, J. Edgar: concern over BSC, 97–
  99; and Confessions of a Nazi Spy, 66–
  69; criticized for civil liberties violations,
  171–74; and Dies Committee, 174–77;
  directed to investigate subversives, 164;
  dispute with Turrou, 57–60; and
  General Intelligence Division, 160–62;
  heads BI, 162; and Japanese internment,
  84–87; and OSS, 170–71; policy toward
  Fifth Column, 6–7, 157–59; public
  comments on Fifth Column threat, 177–
  83; in pulp fiction, 135; and Red Scare,
  161–63, 187; relations with Military
  Intelligence Division, 167–69; relations
  with State Department, 164–67; reports
  to FDR, 141; and sabotage, 132–33;
  suspicion of Soviet Union, 82, 182–83,
  187
Hopkins, Harry, 140
Horn, Werner, 14, 19
House, Edward, 20, 22
House Un-American Activities Committee
  (HUAC): and Bund, 44–45; and
  Communism, 77–79; and FBI, 174–77;
  FDR directs reporters to, 138; and Fifth
  Column, 6; and Moseley, 41; role in
  post-World War II America, 187; on

Index

House Un-American (*continued*)
  vulnerability of U.S. defense plants, 120, 127
Huerta, Victoriano, 15
Hughes, John, 87
Hull, Cordell, 69, 84, 97, 164–65
Hyde, H. Montgomery, 96
Hyphenated Americans, 23

Ickes, Harold, 130, 140, 143–49, 153–54
Isolationism, 6, 9, 95–96, 139–40, 189
It Can't Happen Here, 30–32

Jackson, Robert, 80, 130, 143, 145, 173–74, 177
Joint Chiefs of Staff, 151, 171
Jordan, Jessie, 55–56

Kennan, Joseph, 59–60
Kennedy, Joseph, 101
Khaki Shirts of America, 32, 40–41
Knights of the White Camelia, 41, 46
Knox, Frank: backs propaganda, 130, 145; concern over defense plants, 80–81; and Donovan, 101, 170; and intelligence coordination, 168; and Japanese Fifth Column, 85–86
Knox, John, 61
Kraus, Paul, 51
Krivitsky, Walter, 77–78
Ku Klux Klan, 46
Kuhn, Fritz, 43–45, 66, 140
Kumamoto, Bob, 84

La Guardia, Fiorello, 42, 45, 149
The Lady Vanishes, 103
Lansing, Robert, 18
Lemke, William, 36–37
Le Queux, William, 20–21
Levin, Ira, 185
Lewis, Sinclair, 30–31
Lido, Julio, 128–29
Lindbergh, Charles, 95, 139, 144
Lippmann, Walter, 87
Little Orphan Annie, 134
Long, Huey, 32–34, 40
Lonkowski, William, 50–52
Lothian, Lord, 93, 101
Ludwig, Frederick, 128–29
Lundeen, Ernest, 125–26

McAdoo, William, 17
McCarthy, Joseph, 188–90
McClemore, Henry, 87
McCloy, John, 17, 80, 89, 144–47
McCormack, John, 43
McCormack-Dickstein Committee, 41, 43, 125
MacLeish, Archibald, 145, 149–50, 153
McWilliams, Joseph, 38, 163

Make Europe Pay War Debts Committee, 126
March of Time, 64
Marshall, George, 89, 119, 149, 188
Maverick, Maury, 120
Mellett, Lowell, 146–47, 149, 152–53
Messersmith, George, 164–67
Midway, 89
Miles, Sherman, 119, 167–69
Military Intelligence Division, 119, 141, 166–69, 173
Milton, George, 148
Mola, Emilio, 3
Molly Pitcher Rifle Legion, 7
Moog, Kate, 52, 56, 64–65
Morgenthau, Henry, 139, 148, 168
Morrell, Earl, 95–96
Moseley, George Van Horn, 32, 41–42
Mowrer, Edgar, 96, 101
Mr. Standfast, 102–3
Munich crisis, 74, 111
Murphy, Frank, 68, 164, 166–67
Murray, Robert, viii
Mutual Broadcasting Network, 87, 120, 130

Nasjonal Samling, 114
National Union for Social Justice (NUSJ), 35–36
Nichols, L. B., 68–69
Nicolai, Walter, 52–53
Nightmare in Red, viii
Noordam, 15
Normandie, 131
Norris, George, 173–74
Notorious, 185

The Odessa File, 185
Office of Civilian Defense (OCD), 144, 149, 153–54
Office of Emergency Management, 148, 150
Office of Facts and Figures (OFF), 144, 149–50, 153–54
Office of Government Reports (OGR), 146–47, 150, 152
Office of Naval Intelligence (ONI), 80, 82–84, 141, 165–69, 173
Office of Strategic Services (OSS), 9, 151–52, 170–71, 182, 189
Office of War Information (OWI), 144, 148, 150–154
OGPU, 77–78
The Old Christian Right: The Protestant Far Right from the Great Depression to the Cold War, viii
Operation Barbarossa, 81, 187
Operation Pastorious, 131–33
O'Reilly, Kenneth, 176
Out of the Night, 78
OVRA, 75

Page, Walter Hines, 20
Palmer, A. Mitchell, 160–62, 178
Panama Canal, 52–53, 135
Papen, Franz, 13, 15, 18–19
Paterson, Robert, 80
Paterson, Thomas, 76
Pauley, Bruce, 110
Pearl Harbor, 85–86, 89, 91, 103
Pearson, Drew, 125, 143
Pegler, Westbrook, 87
Pelley, William Dudley, 45–46, 140, 163
Perkins, Frances, 140, 144–45
Pheiffer, Erich, 51–52
"Phoney War," 91–92
Pope, Arthur, 147
Post, Louis, 161
Powers, Richard Gid, viii, 162–63, 182
Prager, Robert, 21, 26
The President Vanishes, 29–30
Production Code Administration (PCA), 31, 63, 68–69
Protocols of the Learned Elders of Zion, 37, 39
Providence Journal, 20

Quadragiesmo Anno, 36
Quisling, Vidkun, 114

Raeder, Erich, 114
Rankin, John, 78, 88
Rathom, John, 20
Rauschning, Herman, 117, 150
Red Scare, viii, 26–27, 159–62, 172, 187–89
Reichsdeutschen, 108, 112
Reichssicherheitshauptamt, 108
Rerum Novarum, 36
Reuper, Carl, 128
Reves, Emery, 93–94, 97
Ribuffo, Leo, viii, 154–55
Ringle, Kenneth, 84
Rintelen, Franz, 14–15, 62
Rivers, E. D., 120
Robinson, Edward G., 64
Rockwell, George Lincoln, 186
Room 40, 19–20
Roosevelt, Franklin Delano: alleged whispering campaign against, 70; announces victory over Fifth Column, 142; and BSC, 95, 97, 99–100; and Churchill, 92; and Communist Fifth Column, 80–81, 163; and Coughlin, 35–39; criticizes FBI, 183; and death penalty for saboteurs, 133; debate over counter-propaganda, 143–55; depicted in Captain America, 134; and Dies, 79, 138, 175–76; directs Hoover to investigate Communists and fascists, 163; fails to support State Department, 166–67; and Fifth Column, 6, 140–41;

and Italian Fifth Column, 75–76; and Japanese internment, 85, 88–89; and Khaki Shirts of America, 40; and lessons of World War I, 27–28; liberalism of as alternative to fascism and Communism, 47; links Fifth Column to isolationism, 139–40; and Huey Long, 33–34; and OSS, 170–71; public speeches on Fifth Column, 137–38; receives complaints from Hoover, 168; relations with Warner, 61; on Rumrich case, 57–59, 61; Steele and Ribuffo on, vii-viii, 154–55
Roper poll, 120
Rosenberg spy case, 188
Rumrich, Guenther, 52–56, 59–61
Rumrich spy case: FDR's response to, 137; Hoover's speeches after, 179; investigation and prosecution, 49–61; media adaptations of, 61–71, 136; State Department revives intelligence coordination after, 165
Ruroede, Carl, 13–14, 19

Saboteur, 103–4
Scheele, Walter, 15
Schlesinger, Arthur, Jr., 28, 36, 154
Schlueter, Karl, 53–56, 64
Schuschnigg, Kurt, 109–10
Sebold, William, 127–28
The Secret Agent, 103
Sedition Act, 25
Seyss-Inquart, Arthur, 109–10
"Share Our Wealth" plan, 34
Sherwood, Robert, 151
Sicherheitsdienst, 108
Silver Shirts, 45–47
Sixth (and Seventh) Column, 182
Skokie, Illinois, 186
Slacker Raids, 159–60
Smith, Art, 40–41
Smith, Bradley, viii, 171
Smith, Geoffrey, viii, 139
Smith, Gerald L. K., 32, 37
Smith, Harold, 144, 148
Social Justice, 36–37
Spanknobel, Heinz, 42–43
Stalin, Joseph, 76, 87, 187
Steele, Richard, vii, 154–55
Stephenson, William, 94–96, 98–99, 105
Stern, J. David, 57–59, 62
Stimson, Henry: FDR discusses Lindbergh with, 139; and Fifth Column in France, 119; and Japanese internment, 88–89; and labor unrest, 80–81; supports centralized propaganda, 144–45, 148; suspects sabotage in U.S., 129
Stone, Harlan, 162
Stout, Rex, 29

Stowe, Leland, 113, 118, 150
The Strategy of Terror, 118
Superman, 134

Tachibana, Itaru, 83–84
Tamm, Edward, 173–74
Taylor, Edmond, 118, 150
The Thirty-nine Steps, 102–3
Thompson, Harry, 83
Thomsen, Hans, 27, 69
*To Save a Nation: American
    Countersubversives from the Great
    Depression to the Cold War*, viii
Townsend, Francis, 32, 36–37
Transocean News Service, 124, 176
Trotsky, Leon, 78
Truffaut, François, 104
Turrou, Leon: played by Edward G.
    Robinson, 64; and Rumrich case,
    50, 55–61; sells story to movies,
    62, 71

Under Cover, 185
Union Party, 36–37
United States Secret Service, 15, 17, 28
U.S. v. McWilliams, 185

Valtin, Jan, 77–79
Viereck, George, 22, 125–25
The Voice of Destruction, 117
Volksbund für das Deutschum im
    Ausland, 108
Volksdeutsche Mittelstelle, 108
Volksdeutschen, 108, 112
Voorhis, Jerry, 177
Voska, Emmanuel, 19–20
Voss, Otto, 50, 56, 59, 61

Works Progress Administration (WPA),
    45, 79
Wallace, Henry, 144, 148
War of the Worlds, 73–74
Warner, Jack, 62–63, 70
Warner, Harry, 63, 70
Warner Brothers, 50, 62–71
Warren, Fletcher, 166
Wedell, Hans, 13–14
Welles, Orson, 73
Welles, Sumner, 96, 166
Western Defense Command, 86–87
Wiegand, Karl, 120–21
Wilk, Jacob, 62
Williams, Wythe, 130
Wilson, Woodrow: establishes CPI, 23,
    144; on German subversion, 11, 13; on
    hyphenated-Americans, 23; on possible
    insurrection, 22; on Prager lynching, 26;
    and slacker raids, 160; and World War I
    intelligence, 165
Winchell, Walter, 96, 130, 185
"Wings of America," 120
Winkler, Allan, 151
Winrod, Gerald, 32, 39–40, 163
Wiseman, William, 20
World War I: anti-German hysteria
    during, 21–27; and British intelligence,
    12, 17–21, 93; British internment of
    suspects during, 100; and Bureau of
    Investigation, 159–60; decline of
    German espionage before, 12; German
    subversion of U.S., 5, 11, 13–19; lessons
    of, 5, 12, 27–28, 137, 144, 158, 163

Zimmermann, Arthur, 21
Zimmermann Telegram, 19, 93